SHORT COURSE SERIES

WORLD TRADE PRESS®

Professional Books for International Trade

THE SHORT COURSE IN INTERNATIONAL TRADE SERIES

A Short Course in International Business Culture

A Short Course in International Business Ethics

A Short Course in International Business Plans

A Short Course in International Contracts

A Short Course in International Economics

A Short Course in International Intellectual Property Rights

A Short Course in International Joint Ventures

A Short Course in International Marketing

A Short Course in International Marketing Blunders

A Short Course in International Negotiating

A Short Course in International Payments

A Short Course in International Trade Documentation

A SHORT COURSE IN

International Intellectual Property Rights

3rd Edition

Protecting Your Brands, Marks, Copyrights, Patents, Designs, and Related Rights Worldwide

Karla C. Shippey, J.D.

Published in arrangement with World Trade Press by

ATLANTIC

PUBLISHERS & DISTRIBUTORS (P) LTD

7/22, Ansari Road, Darya Ganj, New Delhi-110 002
Tel: 40775252, 23273880, 23275880, 23280451; Fax: +91-11-23285873
E-mail: orders@atlanticbooks.com; Web: www.atlanticbooks.com

World Trade Press
800 Lindberg Lane, Suite 190
Petaluma, California 94952 USA
Tel: +1 (707) 778-1124
Fax: +1 (707) 778-1329
USA Order Line: +1 (800) 833-8586
E-mail: sales@worldtradepress.com
www.WorldTradePress.com
www.WorldTradeREF.com (international trade and logistics)
www.BestCountryReports.com (business travel, communications and culture)
www.GiantMapArt.com (Giant maps for building lobbies, conference rooms and education)

A Short Course in International Intellectual Property Rights, 3rd Edition
By Karla C. Shippey, J.D.
Short Course Series Concept: Edward G. Hinkelman
Cover Design: Ronald A. Blodgett
Text Design: Seventeenth Street Studios, Oakland, California, USA
Desktop Publishing: Valentina Pfeil

ISBN 978-81-269-1248-3
First Indian Reprint 2009

This edition is for sale in Indian sub-continent only.

Library of Congress Cataloging-in-Publication Data
Shippey, Karla C., 1957–
A short course in international intellectual property rights: protecting your brands, marks, copyrights, patents, designs, and related rights worldwide / Karla C. Shippey -- 3rd ed.
p. cm. — (The short course in international trade series)
Includes bibliographic references.
1. Intellectual property (International law)
I. Title: International Intellectual Property Rights.
II. Title. III. Series.
K1401 .S528 2009
341.7'58---dc21

2009026778
CIP

Printed in India at Chaman Enterprises, 1603, Pataudi House, Darya Ganj, New Delhi-110 002

INTRODUCTION

A SHORT COURSE IN INTERNATIONAL INTELLECTUAL PROPERTY RIGHTS was conceived for the purpose of demystifying a concept that is intangible at best—the rights of a creator to a monopoly over the creation.

WHY DEMYSTIFY?

Protection of intellectual property (IP) rights, legal constraints on owners and traders in these rights, and wheeling and dealing in these rights have spawned specialized legislation, judicial and administrative departments, and private commercial registries and protective agencies. And (of course) law firms have expanded to provide departments of attorneys with IP expertise. What does all this mean to the average commercial trader who just wants to make a profit? Our first chapter briefly describes what IP means, the second chapter gives you the short answers, and the rest of the book is a guide to making your IP profitable for you. You will find sidebars that emphasize and highlight the issues, checklists for ready access and use in decision-making and record-keeping, a special section on what you can expect in different legal systems and countries, and a glossary defining the technical legal meaning of common IP terms.

WHY WORRY ABOUT THE INTANGIBLE?

You are in business with the intent to make money. Your goods, equipment, building, and other property are assets of your business. Your time and labor are spent in ensuring the best quality and highest quantity of production at competitive prices within a fast changing market. You have a plan, and your plan is bringing (or will soon bring) you a profit. Your services are provided with a smile, and the client is always right. What have you forgotten?

The value of your intellectual property. What's in a name? What's in a new method or procedure? What's in an invention? What's in a web page or software presentation? Your ideas, once presented and distributed, will be the backbone of your business, because it is the presentation of your ideas that will grab your share of the market and keep customers coming back for more and more and more. There is value in the eye-catching design of a new dress, the unusual shape of a bottle containing a new perfume, the formula for the perfume itself, the lyrics and musical score you just wrote, and the logo and name you invented and printed on your stationery. If you cannot protect your rights in your creation, other traders can copy your creation, cause consumer confusion about who is providing the goods or services, and ultimately hurt your sales and market share.

WHAT IS THIS "IP" TERMINOLOGY?

In common US and Western European legal parlance, the term "IP" is taken to mean "Intellectual Property." As a US attorney, the author has adopted this term to refer to all types of creations that anyone can possibly create using his or her intellect, provided the creation has commercial value. The author is using the term "IP" in its broadest interpretation to include not only the traditional concepts of trademarks, copyrights, and patents, but also what some refer to as Industrial Property (intangible creations specifically related to commercial ventures, such as trade names, trade secrets, trade designs, trade dress, industrial drawings and designs, geographical indications, and company manuals and methodologies). Moreover, the author would intend the term "IP" to refer to creations to which legal protection is being extended as this area of law develops, such as ethnobiological IP rights, Internet and software IP design rights, and IP rights in smells, sounds, and three-dimensional shapes.

WHO IN THE WORLD KNOWS ABOUT IP RIGHTS?

As a US attorney, the author admits to some bias toward the highly developed IP laws in the US and other common-law based countries (e.g., Canada, England, Singapore, Hong Kong, South Africa, Australia). However, the author is well aware that the cultures and countries of this world have developed a variety of legal systems, and therefore IP rights are treated differently from nation to nation. In some places, the concept of intangible property does not exist, and therefore rights in IP are not recognized. Where political and legal systems have removed or limited private ownership rights in favor of state and public ownership, rights in IP are considered to be public. In many countries, IP laws have been in force for decades but have not been updated for current commercial practice, and even if laws have been revised, nontraditional IP rights remain beyond their scope. A plethora of international activity is also affecting national IP laws and practices as diverse economic and political interests come together in bilateral, regional, and multi-national trade summits and pacts.

As a trader, you need to be aware of the issues internationally and nationally that will affect your IP rights. Decisions you make today about your IP rights will ultimately affect your future profits in international markets both directly in terms of the labor and cost you spend in establishing and protecting your IP rights, and indirectly in terms of the development of IP that has commercial value and therefore contributes significantly to the international success of your venture. Accordingly, the author has tried to write about IP rights from an internationally generic viewpoint, and therefore she cautions that some of the points may not apply in a particular nation. You should always seek legal counsel to ensure that you understand your IP rights within any particular situation.

DOES THIS "SHORT COURSE" TELL ME EVERYTHING I NEED TO KNOW?

The author does not claim to tell you everything about IP, and quite certainly, you will need to seek other resources, including attorneys, to answer questions about your specific situation. The IP field is extremely diverse and complex, and also very legalistic. Volumes and volumes have been written about each one of the various IP rights, and IP laws vary significantly from country to country. Therefore, this skinny guide cannot do complete justice to every nuance of IP law and practice around the world.

Instead, the author has made a well-considered effort to bring to your attention the issues that you need to know so that you will become aware of your IP interests and can then ask the right questions to get the right answers. The author has also concentrated on giving you a practical how-to guideline from start to finish. Be certain to obtain authoritative legal advice. As the title says, this book is a Short Course.

JUST SAY IT

Forms, forms, forms. Lawyers love written agreements, and you will find many in this book. As the scope of this text is IP rights and the space is limited, the author has provided forms specifically related to IP rights, even if in some instances the forms would typically be included as clauses or sections within more comprehensive agreements, such as a distribution contract or an agreement to sell an entire business. In selecting forms, the author has concentrated on forms that the commercial trader would be most likely to use or review. Forms that are usually completed or prepared by legal counsel, such as applications for registration of IP rights have not been included. You will find sources for obtaining such forms listed at the end of this book.

The author has made a supreme effort to avoid "legalese", but unfortunately some conventions are necessary in the sample forms to indicate alternative phrasing. The conventions are not part of the forms. Alternative phrasing is enclosed within brackets, and inside the brackets additional alternatives are shown within parentheses. The brackets contain italicized instructions for completion; text of the form is always in roman typeface. A slash between two or more words indicates that you should choose one of the words depending on your particular situation.

Karla C. Shippey, J.D.
Irvine, California

TABLE OF CONTENTS

CHAPTER 1

Intellectual Property (IP) Basics

Understanding IP Rights

Intellectual property is a product of the mind, and as such, it is distinct from the usual notions of "property." Land, buildings, vehicles, clothing, even your hat, are all tangible property. You can see and feel them. You can own them, lend them, and pass your ownership temporarily or forever to another person. You can judge their commercial value by looking at them, measuring them, poking about in their dirt mounds, timbers, axles and engines, and fibers. You can do price comparisons with other similar tangible properties.

INTANGIBLE PROPERTY RIGHTS

An intellectual creation, until it is presented in a tangible form, cannot be sensed by someone other than the creator, and it has value only to the creator. It is intangible property, present only in the creator's mind. For many centuries, intangible property rights in creations were not recognized or protected by law. There was an impasse among lawmakers and courts alike over whether and how to protect and value the rights associated with ideas and the presentation of ideas.

With the dawning of the Era of Enlightenment, the economies of the Americas and Europe began overflowing with inventors, authors, composers, publishers, and entertainers, and the political and economic worlds in the West realized that intangible rights in creations needed to be reviewed and come under the protection of the law and the courts. Property rights—such as the right to own, publish, distribute, sell, exchange, or lend—in intangibles had to be recognized if such property was to have marketable value for the creator. Put another way, an idea has marketable value only if you alone, and no one else, can use your manifestation of the idea. Or, marketable value comes from monopoly.

The willingness to recognize property rights in creations is a fairly new concept in relative terms to tangible property rights, which have been long recognized and well developed in the law. Moreover, this concept was first recognized in European and North American countries and in the countries touched by those political powers. In much of the rest of the world, intangible property rights in creations went unrecognized. What is viewed by Western powers as infringement of these rights is in fact not a crime in countries where creations are considered to be the right of the people as a whole. Legislation has been passed in many of these countries, but enforcement of IP rights remains a very difficult problem because of the popular view against recognition of intangible property rights.

Wherever you do business in the world today, be aware that legislative and judicial interpretations, protections, and constraints on the intangible property rights in creations are in a constant state of development and flex. Further, you must keep in mind the public view of IP rights, which can affect where you market and how you choose to enforce your IP rights.

IS MONOPOLY A "BAD" WORD?

A "monopoly" simply means exclusive ownership, possession, or control. Thus, if you own all property rights in an acre of land, you have exclusive rights—or a monopoly—to determine who can enter and cross the land, who can use the land, and how it can be used. This concept is not "bad" in and of itself.

In the context of IP rights, a monopoly is quite favorable, particularly if you are the creator, that is, the holder of the monopoly. If a creator has no monopoly in the creation, there is little or no commercial value in it. If you have designed and built a golf course, you have a monopoly over that design. Until you give up your monopoly, no other person should be allowed to recreate your design at another course or to photograph it for commercial distribution. If you have meticulously splashed color on canvas in your own creative patterns, you have a monopoly over where that canvas may be displayed and who may photograph it until you give up your IP rights. As the creator, you benefit from the monopolistic rights granted by law. Assuming you intend to profit from your creation, be certain that your IP rights—your exclusive property rights—are protected.

The reverse side of monopolistic rights—including rights in property—is that they can be abused to the harm of private parties or the public at large. A monopoly can result in one person controlling a market to the exclusion of all competition. If you want to profit from someone else's creation, the fact that the monopoly rights exist in that creation can hamper your intentions. You may need to purchase those IP rights or obtain a license or other authority to use them. Otherwise, the creator may sue you on grounds that your usage is an infringement of the IP rights.

Whether or not to allow monopolies has always been a conundrum. In many cultures and countries, monopolies go unregulated. Where laws have been enacted to control monopolies, monopolistic rights have merely been limited, not eliminated. For example, a landowner has exclusive rights to use the property, but those rights may be limited if the use causes an attractive nuisance or hazardous condition. Similarly, a creator may be permitted monopolistic rights in the creation, but if the creator stops using the IP or fails to protect the IP rights, the creator may not be able to stop another person's use of the creation.

Because of the view that monopolies are adverse to the interest of the public at large in free competition, IP rights are not considered natural, basic human rights. Such rights are therefore primarily established by statute. The extent to which courts will protect IP rights without statutory requirement or compliance is very limited. Moreover, statutory rights to IP are also limited. Laws regulating IP usually fix a term of years during which monopolistic rights in the IP may exist. In some instances, the term may be extended, typically on a showing that the IP is still used within the jurisdiction. The law also limits monopolistic IP rights by refusing to recognize exclusivity over IP that is merely generic, descriptive, or otherwise not invented or new.

Defining Traditional Forms of IP

Patents, copyrights, and trademarks were the first intellectual property rights to be recognized in law. Because these rights have a longer tradition, most people think of them first when considering IP issues. These three intangible property

Traditional Forms of IP: A Quick Comparison

Although it is difficult to generalize the law of various countries, the following points should provide a framework for understanding the similarities and differences between patents, copyrights, and trademarks.

A PATENT PROTECTS:

1. Inventions (any thing, process or idea), that are
2. not already known generally and currently (novel), that are
3. reducible to tangible form or used in tangible form without too much skill or ingenuity, that are
4. valuable or useful to society, and that are
5. conceived or discovered by the inventor;
6. for a finite term.

A COPYRIGHT PROTECTS:

1. Original (not copied) expressions of ideas, that are
2. creatively produced, and that are
3. fixed in tangible medium (such as paper, tape, disk, canvas, wood, metal, clay);
4. for a finite term (typically life of creator plus 50 to 70 years).

EXTREMELY IMPORTANT CONCEPT: Expression versus Idea. A copyright will not protect the idea, only the expression.

A TRADEMARK PROTECTS:

1. A word, phrase, sign, symbol, shape, or label, that is
2. a distinctive identifier of the goods or services of the creator when placed in commerce, that is
3. used to distinguish goods or services from those of any other person or business;
4. for an indefinite term (provided renewal is made before the term expires).

EXTREMELY IMPORTANT CONCEPT: Classification of Goods and Services. Unlike a copyright or patent, a trademark right is granted only with respect to the specific goods or services claimed by the trademark owner. An exception may be made for famous trademarks, but only if the exception is recognized in the particular country at issue. Thus, the trademark adidas® as used for shoes would not be infringed against by a company that uses the same trademark in connection with tobacco, unless the jurisdiction will recognize the trademark as famous and will accord it protection regardless of the goods or services.

---

rights are quite distinct, and yet they have several aspects in common. Each of these rights is defined here in very broad terms because the definitions will vary from country to country. It is essential to check the specific definition applicable within the country where you are seeking IP protection.

PATENT

- DEFINITION A "patent" may be defined as (1) the exclusive right granted by statute (2) to a party (the inventor) who conceives or discovers (3) a nonobvious and novel invention (4) to use and develop the invention, and (5) to prevent others from manufacturing, selling, or using the invention. The patent right is granted for a limited time, which varies depending on such factors as type of invention and jurisdiction of registration. Patent terms are typically from 14 to 20 years and usually the term cannot be extended.
- STATUTORY RIGHT Patent rights must be granted pursuant to a statute. If a country has no Patent Law, a patent right will not be granted there. Unlike trademarks and copyrights, which may be able to derive some protection from court-made doctrine, patent rights and protection are totally dependent on statute. As a result, the type of invention that may be registered as a patent depends on the law of the country. Be certain to verify with local counsel whether a type of patent is available in the jurisdiction where you seek to patent your invention.

  The following types of patents are commonly found in countries where patent law is most highly developed:

  - UTILITY PATENT is for an invention that can be characterized in one or more of the following categories: a process, machine, manufacture, composition of matter, or an improvement of an existing idea within one of these categories.
  - DESIGN PATENT is for a novel design that is in itself nonfunctional but that is part of a functional manufactured article. For example, a new design for the case of a cellular telephone that gives the product a new look but that does not improve the function of the telephone may be the subject of a design patent.
  - PLANT PATENT is for a new reproducible plant, whether reproduction occurs asexually or sexually (such as a flower).

- CREATIVE CONCEPTION OR DISCOVERY An invention must be conceived or discovered through some creativity on the part of an inventor. Thus, if an inventor "discovers" a pre-existing natural substance, the discovery is unlikely to be allowed patent protection. However, if the inventor has creatively found a way to employ or alter the natural substance so that a new and useful application is developed, the discovery may be protected by a patent. The first date of conception or discovery is the date of the invention, provided further efforts are made to reduce it to practice, such as by filing a patent application or building a working model.
- NONOBVIOUS AND NOVEL INVENTION An invention can be patented only if it is novel and nonobvious. "Novel" means the invention must offer a new development, while "nonobvious" means that the invention must be a surprising or unexpected development when considered by a person of ordinary skill within the particular field of the invention. In other words, the invention must produce both a new and an unexpected result.

A patent examiner will usually make the determination of whether an invention is novel and nonobvious. For this purpose, the patent is assigned to an examiner who has sufficient expertise in the particular field of the invention to know or otherwise review the current state-of-the-art. Because the determination is based on subjective factors, you should offer all possible assistance to the examiner by ensuring that your patent application is carefully and skillfully drafted to state clearly the prior state-of-the-art, why the invention adds something new, and why the new addition gives a surprising or unexpected result.

- USE, DEVELOPMENT, AND INFRINGEMENT Once a patent is granted, its value becomes apparent when other parties seek your permission to license your invention. You hold the exclusive use rights, at least for the limited term of the patent. Moreover, you have the right to enforce your exclusive rights against anyone who uses your invention without your permission. It is important to remember to pay the maintenance fees, also known as annuities, which come due periodically to maintain your patent on the Registry. Otherwise, your patent grant will expire and the invention will become available for public use. For further discussion of maintaining the value of your IP rights, see Chapter 6.

COPYRIGHT

- DEFINITION A "copyright" is the exclusive right of the copyright holder to an original expression or creative work, commonly called "work of authorship." To be protected by copyright, an expression must be (1) original, (2) made or conceived using some creativity, and (3) fixed in a tangible medium. Copyrights generally apply to works that can be characterized as one of the following: literary, dramatic or performance, audiovisual, musical, graphic, or artistic. A copyright has a finite term, typically the life of the author plus 50 to 70 years depending on jurisdiction, date of publication and type of product.

  In most countries, copyright may be sought for the following types of works:

- COLLECTIVE WORKS consist of the independent works of several authors combined to make a single work, but the authors are all given separate credit for their contributions. The works that are included may be within the public domain. If not, the copyright owner of each part must authorize its inclusion in the collective work. The author of a collective work holds a copyright for the presentation—the organization, selection, and design of the work—not for each work itself. If the separate contributions are not presented in a novel way, the collection is not protected by copyright. Examples include encyclopedias and anthologies.

- COMPILATION WORKS consist of preexisting materials, works, and information that are chosen, collected, and presented in a novel fashion. The presentation is an original work of authorship, which is protected by copyright. Collective works are a type of compilation work, although compilation works are broader in concept because many different types of materials and information can be presented, not merely the works of separate authors. For example, an almanac of trade that contains factual information on the geography, demographics, markets, culture, economy, laws, and political history for each country in the world, plus separate works from independent authors giving tips on commercial practices in cross-border trade, would be a compilation work.

- DERIVATIVE WORKS are new works based on old works that were previously copyrighted. A derivative work must have sufficient original work added to render it a new work. Examples include translations of books, a play based on a novel, new renditions of old songs, and abridged versions of books. The right to create and protect a derivative work is included within the exclusive copyright of the original work, and therefore only the original author has the right to create a derivative work. The author may transfer this right by license or assignment. If several authors have created separate works, they may later decide to combine them into a single work, in which event the derivative work would be coauthored.
- FACTUAL WORKS are works that are nonfiction and that contain facts that are in the public domain. The ideas and data in a factual work cannot be copyrighted, but the presentation is subject to copyright.
- WORK MADE FOR HIRE A work that is created by an employee within the scope of the employment or works created by a freelance author under written contract that states that the work is made for hire, provided the work qualifies as one of the following: an atlas, a test, answer material for a test, an instructional text, a translation, a supplementary work, a compilation, a screenplay or other part of a motion picture or audiovisual work, or a work specially ordered or commissioned to be used as a contribution to a collective work. The copyright in a work made for hire belongs to the employer or the party that commissioned the work.

- ORIGINAL EXPRESSION A work must be the original creation of the author or artist for copyright to attach. Facts, ideas, and works that have become part of the public domain are not "original creations" unless the author has added his or her own creative expression. If the work is copied from another person's work, an action known commonly as plagiarism, it is not original and the new author cannot claim a copyright.

NOTE: A copyright protects the expression only, not the thought or idea itself. This is an important distinction that must be clearly understood. For example, the author of this book can write it without infringing the copyrights held by other authors who have already published books on IP rights. Why? Because thoughts and ideas cannot become subject to a copyright. Thus, the author is not infringing prior copyrights, provided the author of this book presents IP rights without copying exactly, or even in a similar fashion, the organization, arrangement, format, or text of previously written books that are still subject to copyright.

- CREATIVITY The work must be produced with at least a modicum of creativity on the part of the author or artist. No hard and fast rule is applied, but a work that is made without any exercise of human intellect is unlikely to receive copyright recognition by administrative or judicial authorities.
- TANGIBLE MEDIUM A creative work must be fixed in a tangible medium before a copyright will attach. This requirement reflects the fact that an idea is not copyrightable, only the expression of the idea. Thus, until the idea is expressed in a tangible medium, no copyright exists.

  In many countries, the copyright will arise at the time the expression is fixed in a tangible medium and registration is not required to claim exclusive rights to the copyright. It subsists by virtue of statute as a privilege or right in a work once that work has been set down in tangible form. For example, when an author has typed a draft of a book on to paper or has saved it to a computer diskette, that work is then protected by copyright. Similarly, when a musician has written a score for a composition, the score is protected by copyright.

It is important to note that a copyright may be lost in some countries if a notice of copyright, such as "© 2010 by Karla C. Shippey," is not included when the expression is fixed in tangible medium. The notice required will vary from country to country. The usual rule is that the notice must be placed in such a manner and location as to give reasonable notice of the claimed copyright, such as on the "verso" page of a book.

TRADEMARK

- DEFINITION If you remember that the word "trademark" is comprised of two words, "trade" and "mark," you will quickly understand the concept of a trademark. First, a "mark" can be any word, letter, or symbol, or any combination of these items. An increasing number of countries have extended this definition of "mark" to include smells, sounds, and 3-dimensional shapes. Second, a "trademark" is a mark that (1) is used in commerce (hence "trade"), (2) to identify a product or service as having been made or provided by the owner of the trademark, and (3) to distinguish the trademark owner's product or service from the products or services of other traders. Once a trademark is registered, the registration may be renewed periodically (usually every 10 to 14 years) for an indefinite number of terms.

  Various types of trademarks are recognized, depending on the law of the country. The most common are as follows:

- ASSOCIATED MARK is one that is identical or so similar to another pending or registered mark that the public would likely be deceived or confused by simultaneous usage of both marks, except that both marks are owned by the same proprietor and are registered for use with the same goods or services. In such event, the mark owner may agree to a statement in the registration that the two marks are associated with each other. For example, if a person owns a registration for the word mark "REKEL" and uses it in connection with soft drinks, the same person may also be granted a registration for a logo that incorporates the same word "REKEL" also for use with soft drinks, provided the second mark registration is associated with the first.

- CERTIFICATION MARK indicates to the public that the products or services on which it is displayed have certain characteristics or qualities such that they meet specific standards set by the owner of the trademark. These standards may include, for example, the regional source, manufacturing method, or the quality of a product or service. For example, the "Good Housekeeping Seal of Approval" is a certification mark. This type of mark cannot be transferred to another individual or company.

- SERIES MARKS are several similar marks claimed by one proprietor. The marks are similar but not identical, meaning they differ slightly such as in their color, in a minor alteration to show different versions (e.g., MACH 1, MACH 2, and MACH 3), or in their usage with similar but not identical goods or services. Each mark may be protected by a separate registration, provided the registrations state that the marks are part of a series and are associated with each other.

- DEFENSIVE MARK can be registered when a proprietor's mark has become so well known that if it were used by someone other than the proprietor for goods or services other than those the proprietor sells, the public would likely be deceived or confused. To protect the distinctive character of his or her mark, the proprietor is permitted to register a defensive mark for goods or services that the proprietor does not in fact provide.

- COLORED MARK is a mark that is limited to a specific color as stated in the registration. If a mark is registered in black and white and no color limitation is stated, the mark is considered registered for all colors and the proprietor is free therefore to vary the color in which the mark is printed.

- USE The use of a trademark in commerce is all-important. In many countries, use of a trademark alone, without registration, can create IP rights in the trademark. If a trademark may not qualify for registration because it is not sufficiently distinctive, it may achieve distinctiveness through use in commerce and therefore become qualified for registration. In some countries, the first party to use a trademark in commerce gains the IP rights regardless of whether the mark has been used and registered by another trader elsewhere in the world.

  In some countries, such as the United States, a trademark registration will not issue until proof of use in commerce is given. Many countries (Cambodia, Canada, China, Laos, Turkey, United States, to name a few) require the trademark owner to submit proof of use during the term of the registration or at the time of renewal. In most countries, a trademark that is not used in commerce is subject to cancellation, and a third party who is interested in using the same or a similar trademark can file a request for cancellation.

- DISTINCTIVENESS A mark is not a "trademark" unless it can distinguish the trademark owner's goods or services from those of another trader. This concept seems to be simple, but it is clouded with so many factors that selecting a mark that will qualify for registration worldwide becomes one of the most difficult, time-consuming, and cost-consuming tasks in IP protection. In general, exclusive rights in a mark cannot be protected and the mark cannot be registered as a trademark, if it is descriptive, generic, in conflict with a prior identical or similar mark, or comprised of any forbidden or reserved matters (such as government crests, flags, or slogans). The selection and registration of a trademark are covered in more detail in Chapter 6.

- IDENTIFICATION OF GOODS/SERVICES With the exception of a few countries (such as Canada), a trademark owner must specify the goods or services that will be identified with the trademark. In most countries, trademarks are subject to a classification system for goods and services (although some countries do not recognize trademarks used in connection with services). An international classification system, originally adopted in a Convention at Nice, France, is most commonly employed, but a few countries retain their own national classification systems. The classification system for trademarks is similar in concept to the classifications used for customs and tariff purposes.

  In many countries, the term "service mark" has been adopted to refer to trademarks when applied to services. Still in other countries, the term "trademark" is considered to apply regardless of whether goods or services are being identified, and if a distinction needs to be made, the phrase "trademark for goods" or "trademark for services" is used.

NOTE: To avoid excessive terminology, the author will adopt from here forward the convention of using the term "trademark" to include trade and service marks. Also, and with apologetic recognition to non-US traders, because worldwide usage of "trademark" (one word) and "trade mark" (two words) is inconsistent, the author will adopt the US convention of using the term "trademark" as a single word.

Classification System for Trademarks

Trademarks are usually registered in connection with a specific class of goods or services, which is a means of limiting the monopoly being granted to the trademark owner. Thus, a trademark owner's exclusive right to use the mark is usually limited specifically to the owner's goods or services. In the first half of the 1900s, countries had begun to develop their own national classification systems, resulting in so much complexity and confusion that protection of intellectual property became an indirect barrier to trade.

Accordingly, country representatives met at Nice, France in 1957 to adopt what is today known variously as the Nice Agreement, Nice Convention, or International Classification of Goods and Services. A majority of countries adhere to the International Classification. The Classification is subject to review and amendment periodically. Countries are allowed to alter the International Classification to some extent in order to suit their own local preferences, and therefore you should verify with local counsel to ensure that you have selected the correct class for your trademark registration.

INTERNATIONAL CLASSIFICATION OF GOODS AND SERVICES (NICE)

CLASSES OF GOODS

- CLASS 1 Chemicals used in industry, science and photography, as well as in agriculture, horticulture and forestry; unprocessed artificial resins, unprocessed plastics; manures; fire extinguishing compositions; tempering and soldering preparations; chemical substances for preserving foodstuffs; tanning substances; adhesives used in industry.

- CLASS 2 Paints, varnishes, lacquers; preservatives against rust and against deterioration of wood; colorants; mordants; raw natural resins; metal in foil and powder form for painters, decorators, printers and artists.

- CLASS 3 Bleaching preparations and other substances for laundry use; cleaning, polishing, scouring and abrasive preparations; soaps; perfumery, essential oils, cosmetics, hair lotions; dentifrices.

- CLASS 4 Industrial oils and greases; lubricants; dust absorbing, wetting and binding compositions; fuels (including motor spirit) and illuminants; candles, wicks.

- CLASS 5 Pharmaceutical, veterinary and sanitary preparations; dietetic substances adapted for medical use, food for babies; plasters, materials for dressings, material for stopping teeth, dental wax; disinfectants; preparations for destroying vermin; fungicides, herbicides.

- CLASS 6 Common metals and their alloys; metal building materials; transportable buildings of metal, materials of metal for railway tracks; non-electric cables and wires of common metal; ironmongery, small items of metal hardware; pipes and tubes of metal; safes; goods of common metal not included in other classes; ores.

- CLASS 7 Machines and machine tools; motors and engines (except for land vehicles); machine coupling and transmission components (except for land vehicles); agricultural implements; incubators for eggs.
- CLASS 8 Hand tools and implements (hand operated); cutlery; side arms; razors.
- CLASS 9 Scientific, nautical, surveying, electric, photographic, cinematographic, optical, weighing, measuring, signaling, checking (supervision), life-saving and teaching apparatus and instruments, apparatus for recording, transmission or reproduction of sound or images; magnetic data carriers, recording discs; automatic vending machines and mechanisms for coin-operated apparatus; cash registers, calculating machines, data-processing equipment and computers; fire-extinguishing apparatus.
- CLASS 10 Surgical, medical, dental and veterinary apparatus and instruments, artificial limbs, eyes and teeth; orthopedic articles; suture materials.
- CLASS 11 Apparatus for lighting, heating, steam generating, cooking, refrigeration, drying, ventilating, water supply and sanitary purposes.
- CLASS 12 Vehicles; apparatus for locomotion by land, air or water.
- CLASS 13 Firearms, ammunition and projectiles; explosives; fireworks.
- CLASS 14 Precious metals and their alloys and goods in precious metals or coated therewith, not included in other classes; jewelry, precious stones; horologic and chronometric instruments.
- CLASS 15 Musical instruments.
- CLASS 16 Paper, cardboard and goods made from these materials, not included in other classes; printed matter; bookbinding materials; photographs; stationery; adhesives for stationery or household purposes; artists' materials; paint brushes; typewriters and office requisites (except furniture); instructional and teaching material (except apparatus); plastic materials for packaging (not included in other classes); playing cards; printers' type; printing blocks.
- CLASS 17 Rubber, gutta-percha, gum, asbestos, mica and goods made from these materials and not included in other classes; plastics in extruded form for use in manufacture; packing, stopping and insulating materials; flexible pipes, not of metal.
- CLASS 18 Leather and imitations of leather, and goods made of these materials and not included in other classes; animal skins, hides, trunks and traveling bags; umbrellas, parasols and walking sticks; whips, harnesses and saddlery.
- CLASS 19 Building materials (non-metallic); non-metallic rigid pipes for building; asphalt pitch and bitumen; non-metallic transportable buildings, monuments, not of metal.
- CLASS 20 Furniture, mirrors, picture frames; goods (not included in other classes) of wood, cork, reed, cane, wicker, horn, bone, ivory, whalebone, shell, amber, mother-of-pearl, meerschaum and substitutes for all these materials, or of plastics.
- CLASS 21 Household or kitchen utensils and containers (not of precious metal or coated therewith); combs and sponges; brushes (except paint brushes); brush-making materials; articles for cleaning purposes; steel wool; unworked or semi-

worked glass (except glass used in building); glassware, porcelain and earthenware not included in other classes

- CLASS 22 Ropes, string, nets, tents, awnings, tarpaulins, sails, sacks and bags (not included in other classes); padding and stuffing materials (except of rubber or plastics); raw fibrous textile materials.
- CLASS 23 Yarns and threads, for textile use.
- CLASS 24 Textiles and textile goods, not included in other classes; bed and table covers.
- CLASS 25 Clothing, footwear, headgear.
- CLASS 26 Lace and embroidery, ribbons and braid; buttons, hooks and eyes, pins and needles; artificial flowers.
- CLASS 27 Carpets, rugs, mats and matting, linoleum and other materials for covering existing floors; wall hangings (non-textile).
- CLASS 28 Games and playthings; gymnastic and sporting articles not included in other classes; decorations for Christmas trees.
- CLASS 29 Meat, fish, poultry and game; meat extracts; preserved, dried and cooked fruits and vegetables; jellies, jams, fruit sauces, eggs, milk and milk products; edible oils and fats.
- CLASS 30 Coffee, tea, cocoa, sugar, rice, tapioca, sago, artificial coffee; flour and preparations made from cereals, bread, pastry and confectionery, ices; honey, treacle; yeast, baking-powder; salt, mustard; vinegar, sauces (condiments); spices; ice.
- CLASS 31 Agricultural, horticultural and forestry products and grains not included in other classes; live animals; fresh fruits and vegetables; seeds, natural plants and flowers; foodstuffs for animals, malt.
- CLASS 32 Beers; mineral and aerated waters and other non-alcoholic drinks; fruit drinks and fruit juices; syrups and other preparations for making beverages.
- CLASS 33 Alcoholic beverages (except beers).
- CLASS 34 Tobacco; smokers' articles; matches.

CLASSES OF SERVICES

- CLASS 35 Advertising; business management; business administration; office functions.
- CLASS 36 Insurance; financial affairs; monetary affairs; real estate affairs.
- CLASS 37 Building construction; repair; installation services.
- CLASS 38 Telecommunications.
- CLASS 39 Transport; packaging and storage of goods; travel arrangement.
- CLASS 40 Treatment of materials.
- CLASS 41 Education; providing of training; entertainment; sporting and cultural activities.

- CLASS 42 Providing of food and drink; temporary accommodation; medical; hygienic and beauty care; veterinary and agricultural services; legal services; scientific and industrial research; computer programming; services that cannot be placed in other classes.

COUNTRIES EMPLOYING INTERNATIONAL CLASSIFICATION

Algeria, Argentina, Australia, Austria, Barbados, Belarus, Belgium, Benin, Bolivia, Bosnia and Herzegovina, Brazil, Cambodia, China, Costa Rica, Croatia, Cuba, Czech Republic, Denmark, El Salvador, Estonia, Finland, France (and Overseas Departments and Territories), Germany, Greece, Guatemala, Hungary, Iceland, India, Indonesia, Ireland, Israel, Italy, Japan, Korea (South and North), Kyrgyzstan, Laos, Latvia, Lebanon, Liechtenstein, Lithuania, Luxembourg, Malawi, Mexico, Moldova, Monaco, Morocco, Myanmar (cautionary notice), Netherlands, Nicaragua, Norway, Poland, Philippines, Portugal, Republic of Macedonia, Romania, Russian Federation, Singapore, Slovakia, Slovenia, Spain, Suriname, Sweden, Switzerland, Taiwan, Tajikistan, Thailand, Trinidad and Tobago, Tunisia, Turkey, Ukraine, United Kingdom, United States, Uruguay, Venezuela, Federal Republic of Yugoslavia

COUNTRIES EMPLOYING NATIONAL CLASSIFICATION SYSTEMS

Anguilla, Dominican Republic, Iraq, Somalia

COUNTRIES WITHOUT SERVICE MARK REGISTRATION

Albania, Anguilla, Antigua, Bahamas, Bangladesh, Cyprus, Dominican Republic, Fiji, Gambia, Gaza District, Ghana, Greece, Guinea, India (enacted but not in force at time of publication), Iran, Iraq, Ireland, Jamaica, Jordan, Kenya, Libya, Malawi, Malta, Mauritius, Montserrat, Netherland Antilles, Nigeria, Pakistan, Poland, Rwanda, Saint Kitts and Nevis, Saint Lucia, Seychelles, Sierra Leone, Solomon Islands, Somalia, Suriname, Tanganyika, Tonga, Trinidad & Tobago, Turks & Caicos Islands, Uganda, Western Samoa, Zambia, Zanzibar

Defining Non-Traditional Forms of IP

Intellectual Property today is bursting traditional boundaries in a frenzy of evolution and exploitation. Wherever value is perceived in an intellectual creation, someone is seeking exclusive rights in it. In the absence of protection for those exclusive rights—in effect, without the creation of at least a limited monopoly—intellectual pursuits and endeavors would become public property, which may be fine for dreamers, but is completely without merit for entrepreneurs. How far IP rights may be stretched is limited in two ways: the capacity of the creative human intellect, and the willingness of society, legislators, and courts to recognize the property value in diverse creative endeavors.

The awareness of IP rights is constantly evolving, and IP rights today are expanding to protect trade secrets, trade names, brand names, indigenous knowledge, domain names, website screens, business methodologies, and distinctively marketable tastes, smells, and sounds. Virtually any intellectual pursuit that yields a product of value to the marketplace—that is, to the global marketplace—should be thought of as intellectual property. If your creation is on the cutting edge of recognized rights, be

Chart of IP Rights Protecting Specific Creations

The following chart is a general guide to the categories of creations that are protected by traditional IP rights (patents, copyrights, and trademarks). The parenthetical notations give examples of creations that may fall within each category for purposes of illustration only. It is interesting to note that some creations can be protected by more than one IP right, and dual protection can be particularly advantageous for enforcement purposes. See Chapters 6 and 10 for further discussion.

CREATION	PATENT	COPYRIGHT	TRADEMARK
Artistic Works (drawings, painting, photographs, sculptures, cartoons, etchings, stained glass, pottery)		X	
Audiovisual Works (videotapes, movies, television programs, documentary films)		X	
Commercial Works (advertising slogans and copy; company names; brand names; magazine titles; product and service names)		X	X
Computer Programs	X	X	
Design Inventions (clothing, textile, and carpet designs; shapes, containers, and covers without function for appliances and accessories)	X	X	
Graphic Works (architectural, engineering plans; flowcharts; designs for goods such as clothes, jewelry, rugs, hardware, wallpaper; cartoons)		X	
Literary Works (books, articles, indexes, factual reference guides, newsletters, dramatic performances, poems, translations)		X	
Musical Works (sound recordings, music scores)		X	
Performance Works (stage, television, movie, radio performances)		X	
Plant Inventions (new rose hybrids, improved vegetable and fruit hybrids)	X		
Utility Inventions (biological envisions, computer hardware, chemical formulas and processes, medicines, medical devices, tools, machines, sports equipment, electronic circuits)	X		

patient. Society and the law will catch up with you, and probably sooner than later as the international trend is toward the liberalization of IP rights.

The following are definitions and descriptions of non-traditional forms of IP:

- TRADE NAMES The distinctive name used by a business owner to identify a business entity and to distinguish it from the companies of other business owners. A business owner can claim rights in a trade name only if the name is regularly and consistently used when doing business, although it does not have to be used in direct connection with the owner's products or services. For example, a company that sells perfumes under the trademark POIVRE may imprint its packaging with the additional information that it imports products as the Asian Green Tiger Trading Company. The company name is a trade name, not a trademark, because the company is using it to identify its business but not its goods.
- TRADE SECRETS Creative works and compilations of information that give the creator or compiler a competitive advantage over other traders who cannot develop the same information without great difficulty (or a clandestine theft) are trade secrets, but only so long as steps are taken to maintain confidentiality and to prevent public disclosure. This term is extremely broad, covering for example:

- customer and mailing lists
- information about customer characteristics
- information about prospective business opportunities
- sensitive marketing manuals and materials
- price and fee schedules
- supply sources
- business records, systems, and practices
- information on the effectiveness of personnel
- technical know-how such as formulas, recipes, magic tricks, and even ideas such as a conceptual plot for an as yet unwritten novel or movie.

If information could be easily compiled independently, it will not usually qualify for treatment as a trade secret. For example, a manual explaining employee policies required by labor laws is not a trade secret. Likewise, a manual on compliance with statutory shipping requirements would not be a trade secret.

The important feature of trade secrets is that their value is dependent on nondisclosure. The holder of a trade secret has a potential to gain greater market share and to earn higher profits than the trader next door. Accordingly, contracts forbidding employees to disclose the trade secrets of a company have become part of the new-hire routine in today's business world.

- BRAND NAMES The name that you have given to your product or service is a brand name. In practice, the terms "brand name" and "trademark" are used interchangeably, and indeed, a brand name may be or may become a trademark or service mark. However, the term "brand name" encompasses more than the rights represented by a trademark.

In a broad sense, the term "brand" refers to any mark intended to signify some kind of connection between the item branded and the person doing the branding. Thus, a steer is marked with a brand by a ranch hand, and a diverse line of products, each with their own trademark, can also display a store brand to indicate the origin of manufacture. That brand may or may not be registered as a trademark. All cars made by Ford will carry the FORD brand (which is also a trademark), but each car will also display a distinct trademark, such as MUSTANG, TAURUS, or MERCURY. Products sold in grocery stores as generic brand products display no trademark, but merely have distinctive packaging with a name that is directly descriptive of the product.

- TRADE DRESS A form of IP that is rarely protected by statute but often protected by court law is "trade dress." This IP right encompasses the "look" of your product, namely, the color, shape, and type of packaging or sales presentation. Infringement by imitation of trade dress is a fairly common problem. For example, you might sell a frozen food under the trademark "MRS. CHIPS" spelled in a cursive dark green arch set against a tan background across the top of the packaging with a very delicious looking photograph of the heated dish beneath the arch surrounded by three concentric circles of green, tan, and green. Company VEGY chooses the exact same colors, the same cursive lettering, the same arch and concentric circles enclosing an enticing photograph of their own frozen entrée, but they use the trademark "MRS. VEGYS". Arguably, you would have a claim of infringement because the trade dress is so similar to your own product as to cause confusion in the marketplace. However, trade dress infringement claims can only be brought in jurisdictions where trade dress rights are recognized.

- DESIGNS A "design" refers to a shape, configuration, pattern, or ornament that is applied to an article by any industrial process or means and that is a feature that appeals to or is judged solely by the eye. It is not a method or principal of construction, nor is it a feature that depends on the function of the product.

  In the past, designs have primarily been protected by copyright. However, a design does not necessarily fit within the definition of works that are subject to copyright. For this reason, a growing number of countries have enacted laws that deal particularly with the protection of designs.

- DOMAIN NAMES The awesome magnitude of the Internet is giving rise to a new IP genre: domain names. These names are simply the little word that you create to identify your own, unique website address. In just a few short years, an entire industry has grown up around domain names. Seminars, lobbyists, international trade sessions, television and magazine exposes, legislative committees, private and public enterprises are all trying to explain, understand and organize the tremendous number of issues that have arisen with the advent of the domain name: how to register and regulate use, who has the right to register, who has the right to enforce prior IP rights, and how to protect against infringement. The laws have not kept up with the technology, and the technology is having a difficult time keeping up with the sheer number of domain name registrants. Public awareness and respect for IP rights is being put to the test in the domain name arena.

- APPELLATIONS OF ORIGIN Some confusion exists internationally with regard to whether appellations of origin are in fact intellectual property rights, and therefore they are treated here briefly. An appellation of origin is a name of a geographical place that is used in connection with a product or service sold in commerce to indicate the place from where that product or service originates. Thus, appellations of origin are not "intellectual property" in the sense that they are not derived from intellectual pursuit and commercialization of novel and unique creations. In fact, the intellectual property laws of most countries prohibit the registration of geographical place names as trademarks and service marks because of the tendency to deceive or confuse the public into thinking that the goods or services originate from that locale. Furthermore, there are separate registries for appellations of origin. Conflicts can arise among parties who are using registered marks that are similar to registered appellations of origin.

- INDIGENOUS KNOWLEDGE One of the most recent IP rights to be recognized is affecting the way in which we view the property claims of various cultures to their arts and practices. Indigenous people, supported by their countries and business communities, are seeking recognition and protection as IP rights their cultural arts, medical practices and procedures, and various other types of indigenous knowledge. Although not yet encompassed specifically within the IP laws of most nations, there is a trend on the international level to recognize these rights and to provide specific protection.

CHAPTER 2

The Role and Value of IP in International Commerce

THE RECOGNITION OF INTELLECTUAL PROPERTY RIGHTS is an important key to converting creativity into a marketable product with positive cash flow. Creativity is essential to economic growth. Consumer sales depend on attractive, efficient, safe, innovative, and dependable products and services, and these qualities are built on intellectual property. The IP rights of a business are among its most valuable assets. The protection of those IP rights can promote creativity, distinguish a business and its products or services, and increase its profitability and endurance.

Understanding the Significance of IP Rights

GIVING IP RIGHTS A PRACTICAL CONTEXT

To understand the role of IP rights in practical terms, you must first appreciate the purpose of IP laws. Although IP laws will differ in detail from country to country, they have the same basic purpose, which is also reflected in international and regional agreements. In broad terms, exclusive rights in intellectual property are usually granted pursuant to laws that are intended to do the following:

- Define the monopolistic rights, namely, exclusive ownership rights that belong to the holder of the IP and are transferable to another holder in certain situations.
- Define the limitations on the monopoly, such as by restricting the application of exclusive rights to an invention, presentation, or specific goods only, by making exceptions to exclusive use for permitted acts (e.g., authorizing single copies for educational purposes), and by setting terms of duration.
- Define the remedies for violation of IP rights.

In other words, IP laws create affirmative rights, but not an absolute defensive shield against infringement. They give the owner of the IP the right to stop other persons from using the IP in a manner that is not permitted by the law. Unless the IP owner takes affirmative action, an infringement of IP rights may continue unchecked by any other authority. This concept is extremely significant: mere registration of IP rights is not alone sufficient to protect those rights against unauthorized use. If you are going to spend the money and labor to register your IP claim, you must be also willing to spend the money and labor to enforce your claim.

To manage your IP rights in international commerce most effectively in terms of cost and labor, you must keep in mind the rationale underlying IP laws. At a fundamental level, your claim to IP rights is adverse to the public interest in free information. While IP rights may encourage innovation and creativity, they can also limit it by removing from public use creations that could otherwise lead to more creations. For this reason, monopolistic rights in IP are limited and must be affirmatively asserted.

In the face of such a strong public interest, you should assess your claims to IP and seek enforcement where the costs balance against the importance of keeping your IP out of the public domain. For example, you may find that your advertising and distribution channels are so cheap that you have sufficient return on your products or services without needing to sue every small infringer in order to collect every potential royalty. On the other hand, if your IP could become public domain property such that its value to you is largely lost, you might decide to fight for it. You should also keep registration and enforcement in mind when you first create your IP, because acquiring and maintaining your monopoly will be much more expensive and time-consuming if your IP may already be in use, even in part, by the public at large. These concepts will be revisited in more detail in later chapters.

WHAT CAN IP RIGHTS DO FOR YOU?

Your IP can be one of your most useful and most used business tools. If you own patents, copyrights, designs, or similar IP, you will realize value from utilizing them in your own exclusive manufacture or production. If you own marks, you will use them to distinguish your business and your products or services, to grow its customer base, and to promote its goodwill and reputation. If you own trade secrets, specialized mailing lists, secret recipes or processes, and similar IP, your business can provide distinctively unique services in contrast to your competition. In all instances, you may also realize substantial value from licensing or transferring ownership of your IP rights.

In the international context, you will realize value from your IP rights in the same fashion as on a local level, but now your markets have expanded and your potential revenue is far greater. Thus, a larger population of consumers will buy from you or will pay your royalties. Instead of a few licenses within a single country, you may license your IP rights to persons in various countries. A change in language between countries may mean that you can license translation rights.

When you take your IP international, you also gain another advantage that is not present if your business is local only. Your IP becomes famous. Your book—and your name as author—becomes world-renowned. Your mark is known in the farthest reaches of the planet and makes the top 100 well known brands list. Your painting or movie or patented process makes it onto satellite news, and you are invited to show it, license it, talk about it, and promote it. The value of your IP grows exponentially, and your IP becomes one of the most valuable assets of your business. It can even carry your business onto a public stock exchange.

EXAMPLE: In the mid 1990s, demand in Hong Kong for locally produced television news and entertainment shows was very high. The original programming produced by the local company, TVB, was so successful that it began exporting. In 1995, its revenue from licensing and distribution was more than HK$320 million. As of the year 2007, Hong Kong's film industry ranks third in the world in terms of value of annual exports, just behind Hollywood and Bollywood.

WELL KNOWN IP COMMANDS CONSUMER LOYALTY

Well known IP has clout with the consumer, and the clout gained is reflected in the value of the IP. Intellectual property is well known when it becomes so recognized by the public at large that it attracts a large number of consumers, gains repeat consumers, and continues to grow in consumer acceptance. Consumers most frequently purchase goods and services based on recognition of the brand. They will line up sometimes for days to buy tickets to the latest movie in a famous series. Millions of dollars are collected in pre-release sales of books written by the most popular authors.

To a consumer, well known IP means the following:

- High quality product, service, book, movie, design, or other item with which the IP rights are associated.
- Responsiveness of the company holding the IP rights to the consumer, whether by means of customer service, product replacement, expense refunds, product modification, or otherwise.
- Dependability of the company to stay in business and to continue producing IP of high quality or associated with products or services of high quality.
- Premium pricing: "you pay for what you get" is a typical American phrase meaning if you want top quality, you must pay the premium for the well known IP or items sold in connection with the well known IP.

To the trader, well known IP could mean a substantial market share. It could also mean repeat business and steady growth in market share. Once IP becomes so well-known as to enter the upper echelons of the world's top ranked IP in terms of consumer recognition, it is likely to stay there. For example, among the top marks existing in the North American market in 1925, the following are still with us today: EVEREADY, KELLOG, IVORY SOAP, GOODYEAR, DEL MONTE, CRISCO, BUDWEISER, KODAK, LIPTON, WRIGLEY'S, SHERWIN-WILLIAMS, COCA-COLA.

To the owner, well known IP offers yet another commercial promise: it can be licensed or sold for a substantial sum. Corporations often merge in order to acquire a well-established mark or the patent technology of another company. The cost of launching a new product or developing a new invention can sometimes be so costly that licensing or merging with another company is less expensive. When selling a business, the valuation of assets should always include the value of all IP rights held by the business.

HOW VALUABLE CAN IP RIGHTS BECOME?

There are no limits on how valuable IP rights may become. The value of your IP could double your company's value. Your IP may become the most valuable asset in your business. You business may even be or become the exploitation of your IP rights through licensing or other similar arrangements.

For example, copyrights generate lucrative license fees and royalties. Publishers, authors, music makers, record companies, entertainers, sports figures, television and movie studios make millions from IP protected by copyrights. A famous person can command millions for an appearance, and can sue for millions for unauthorized use of his or her famous name or likeness.

Companies holding patents can gain substantial market share while other companies are trying to find another way to replicate the same result. Small inventors and large companies alike often license patented technologies for substantial fees. It has been reported by the *Asian Wall Street Journal* that an inventor who has filed more than 500 patents in the United States in the last 35 years has made more than US$500 million without directly engaging in any industrial application of the invention.

Intellectual property rights can become worth more than the physical assets of a company. For example, the IP produced and acquired by Microsoft Corporation is valued at more than the company's physical assets, and the company itself has been valued at more than the value of General Motors Corporation, despite the latter's significant physical assets. Similarly, the Internet company Yahoo, Inc., has been valued at more than the value of New York Times, Inc., based on the IP rights developed and acquired by the former.

As further examples, take a few famous trademarks:

ESTIMATED VALUATION OF TRADEMARKS	
MARK	VALUED AT
MARLBORO	More than US$40 billion
COCA COLA	More than US$33 billion
INTEL	More than US$18 billion
KELLOGG	More than US$10 billion
NESCAFE	More than US$9.2 billion
BACARDI RUM	More than US$5.5 billion
NIKE	More than US$3.5 billion
TROPICANA	More than US$1 billion

The acquisition of IP rights, whether through merger or other arrangements, can run into the billions. Thus, Phillip Morris gained control of a family of famous consumer brand names when it purchased Kraft, Inc. for US$13 billion. In the US$25 billion take-over of Nabisco, 80 percent of the acquisition price was attributable to the purchase of trademarks and other intangible assets.

The value of IP can even be a significant marketable resource for a country, and this value is what has spurred indigenous populations throughout the world to begin lobbying for international recognition of IP rights in traditional knowledge. In countries where an extremely high percentage of the population is living in poverty, IP rights over such properties as medicinal innovations and culturally distinctive art, music, dramas, and stories of the people can raise significant funds through licensing and sales of those rights. The value placed on these rights is tremendous, so much so that representatives of developing countries have been sent regularly to international conferences and forums to seek recognition of this form of IP.

IS THERE STILL ROOM AT THE TOP?

Consumer demand for the new and original plus market dynamics leave plenty of room among the famous for your IP to rise to the top. An excellent illustration of the power of IP can be observed in the general popularity of "store brands." The popularity of generic and store brands has been rising for decades. Generic products appear on shelves and racks in many retail outlets throughout the United States. These brands are sold with descriptive names and minimally attractive packaging. Consumer response has been favorable, particularly for products where the price differential is substantial and the product quality is comparable or less important. As a result, generic brands have taken on a significant share of the market.

In view of the popularity of generic brands, many stores today carry products labeled with the store's own mark. Private store labels are popular with consumers, offering them an alternative to the famous brands. For example, private store labels hold nearly 20 percent of the supermarket sales volume in the United States. Similarly, private store labels in the clothing industry have gained significant footholds as against designer labels.

Even if your business is not making billions in profits, your IP rights add substantial value to your business. Whether you have developed a catchy name and own only one retail outlet or service center, whether you have painted a few canvases in your atelier, or whether you are a yet to be discovered author, your IP rights have commercial value when you exploit them in the market.

- Your customers are attracted to your name and continue to return to you because your name represents the quality of products and services your provide, and as a result your goodwill and reputation is likely to spread.
- Sophisticated art collectors or corporate clientele may seek your canvases after seeing one or two media clips.
- You can command at least same price for the outright sale of your copyrighted manuscript, or perhaps a royalty back on transfer of the copyright. If your book becomes the basis for the next hit on Broadway or makes the top ten on the Best Seller List, the copyright on your next book will have gained substantial value.
- You can sell your patented invention instead of licensing it.

Valuing IP Rights

ROLES IN VALUING IP RIGHTS

The value of your company's IP rights is a substantial asset for your company. Each IP right should be valued periodically by a knowledgeable appraiser or accountant. The value of each IP right belongs in your balance sheet.

Although valuation is best left to professionals, you should be aware of the typical valuation methods and the special factors that make IP valuation different from appraisals of tangible property. You know your business and your industry, whereas your appraiser or accountant may be unaware of some of the complexities that are likely to affect the value of your IP rights. You will need to provide your appraiser or accountant with information about your business and industry in order to obtain as accurate an assessment as possible.

In addition to knowing the factors that complicate the value of your IP rights, you hold the key to identifying other intangible assets, which may be taken into account in combination with your IP rights or as separate assets. Before obtaining a valuation, you should identify all assets that add value to your business by contributing to its financial success. Remember to include any of the following:

- Intellectual property, namely patents, trademarks, trade secrets, trade dress, company and domain names, and all other forms of such property.
- The workforce that has been assembled and trained.
- Business, management, compliance, and accounting policies and procedures.
- Marketing and sales campaigns.

METHODS OF VALUING IP RIGHTS

Experts in valuation have developed formulas to assess the value of tangible and intangible property. The methods of valuation applied typically differ depending on whether the valuation is being made for purposes of selling the property, obtaining a secured loan, fixing estate value, declaring taxable or dutiable revenues, or some other purpose.

- **MARKET VALUE** One of the most common methods for valuing tangible property is based on market value, namely the price that a person would pay under prevailing market conditions, such as supply and demand. Often the value of a tangible asset can be determined by comparison to another recent arm's length transaction for the same or a similar asset.
- **COMPARABLE MARKET VALUE** Comparable market value can also be applied when valuing intangible property, and therefore you should first consider whether you have any evidence of market value in relation to your IP rights. For example, you may have a previous or existing license agreement for similar rights, or you may have sold similar IP rights recently. These transactions can suggest the market value of your existing IP rights, provided you make adjustments to account for distinguishing factors such as geographical or other limits on the previous license and rising popularity of your IP rights.
- **ALTERNATIVE VALUATIONS** Unfortunately, different methods of valuation must often be employed to value intangible property because comparable market data is frequently not available. Even if it is, the uniqueness of this type of property makes comparable assessment difficult and inaccurate. Therefore, valuation experts often use alternative methods, depending on the circumstances presented.

Various alternative methods are available, and the choice of method is usually best left to the experts. These may include the valuation of IP rights:

- By considering the market value for a monopoly (assuming the IP rights in fact extract higher prices than your competitors),
- By identifying IP rights with revenue from particular products or services and totaling the incremental values (assuming the IP can be specifically associated with certain products or services), or
- By determining your company's value based on its current stock price, subtracting

the value of its tangible assets, and applying a formula to the residual value to allocate a portion to the IP rights (assuming your company is listed on a stock exchange).

Unfortunately, all of these methods are somewhat unsatisfactory, and usually factors have to be added to the calculations to account for special circumstances existing in your industry, trade, or business. You will need to work closely with your accountant and appraiser to reach a figure that estimates the worth of your IP rights. The figure you eventually arrive at should be adjusted periodically to account for changes in the value of your IP, as your business and market expands or contracts.

CHAPTER 3

Issues Affecting IP Rights Internationally

Cultural Issues

CULTURAL ACCEPTANCE

It is important to recognize and respect the culture of other people when you develop your IP rights. Cultural differences will affect whether your IP will be accepted, will gain in value, and will bring an increase in market share. The mark that you introduce in connection with your goods or services, the book, art, or music that you choose to create, or the invention that you decide to develop must have attraction to the culture where you intend to market it. Otherwise, your IP rights will have little or no commercial value.

Culture determines what is acceptable in daily life, work, health care, and recreation. You must be aware and sensitive to other cultures so that you can adapt your IP to their preferences and succeed in foreign markets. If you are not planning to adapt your IP to differences in culture, your cultural awareness is still important for purposes of identifying the markets where you will succeed and those where your IP will not gain a share.

In identifying cultural preferences, always remember that culture applies to people, not nations. In today's fast moving world, it is nearly impossible to identify a single culture for a particular country. Many subcultures are likely to exist within a country because the rate of cross-border travel is on the rise, populations are mobile, and people in all corners of the globe are discovering how other people live through the ever-expanding web of mass media. Do not cling to preconceived notions of culture, but rather learn to recognize and accept the differences within the peoples of one nation.

Cultural awareness is important when you first begin to develop your creation, since acceptance in the marketplace is what gives your IP commercial value. If you choose to create artwork that will not be acceptable because of content or color in some cultures, you have limited your market. If you develop a vaccine based on Western medicine, it may be less acceptable in countries where herbal remedies are preferred. If your trademark has a negative meaning in some cultures, your products or services will not gain a market share.

CULTURAL RECOGNITION

Once you have developed your creation, cultural awareness will next come into play when you decide how to commercialize your creation and where to protect and enforce your IP rights. At this point, cultural recognition of IP rights becomes as important as cultural preferences. While you must continue to pay attention to cultural preferences in marketing your creation, you must also be acutely aware of whether the people in those markets accept and respect the private ownership of IP rights.

Cultural recognition of ownership rights in IP will affect your decisions on how to protect your IP rights and how much cost will be involved in enforcement. In countries where IP laws are just developing, the concept of IP is new and enforcement of your own rights against infringement could be difficult and expensive. In countries where IP laws are well developed but commercialization and capitalism are also extremely strong, you may also have to spend substantial funds protecting your IP from piracy. As an IP owner, part of your responsibility may be to educate your potential buyers and clients on the importance of respecting IP rights. You may also need to develop cost-effective strategies to prevent or at least minimize infringement of your IP rights, as will be discussed in a subsequent chapter.

Trends toward Globalization and Uniformity

National differences in the treatment of IP rights are indirect barriers to trade. For this reason, many nations of the world have banded together to try to harmonize their treatment of IP rights. Many of the international and regional trade treaties—General Agreement on Tariffs and Trade (GATT), European Union (EU), North American Free Trade Agreement (NAFTA)—include provisions requiring member countries to harmonize the registration and protection of IP rights. In addition, landmark conventions of national representatives have resulted in IP-specific treaties, such as the Nice Convention (establishing the International Classification of Goods and Services), the Berne Convention (protecting copyrights), the Paris Convention (protecting marks), the Madrid Convention (protecting marks and appellations of origin), and the Patent Cooperation Treaty (PCT). Refer to the glossary for more information on these treaties.

As you enter the global marketplace, you will find a changing IP scene. Although some countries have not yet eliminated barriers to IP protection, most countries have come to recognize the importance of IP rights to the growth of their economies. The existence of mechanisms for protecting IP rights can be a primary factor in attracting foreign investment. To be most attractive, those mechanisms must also be effective and in harmony with international practices.

In addition, many countries are now recognizing the value of IP rights to their own populations. Accordingly, they have instituted educational campaigns among the people in addition to strict enforcement measures to raise awareness of IP rights not only of foreign companies but also of nationals. Thus, more and more of the world's consumers would rather have "the real thing" than a "knock-off" infringement, and more and more of the world's businesses are learning the value of licensing and selling their IP rights.

As trade barriers continue to fall and awareness of the value in IP rights continues to rise, the trend toward global harmonization of IP laws and regulations is likely to continue. A primary factor in this trend is that IP rights themselves tend to be a barrier to free trade, depending on one's point of view. There are some who argue that if a person is allowed to claim and enforce IP rights, trade is stifled by a monopoly. The contrary argument is that without IP protection, creativity would be stifled for lack of commercial gain, which will in turn hurt an economy. Regardless of which side you may take, the concept confronting our global leaders is to achieve harmonization of IP laws and regulations in such a way as to have the effect of facilitating cross-border trade and maintaining respect for IP rights.

The trend toward globalization of IP rights is being pushed forward by two factors: private business and the information age. These factors are in conflict with each other, and the need for a solution is growing exponentially. Private business seeks to retain its monopolistic hold over IP rights, while free exchange of information—particular on the Internet—is a rising demand among consumers. As a result, enforcement of IP rights by existing legal measures is becoming more difficult and more expensive. Likewise, the difficulty and expense of educating consumers to respect IP rights is increasing because the ability to exchange and pass on information has become so easy. A new approach is needed soon on a worldwide basis.

Role of Politics

When you are considering where to go in the global marketplace, an important factor to look at is the political climate of a country. Political events will inevitably affect the markets and economy of a country. No one wants to sell to an unstable market, while profits can be reaped in a country with a stable government and populace. Poverty tends to create political turmoil within a country, while a strong and expanding economy tends to have a calming effect. Government regulation of private business, whether minimal or invasive, is most likely a permanent feature because political and economic stability are tightly tied together.

Political influence over international trade is in part exercised through direct and indirect trade barriers imposed by countries to regulate cross-border and domestic trade and competition. With respect to IP rights, the political climate of a country has particular significance because IP treatment can be an indirect trade barrier. Thus, if IP protection is unavailable or too difficult to obtain, foreign companies will be less interested in cross-border transactions and local nationals will be unable to protect their rights within their own country, thereby adversely affecting trade. Furthermore, a country without sufficient trademark protection often gains a reputation for harboring infringers, and once gained, such a reputation will require a substantial public relations effort to reverse it.

TIP: You should keep aware of changing political situations and the developing IP rights in many countries. You could lose your IP rights to someone else who registers or uses the mark first in a particular country. If protection is available, even through a published notice, you should apply.

Regulatory Laws

You are responsible for knowing the laws in the country where you do business, even as those laws are changing. If a law for protection of IP rights exists but you have not followed it, you can lose your rights to another party who has complied. Lack of knowledge is not a defense in an action for infringement, a suit for unfair competition, or a criminal seizure and counterfeit proceeding. You must know the import and export restrictions, the marking requirements for goods or services, and the laws related to publication and public domain. An attorney who is well versed in international IP law can offer valuable advice and assistance in creating a strategy for global IP protection. The attorney can also inform you about the effect of newly enacted laws, modified regulations, and impending legislation.

Internet Issues

The Internet has evolved into a tremendous marketing and sales tool, allowing consumers and companies to transact business near and far without having to establish branch offices or stores, hire personal sales agents, or otherwise incur overhead expenses of keeping local contacts. In the IP context, however, the Internet is considered public domain. If you put material on the Internet, be certain to protect it first, to monitor usage, and to secure usage on the Internet against unauthorized copies.

The Internet has made information transfer so easy that holders of IP rights are now lobbying for controls against a growing number of infringements. The difficulty is twofold. First, companies are unable to monitor and enforce effectively their IP rights on a system that is exceedingly large and increasing daily. Second, the public often fails to understand and respect the IP rights of others when access to information exchange is so effortless.

Several international task forces are at work on proposals to protect IP rights on the Internet. A number of countries, including the US, have taken the lead in enacting at least provisional legislation to handle infringement claims. Courts in national and international forums have begun deciding cases generally in favor of enforcement. The registries for domain names have also developed complaint and cancellation procedures if a legitimate claim is made.

CHAPTER 4

Parties to IP Rights, Part I: Owner, Consumer, Authorized User, Licensee, Attorney

COMMERCIAL TRANSACTIONS INVOLVING IP RIGHTS occur between the owner of the rights (who may be, but is not necessarily, the creator or inventor) and another party. The identity of the other party depends on the type of transaction. The owner may sell copies of the IP created to other traders in the industry or the public at large, all of whom are considered consumers of the IP. The owner may also sell, exchange, license, or otherwise transfer the IP rights themselves to another party. If the owner transfers the ownership rights in the IP entirely, there is a new owner. The transfer transaction is usually in the form of an assignment, and the former owner is called an assignor while the new owner is an assignee. If the owner transfers rights to use the IP only, the arrangement is referred to as a license, and the owner is then a licensor while the other party is a licensee or authorized user. When IP rights are transferred in part or in whole, the parties to the transaction should seek legal advice, particularly if the transaction is cross-border.

Owner/Creator

THE OWNER AS CREATOR

A creator generates IP, whether in the form of material that can be patented, copyrighted, trademarked, or simply protected as trade dress, trade secrets, or otherwise. The creator may be, for example, an inventor, artist, author, playwright, songwriter, musician, performer, sports figure, or movie producer. In any event, as a creator you are at the beginning of the chain of IP rights. Without your creation, no IP rights would exist. Unless and until you give away your rights, you own them.

Two or more parties who have contributed to a creation and its form of expression are co-creators, and they can obtain joint ownership. Joint ownership usually results in each party holding an equal share, unless the parties have agreed by contract otherwise. In the absence of contractual provisions, each coauthor may use the IP without the permission of the others, but each must also account to all of the other owners and must equally share the profits derived from the IP.

THE OWNER AS EMPLOYER OF THE CREATOR

If you are employed for purposes of generating IP for the use of an employer, you usually give up all ownership rights in the IP to the employer. Similarly, if you are employed as a freelance or independent contractor, the employer commonly owns the rights to the IP created. An exception may be made by your contract with your employer to allow you to hold the IP rights solely or jointly with the employer, but this situation is rare because creators do not usually wield sufficient weight at the bargaining table to gain the IP rights.

While you may give up IP rights when working under an employment or freelance contract, such an arrangement ensures you of a source of income. However, the income received is typically not commensurate with the value of the IP produced, again usually because you have minimal bargaining power. On the other hand, the employer, not you, is responsible for the overhead expenses incurred during the creation process and the costs of marketing and maintenance. The employer also takes on the risks of ownership, such as responsibility for defective products and for production of materials that are not commercially viable. Even a freelance creator, as opposed to an employee, can pass some of these expenses and risks to the employer.

THE OWNER AS ASSIGNEE

You can acquire IP rights from another owner, in which case you become the new owner of the IP. Acquisition of IP rights means that all of the rights in the IP are transferred to you, including title and ownership rights, exclusive use rights, and the right to license or transfer the IP to other persons. You hold the right to make copies and to prevent others from infringing on your IP rights. The transaction is usually called an assignment, and the former owner is the assignor while you as new owner are the assignee.

The acquisition of IP rights has become a significant factor in the selection of business partners in today's world. Company mergers and acquisitions include valuable IP rights, and often the choice of business partners hinges at least in part on the value of the IP rights held by each company. The right choice can combine the strengths of two companies built on well-known IP rights, resulting in one company expanding into the pre-made market of the other, or even taking over that market and eventually closing down a competitor.

THE GOALS OF THE OWNER

As an owner of IP rights, your first goal is to secure exclusive rights in the IP—that is, to ensure that you alone have the right to use, copy, transform, transfer, license, or otherwise determine how that IP will be exploited. To achieve this goal, you will need to do two things. First, you must ensure that your IP is unique and distinct from the IP of others. Second, you must consistently protect your IP from infringement by others and from becoming generally used by the public. In other words, you must select IP that can be protected and then you must protect the IP that you have selected. These concepts are discussed in further detail in the next chapters.

A second goal of the IP owner is to create or acquire commercially viable IP. Creation for creation's sake is a laudable ideal, but it will not generate income unless and until you can sell it to a consumer. To attain this second goal, you must have an understanding of the market for the creation, as well as some sense of business ownership and risk. An IP owner should always be seeking the best price for the original creation or the top market price for copies of the creation, while at the same time keeping the production costs for it to a minimum.

Similar goals apply regardless of whether the owner is also the creator of the IP. The owner will want to have unique, marketable IP. For example, if you are an employer, you will want your employees to develop work-for-hire IP that is novel, unique, and valuable within the marketplace. If the IP has no commercial application, you are likely to demand a change in the creation or even to replace your employees with other creators. As an employee, your goal is to keep your employer happy by providing cost-efficient development and an end result that commands a competitive price.

THE HIDDEN COSTS OF IP DEVELOPMENT

When deciding the value and cost of IP, you must remember to account for the hidden expenses of creating and maintaining it. What did the IP actually cost during development? What is the actual cost of copying and maintaining it? Will you be able to recover the entire cost plus make a profit, or are you creating IP just for the fun of it or for its social value? Your hidden expenses might include a few of the following items:

- RESEARCH AND DEVELOPMENT COSTS When developing a creation, you may have to do substantial research, which may require for example travel, interviews, translations, library or laboratory access fees, and reproduction costs. You may spend days staring at the walls to allow your subconscious freedom to ramble. It might be wise to conduct or study market surveys to learn consumer reactions, and you may decide to test the market for receptivity to your presentation or invention. These are all hidden costs of R&D, and they can be substantial.
- PRESENTATION COSTS Your creation will not be commercially valuable unless you can sell it. To sell your creation, you will have to present it to a prospective client or to your employer. The form and content of your presentation can be a deciding factor in whether your creation is accepted or whether you are told to go back to the drawing board. For this reason, you should plan your presentation carefully for your audience. This may require taking time to research the background of the person or company you are approaching and putting together a technologically appealing portfolio. The time and cost you spend on your presentation may gain you a sale, but is an expense as well.
- PRODUCTION COSTS This includes the materials, the labor, the site, the machinery, and all of the various factors that go into producing your creation and copies of your creation for sale. Even if you build a prototype only and then sell or license your creation to another person who takes on the production costs, you will have some production costs. If your creation is one of a kind and copies will not be made, you must still consider your own production costs. Production may also include installation of your completed creation.
- GOVERNMENT COMPLIANCE COSTS The development, presentation, production, and installation of your creation may be subject to regulation by the government. You may be working with hazardous materials, you may need a special permit to install your work at the intended location, or you may have to meet certain consumer or regulatory standards. Once your work has been created, the government will assist in protection of your rights, provided you have

complied with registration requirements. The compliance costs will vary from country to country, but you will encounter them in most every country.

- MARKETING, DISTRIBUTION, TRANSPORT, AND INSURANCE COSTS If you are reproducing your own creation for sale in your own country or worldwide, you will incur the typical costs that any business owner faces when marketing, distributing, and transporting goods or services. These expenses may include the costs of transport, customs clearance, government value added taxes, transport permits, insurance against damage or loss, temporary storage costs, and expenses that arise because of a delay in delivery. You are also likely to have to advertise, market, entertain prospective customers or clients, and otherwise promote your creation to the industry or the public.

Consumer

THE CONSUMER AS A PURCHASER

A consumer acquires or observes a creation or a copy of a creation protected by IP rights, usually in exchange for compensation to the owner of the IP rights. The consumer may be in the middle of the consuming chain, in which event the consumer resells or otherwise transfers the creation or copy to other consumers. Alternatively, the consumer may be at the ultimate end of the chain, using or observing the creation or copy without transferring it to other consumers. For example, a museum that purchases paintings would be a consumer in the middle of the chain, while the public that visits the museum to view the paintings would be at the end of the chain. The people in the audience at a musical show are end-consumers, but a retail bookseller is in the middle of the chain and sells books to consumers at the end of the chain.

THE PURCHASE OF A COPY

The sale of a work that is protected by IP is not the same as the sale of the IP rights. This concept is extremely important to understand because it is one of the basic tenets of IP law: there is a distinct separation between ownership of the IP rights and ownership of the physical IP itself. This concept affects the rights of a consumer in two ways.

First, the owner of the IP rights continues to own exclusive rights to use the IP. Mere sale of a work does not include the transfer of the IP rights unless the owner expressly contracts with the buyer for a sale or other transfer of the IP rights. This means that a consumer of a creation is not allowed to reproduce and distribute the creation or to otherwise exercise any of the rights of the owner of the IP rights without permission.

Second, the owner of IP rights does not retain ownership control over copies of the work sold. If IP is copied and sold, the owner of the IP rights relinquishes all control over that physical copy. The consumer is free to resell, rent, lend, or otherwise transfer that specific copy to the public at large, although the consumer must not reproduce and distribute additional copies. For this reason, many companies, and in particular software companies, demand that consumers enter into a license with the company rather than a purchase agreement because the owner of the IP rights then retains ownership of the physical copy of the IP as well as the IP rights. In such event, the consumer is required to return the IP to the owner when use is discontinued or the license is otherwise terminated.

Authorized User/Licensee

THE ROLE OF AN IP LICENSEE

A license is a contract made between two parties: the licensor (owner of IP rights) and licensee (user of the IP). In a license, the licensor transfers some but not all of the IP rights to the licensee. A licensee of IP is typically authorized to use the IP within the terms of the license contract. In other words, the licensee does not own all rights in the IP but may exercise only those rights permitted by the license contract. For example, the licensee may be entitled to exclusive or nonexclusive use of the IP within a certain territory, for a specified period of time, or in respect of certain types of manufactured products. The licensee is usually entitled to protect the IP against infringement by third parties if the licensor fails to act against violators.

The licensee will typically have certain obligations under the license contract that are intended to protect the IP ownership rights of the licensor. These obligations may include quality control provisions, by which the licensee warrants that all copies of the IP will meet the standards of quality established by the licensor. The licensee will be prohibited from interfering with the ownership rights of the licensor, including the right to register as owner of the IP. The licensee will also be required to compensate the licensor for the use of the IP, to account for all sales, and to sell copies of the IP only with the knowledge and approval of the licensor.

THE ROLE OF AN IP LICENSOR

The licensor of IP rights retains ownership rights, and the licensor's good will and reputation is closely tied to the use of the IP rights. Therefore, the licensor should personally continue to secure those rights against infringement and unauthorized or substandard use. If the value of the IP rights is to be maintained, exclusivity and quality of use must be enforced.

Accordingly, the licensor should never allow the licensee to protect and register the IP rights because the ownership rights must stay with the licensor. The licensor should avoid even the potential that the licensee may try to claim ownership rights in derivative or associated works. Similarly, the licensor should always take on the burden of defending the IP rights against infringement because this defense is of ultimate importance to the ownership and reputation of the IP rights. The licensor must additionally monitor the production of the licensee for quality, quantity, and adherence to the license contract terms.

Attorney

Any of the parties involved with IP rights may seek legal advice at any time during the course of creating, transferring, purchasing, licensing, using, or otherwise dealing with IP. An attorney can offer insights into the legal requirements and issues that will be encountered at any stage of the IP creation process, and the attorney's advice could affect the process from start to finish.

WHY SHOULD YOU CONSULT AN ATTORNEY?

Basically, your actions are subject to the law. You must be aware of your legal obligations. Moreover, you presumably wish to use the law to protect, enforce, and define your IP rights. Therefore, you must respectfully act within the law when you create, transfer, acquire, license, or use IP.

Your innocence or ignorance of the law can lead to substantial financial and legal troubles, even to loss of IP rights or the need to file court actions to stop infringement. Even if you think you know your legal rights within your own country, if you choose to use the Internet or to expand otherwise into the global marketplace, the legal complications will multiply exponentially. Your creations and IP transactions will become subject not only to the laws and regulations of other countries, but also to international standards. What you don't know can hurt you.

Whether you are a creator or trader of IP globally, you will be subject to government authorities that seek to protect what they view as the interest of the public in accordance with the policies and practices of that particular regime. Significant penalties, including criminal ones, can be imposed if IP is created, transferred, or used wrongfully, fraudulently, in bad faith, or in a manner that amounts to IP infringement or a violation of fair trade or anti-trust laws. A breach of law in a foreign country can subject you to legal proceedings before an administrative agency or a judge in an unfamiliar and confusing place.

When you are considering whether to seek legal advice, ask yourself these questions:

1. How much time, money, and labor have I already invested, or do I plan to invest, in developing or acquiring the IP? Do I mind losing my investment because I have not sought or maintained the legal protections available?

2. How much time, money, and labor have I spent in preliminary market research, market testing, and marketing the IP that I have created or acquired? Would it bother me to lose that investment?

3. How much would it cost me to change my IP if protection is no longer available or enforcement becomes too expensive? Would it bother me to lose my IP rights and to have to create or acquire new IP? What would the effect be on my business?

4. Is my IP worth more to my business than the cost of registration and maintenance?

5. If the value of the IP that I have acquired or created is lost or reduced, does it matter to me? Will it affect me financially? Could I become legally liable for the loss or reduction of value, and if so, how much will that cost me in legal fees and other costs?

LEGAL ADVICE FOR THE OWNER/CREATOR

An attorney can provide crucial advice as to the rights you have when you are creating IP or when you have acquired another person's IP. The attorney can give you an opinion on the breadth and limits of your legal and contractual rights, the steps you must take to protect and enforce those rights, and the alternatives that you have for transferring or using those rights. The attorney may be able to assist you in valuing IP rights and in increasing the value of your IP rights. From the very start of creation, you must be aware of your rights, obligations, and risks if you intend to keep your exclusive rights and reap the value of the creation.

An attorney will be able to assist you in the actual registration process for your IP rights and in maintaining them thereafter. In many countries, the owner or creator of IP is entitled to seek registration of the IP directly, without the assistance of counsel, provided the owner or creator is resident or at least has a service address in the country. In some countries, agents (usually licensed but not as attorneys) can file applications to register your IP rights, and their fees are likely to be less, at least at first. These may be ways to save money—for now.

So why bother to seek advice of an attorney for something so simple as the registration of your IP rights? Precisely because:

1. Nothing is ever so simple. Your application for registration can be rejected for any number of formal and substantive reasons—it is filled out improperly, your claimed IP rights conflicts with other IP rights previously registered by someone else, your IP is not novel, distinctive, or otherwise unique within the meaning of the law, etc.

2. Registration is an extremely important process to complete. By registering your IP rights, your rights gain value and you gain remedies available only through the registration statutes. Most of the time, you won't know that there is an objection to your registration for months, and in some countries for two or more years. If you begin using your IP in reliance on protection from the date of your application for registration, but your application is later rejected, your investment of labor and money may be for naught.

Advice from your attorney on the technical, formal, and substantive requirements to keep in mind when creating IP will make you aware of the factors needed to ensure that your creation can be protected. Your attorney's assistance in filing the registration will allow you to anticipate the likely objections that might be made to your registration. As the application proceeds through examination, your attorney's advice will be invaluable in replying to objections and persuading the examiners to accept your IP registration. Once you have sought registration, your attorney can reference your pending or finalized registration to fight infringers more successfully, and often more cheaply because you will own the rights on the public record.

If you are not yet convinced about the value of legal advice to the creator or owner of IP, keep in mind the following: A single litigation to enforce IP rights or to defend against infringement in the US can cost upwards of US$150,000, while the simple process of registration will usually cost less than US$10,000 for a patent, less than US$2,000 for a trademark, and less than US$1,000 for a copyright. While costs vary from country to country, the concept remains the same: It is substantially less expensive to protect registered IP rights than unregistered ones, and there is a greater risk of losing unregistered IP rights to the public.

LEGAL ADVICE FOR THE CONSUMER

As a purchaser or user of a copy of IP, you should be aware of the importance of respecting the owner's IP rights and the economic and legal realities and consequences of violating those rights. Sharing copies of other copies of other copies may seem like the cheap alternative to purchasing legitimate copies of the IP, and, you say, the only party adversely affected is the owner of the IP rights. This is simply not so.

By infringing IP rights, you actually undermine the value of your own property rights in the copy of the IP. That is, by violating the rights of the IP owner, you are also cheapening the value of the copy of the IP that you have acquired plus all other copies of the same IP. The IP could eventually become generic, that is, part of the public domain, in which event the exclusive IP rights will be lost along with any value inherent in those rights. While the owner of the IP rights will obviously be adversely affected by such a result, your own copy or copies of the IP will at the same time be devalued. You will no longer be able to sell copies, whether legitimate or illegitimate, for a premium price because other consumers will no longer respect the value.

Moreover, if you acquire IP pursuant to a license agreement, you do not acquire full ownership rights in the copy of the IP. You merely have a right to use the IP copy within the terms of the license. If you make unauthorized copies of the IP, you are breaching the contractual terms of the license and cheapening the value of the IP.

Although economic realities are likely to prevent the owner of IP rights from enforcing those exclusive rights against every possible infringement and breach of license, the owner of IP rights has a legal privilege to do so. Whether to take action, and the choice of action, is entirely at the discretion of the owner of the IP rights. The IP owner is likely to take action against you if your infringement or breach is causing or threatening to cause significant harm to the value of the IP rights; a zealous owner of IP may act against even small infringements and license breaches. If you do not respect IP rights, you take the risk of being enjoined by a court and being held liable for damages, penalties, and possibly attorney fees.

Therefore, to avoid adverse legal claims and penalties, you should be aware of the scope of your rights and your legal obligations related to those rights. Of course, each time you make a purchase or a copy of IP, you need not obtain legal advice. However, if your use of the IP is not within the concept of "fair use," you may need to seek a license from the owner of the IP rights. If you decide to start making and distributing copies of the copy, you may be subject to infringement and breach of contract claims. Before taking such actions, you should spend a little time and money on legal advice. Otherwise, you may end up spending substantial time and money for legal defense.

LEGAL ADVICE FOR AN AUTHORIZED USER/LICENSEE

As user of IP that is licensed from the owner of the IP rights, you are also a consumer of the IP. That is, you have acquired a copy of the IP with the intent of using it. You have the same obligation to respect the IP owner's rights and the same liabilities if you do not. If you do not know your rights and liabilities as a consumer, you should take the time and spend money for initial legal consultation.

In addition to being a consumer, as a licensee you're also subject to the terms of your license contract. This contract has most likely been prepared and handed to you by the owner of the IP rights or his or her representative. It will probably state that the owner is still the owner and you are merely a licensee of the IP rights. It will probably require that you meet quality control standards set by the owner of the IP rights. It will probably set strict limits on production, distribution, and use of the IP. And, of course, it is likely to provide for remedies in case there is a breach of the license.

A license contract is a legal document, and once you sign it, you will be bound by its terms. Although those terms have been decided by the licensor, you do have some bargaining power to change provisions that are particularly burdensome to you because, after all, the licensor has sought after you and qualified you to be a licensee of the IP. Whether you are an experienced licensee or a novice, you would therefore be most wise to obtain the advice of a legal professional, who will be able to point out the potential pitfalls and advantages of the contract before you fall prey.

WHEN TO CONSULT AN ATTORNEY

- IN THE BEGINNING The best time to consult an attorney is before you need to consult an attorney. You should consult your attorney before you come into possession of IP rights or a copy of the IP because the answers to your questions will affect your course of conduct. This means that, as a creator, you should seek legal advice before fixing your ideas in a tangible medium; as a consumer, you should know whether your intended use of the copy of the IP is legally permissible, and if you have any doubt, you should ask your attorney before you spend your money to acquire the IP; and as a licensee, you should have your attorney review the contract before you agree to the terms and give up whatever bargaining power you may have to insist on protection of your rights. Once you possess IP rights or a copy of the IP, your attorney can only provide you with defensive advice–how to regain your prior exclusive rights from an intervening party or seek co-existing rights with them, how to renegotiate, repudiate, or otherwise avoid an acquisition or license contract, or how to minimize your losses from a bad deal.
- DURING CREATION OR ACQUISITION Whether you consult your attorney during the creation process depends on the complexity of your particular situation. In general, a creator who has obtained legal advice in the beginning will probably not need to contact counsel until the creation is finalized. However, if protection of the creation depends on its novelty, distinctiveness, inventiveness, or uniqueness, the creator may not be able to finalize the creation without assistance of an attorney, who can perform a prior use check and advise on potential conflicts. If the creation process itself is subject to complicated legal requirements, as is the case in patent drafting, your attorney will have to play a greater part.

  The same rule applies during acquisition of IP rights or a copy of IP. That is, most consumers of IP do not need legal advice because their use of the IP is personal or otherwise within fair use and therefore is not infringing. But if the acquisition involves the transfer of all ownership rights in the IP or a license to use the IP, legal advice during the transaction is certainly warranted, if not essential. In fact, your wisest course of action may be to allow your attorney to negotiate the contract or at least to be present with you during negotiations.

- WHILE IN POSSESSION Your need for an attorney's advice does not end when you have completed your creation or acquisition of IP. Unfortunately, possession of IP rights, whether through creation or acquisition, is not nine-tenths of the law. If you fail to register, maintain, renew, or enforce your IP rights, you are likely to lose them. That is, you must assert your IP rights if you wish to keep them. Furthermore, you must assert them worldwide or risk the chance of having the value of your IP rights undermined by third parties who use or register your IP in another country before you get there.

  In simple terms, you will still need an attorney, and you would be wise in the beginning to ask your attorney about the continuing costs for ensuring the protection of your IP. The good news is that, if you take advantage of the available means for protecting your IP, your costs will be relatively less than if you have to fight infringers without having first registered your IP rights. Your attorney can advise you on the best means of ensuring that the weight of the proof—who has better rights to the IP—is on your side.

  If you have acquired IP rights, you may also be faced with enforcing or renegotiating the agreement for the license or other transfer, and again you will need the assistance of counsel. Your attorney can review your particular circumstances, point out your strengths and weaknesses in your bargaining position, and explain the risks and liabilities you would probably encounter by choosing one course of action as opposed to another. To keep you out of further trouble, you might ask your attorney to represent you through the entire renegotiation or settlement process. Although this decision may depend on such factors as the cost of legal advice versus the value of the contract, your familiarity with the legal system, and the strength of your relationship with the other party, it is always wise to seek at a minimum your attorney's review and advice on any agreement before you sign it.

- FUTURE CREATIONS OR ACQUISITIONS Once you have been through the creation or acquisition process with your attorney's advice, you will be familiar with the legal requirements, rights and obligations, and available provisions for protection and enforcement. If you undertake future creations or acquisitions, you may find that you need less legal advice unless your new creations or contracts substantially differ from the previous ones. You should not, however, forego legal advice completely because each creation or acquisition has its own peculiar characteristics. Your investment in up-front legal review and advice is relatively less expensive than your investment in creating or acquiring IP, developing a market for the IP, and protecting and enforcing your rights in the IP.

HOW TO SELECT AN ATTORNEY

Finding an attorney is as easy as consulting a telephone or legal directory, calling an attorney referral service, asking friends or family for a recommendation, or seeking out a relative who just happens to have a law office in your hometown. Once you have narrowed your choices, pick the attorney who is:

1. Knowledgeable about IP rights and your country's laws regulating IP rights,

2. Knowledgeable about international IP and business law, or at least willing to learn the relevant international aspects without costing you too much extra for the research involved,

3. Knowledgeable about practical, administrative, customs, and judicial processes and procedures for the maintenance and enforcement of IP rights,

4. Connected to legal associates abroad, or at least willing to make those connections and to take an active role in on obtaining IP registrations worldwide,

5. Frank in advising you to contact other professionals, such as foreign legal counsel or IP agents, consultants with technical skills, appraisers, accountants, and advertising, public relations, or market survey consultants, for assistance with issues that are not legal, and who is willing to liaise with those professionals on your behalf, and

6. Diplomatic, culturally aware, understanding of the difficulties involved in negotiating across country borders, and excited to be part of the international trade arena.

As a note of caution, two parties to a contract should never use the same attorney. Even if the parties are best friends, each of them holds an interest in the contract that is adverse to the other. One party seeks to acquire the broadest scope of IP rights possible for the least amount of compensation, while the other offers to sell IP rights or limited IP rights for the highest price. If a single attorney represents both parties, there is a distinct potential for conflict of interest because the attorney is bound ethically and morally not to give conflicting advice to parties within the same transaction.

HOW TO WISELY SPEND YOUR ATTORNEY'S TIME

From the first telephone call, to the initial in-person meeting, and in all subsequent contacts with your attorney, adequate preparation is to your benefit because your attorney's time will cost you money. Before you speak to your attorney:

1. Review the issues and the answers that you need to have to lead you to the next stage in your creation, acquisition, or protection of your IP.

2. Collect and organize all facts, documents, correspondence, marketing information, IP evaluations, and any other items that you think might be relevant to your discussions, and

3. Consider your IP from a global viewpoint: where will your IP be used, licensed, transferred, or sold, where will you need to protect it, and where is infringement most likely to occur?

ADVICE AN ATTORNEY CAN PROVIDE

Your attorney's advice will be most helpful, and you will get the most for your dollar, if you inform your attorney of the information relevant to your IP rights in an orderly and well-considered manner. In the preliminary stages, you should ask your attorney about the following topics:

- COUNTRY LEGAL SYSTEMS Few people understand fully the legal system in their own country, let alone the legal systems in other countries. An experienced attorney can offer invaluable insights.
  - Can I protect my IP in all of the countries in my business plan?
  - What types of protections (e.g., IP registrations, cautionary notices, customs registrations) are available in these countries?
  - What types of remedies are available for enforcement of my rights and which remedies are in fact recommended?
  - If I do not protect my IP simultaneously in all countries, do I risk losing my IP rights in any particular countries? If so, in which countries?
  - Which countries are members of international treaties that cover my type of IP rights? What is the procedure for gaining recognition under these treaties?
- IP RIGHTS GENERALLY Before you create or choose your IP, you should consider what would be most easily registered and enforced. Your attorney can explain the factors considered by administrative examiners and judicial tribunals.
  - What are the substantive requirements for registering my IP? What characteristics and properties does my IP have to have in order to complete the registration?
  - What does "derivative" mean? Can I base my IP on the IP of another person? How distinct or different must my IP really be from the IP belonging to some else?
  - Why should I bother getting a registration at all?
  - Should I protect my IP through different types of registrations, such as a copyright and a trademark registration? What would be the advantages? What would be the disadvantages?
  - What does due diligence mean in relation to the registration of IP rights? Why should I request a due diligence check?
  - When do my IP rights become effective and what can I do with my IP rights while the application for registration is pending? Can I transfer them? Can I use them? How can I protect them?
- CONTRACTS Even a simple transaction for the license or transfer of IP rights can have a complicated contract. An attorney's expertise is needed to understand the nuances and implications of most contracts.
  - Is there freedom of contract in each of the relevant countries? In terms of IP specifically, what limits are placed on the rights of parties to contract in particular countries?
  - Why should I sign a written contract?
  - Is a memorandum sufficient evidence of the transaction?
  - Why should I have a written contract reviewed by my own attorney when the other party's attorney has already prepared it and the terms are fixed? Why shouldn't I simply rely on the other party's attorney?
  - When does an agreement become binding? What is mutual understanding?

- ENFORCEMENT OF IP RIGHTS Your attorney should be able to advise you in the beginning about your enforcement obligations. Registration and protection of your IP are only a start, and the investment you make in development of your IP and your markets will be lost if you do not follow through with adequate enforcement.
  - How do I locate infringements? Are there any inexpensive means for finding infringements of my IP rights? For each method, what is its scope and how reliable is it?
  - Should I rely on my agent, licensees, and other similar representatives in the country to find infringements?
  - What alternatives do I have for stopping infringements? What costs can I expect to incur for each of these alternatives?
  - What would be the effect of settling with every infringer that I find?

ADVICE AN ATTORNEY TYPICALLY WILL NOT PROVIDE

You may certainly ask your attorney about subjects that are usually outside the realm of the attorney's advice. However, an attorney's time may be extremely valuable, and you will pay the price. Most likely the attorney will inform you that you should contact other service providers for this advice.

- FOREIGN IP COUNSEL OR AGENTS Any attorney can provide you with advice on the laws, procedures, and practices of any jurisdiction in the world, except when prohibited by the laws of a particular country (although your attorney may charge you a premium for the research required). However, an attorney is generally not permitted to represent you before a court of law, and sometimes before administrative agencies, in jurisdictions where the attorney is not admitted to practice law. If IP issues become complex in a foreign country, such as when an infringement action must be filed in court, you should request your attorney to assist you in selecting local counsel and to act as a supervising lawyer for purposes of coordinating and liaising with the local counsel.
- CONSULTANTS WITH TECHNICAL SKILLS Your attorney is supposed to give you legal advice, not technical advice about the formal or substantive content of the IP. Although many attorneys, particularly in the patent realm, are also qualified in scientific, computer, and other technical fields, their primary focus is on the legal aspects of the IP. They will not advise you on engineering weaknesses in your invention, editing changes in your manuscript, or rhythmic flaws in your musical scores. Therefore, you would be wise to consult with a person whose specific occupation is in the technical field relevant to your IP.
- ADVERTISING, PUBLIC RELATIONS, OR MARKET SURVEY CONSULTANTS Attorneys are not experts on the marketability of your IP. They may be able to refer you to advertising, public relations, or marketing firms that can assist you in developing your IP so that global cultural, language, climate, and other similar considerations are taken into account.
- APPRAISERS OR ACCOUNTANTS The majority of attorneys are not skilled in valuation or appraisal methods for IP rights. To obtain an appraisal of your IP rights, you should consult an appraiser or accountant who is knowledgeable in the methods commonly applied to determine the value of intangible property, and specifically IP rights.

CHAPTER 5

Ensuring the Value of Your IP Rights: At Creation

WHEN YOU HAVE A CREATIVE ITCH, you are probably also thinking: "I wonder what this might be worth?" To ensure that you gain the full value of your IP, you must recognize at the very start that you are in fact creating IP rights. You must also be aware of how easy it is to lose those rights and how to keep them. If you develop a well-considered IP portfolio strategy in the beginning, you can realize significant profits from your creation and save substantial sums in enforcement as the world comes to know, and then desire, your IP. If you fail to consider what will make your IP rights valuable, you are likely to encounter reversals and losses at a later stage when you try to market or protect your creation.

Adding IP to Your Business Plan

A successful and healthy business is usually based on a business plan. Whether you are just starting a business, acquiring a business, or operating a going concern, an ongoing business plan is essential. Your plan should begin with three short Statements of Commitment that answer the following questions:

1. STATEMENT OF VISION: What direction do you see your business going? Where do you want your business to be within your industry or trade? Within the world? By what year do you want to be there? What will your business be doing and what financial returns do you expect for your business?
2. STATEMENT OF MISSION: What three or four things will your business need to do in order to achieve the Vision? Do you need a certain public or market image? Do you need certain qualities in your employees? Do you need certain clients or a specific type of financial backing?
3. STATEMENT OF UNDERTAKING: What steps will you implement in your business to accomplish the Mission? What policies and practices will be established to meet the Mission and achieve the Vision?

TIP: The Statements of Commitment are intended to focus your business plan on one of the keystones to success: consistent branding. In this sense, "branding" means the entire image or whole experience that you would like to create for your business. Your business vision should be like a house that is raised on a single, solid foundation. A consumer who visits your "house" will be more impressed, and more likely to remember it, if it is built on a core image throughout—in its business identity, media and public communication, products and services, and business practices and policies. Brand loyalty is a prime factor in a company's success and ability to achieve long-lasting presence in today's markets.

Once you have carefully drafted, redrafted, and finalized your commitment statements and decided on your company's brand image, you will need to expand your business plan to cover the operational details. A common practice is to make a short-term (say, 5-year) and a long-term (say 15-year) plan aimed at accomplishing even longer term goals. If you need assistance, business consulting companies and business planning software are available to ease this task.

Before you expand your plan, it is essential to stop and think about the legal consequences of your actions. At this point, you have already created valuable IP—the foundations of your company's brand image—and you should recognize and begin to protect it. Your company's IP, even though it is intangible, is likely to be or to become one of the most valuable assets of your business. Therefore, the development of an IP policy should be at the top of your list, and you should implement the first stage of protection immediately through confidentiality agreements and trade secret identification.

During the development of your business plan, be certain to expend significant efforts on creating an IP strategy. Your IP strategy should support, encourage, fortify, and extend the IP policy you initially adopted. It should also reach into every aspect of your business and ensure that all IP rights will be protected. A well-planned IP strategy will preserve the value of your investment not only in your creations but also in your business as a whole. Remember that "brand image" is the creation of a whole experience.

Developing an IP Strategy

To develop an IP strategy that is practical and effective for your business, you will need to consider the topics discussed in the rest of this chapter and in the following chapter as well. It is recommended that you read through these chapters once for purposes of identifying the areas that are relevant to your specific IP situation. You should then be in a position to develop a general IP strategy, and you can return to each topic for more detailed review as you begin to implement your plan.

IDENTIFYING YOUR IP

The simple truth of the matter is that you can protect your IP rights only if you know about them. As part of your business plan, you should have a written list of your current IP and the IP that you intend to develop. Each IP that you identify should then be entered into a project tracking system, through which you can record the status of those rights from development through maintenance.

TIP: Your list should contain all the traditional IP that you have or intend to develop: each and every trademark, patent, and copyright. You should add the nontraditional IP associated with your business, which may include designs, trade names, mailing and client lists, business methods, trade dress, trade secrets, and so forth. Also remember the IP associated with the computer era—software created for your business, websites, domain names, presentations in electronic media and the like.

Once you think you have identified your IP, seek confirmation from your attorney. In a brief meeting with your attorney, you should outline your business plans and request your attorney to give his or her initial reaction and advice. Of course, at the early stages your plans are probably still flexible and unsettled, but this is the perfect time for a bit of legal counsel. Your attorney should be able to help you focus your plans by pointing out the consequences of certain actions and the means of avoiding the pitfalls. Be certain to discuss generally the protection of your IP rights, since those rights will likely become a valuable asset of your new company.

Your attorney will be able to best advise you only if you first provide information on the industry, trade, operations, plans, and goals of your company. In this regard, collect and organize a packet of materials about your proposed business for your attorney's review prior to your meeting. Use the checklist that follows in the next section to assist you in this process.

Evaluating Your IP Needs: A Checklist

Assuming you have identified at least most of the IP that your company has or intends to create, the next step is to evaluate the nature and the scope of your company's IP needs. This step cannot be taken in a vacuum: it is tightly related to your company's overall business structure and strategy. While evaluating your IP needs, you will also be solidifying your company's short- and long-range goals. During this process, you may discover that you will need more or less IP than what you have already identified, and you can then adjust your plans.

The extent to which you develop and protect your IP rights must fit your business plans and goals. The list of questions that follows are intended to start you thinking about your IP needs in terms of your overall business strategy. These questions are general because it is impossible to consider the circumstances specific to every business. Therefore, you should adapt, add, and delete questions to fit your own particular situation.

NOTE: Record and keep your answers to these questions, together with the data that you compile and consider. These materials can become the core of your business portfolio and will be very helpful in explaining your business to your attorney when you seek legal advice on your IP needs. To evaluate your IP needs, your attorney will be asking you many of these same questions.

WHAT IS THE NATURE OF YOUR CORE BUSINESS?

- QUERY: DO YOU SELL PRODUCTS OR PROVIDE SERVICES?

- SIGNIFICANCE: If the products, and even the machinery that make them, qualify as inventions, your exclusive rights can be protected by patents, allowing you to gain an edge over your competition. If you sell services, you will need to carefully preserve your trade secrets and you should consider whether your works are protected by copyright. If you use a trademark for your service business, you may not be able to register it in some countries, and therefore you may need to develop a product line for use with your services to ensure protection of your mark worldwide.

- QUERY: ARE YOU IN THE BUSINESS OF CREATING IP?

- SIGNIFICANCE: If the creation of IP is your business, you should place high value on the protection of your IP rights. For each creation, you should ensure that protection is in place before releasing it to the public. If you create IP on commission, as an employee, or otherwise for someone else, who owns the IP? Before the creation is completed, ownership rights should be clarified by means of agreement, such as an assignment, license, or work for hire contract.

- QUERY: DO YOU SELL ONE PRODUCT OR SERVICE, A LINE OF CLOSELY INTERRELATED PRODUCTS OR SERVICES, OR A VARIETY OF PRODUCTS OR SERVICES?

- SIGNIFICANCE: Each invention should be protected by a separate patent, each design and mark by a separate registration, and each work by a separate copyright. If you sell many products or services or a line of products or services, you might create names and marks for each product or service, and you may add more and more names and marks as your products or services change or expand. But remember that the most successful companies keep a consistent brand image. To ensure repeat customers and brand loyalty, you should develop a strong, core name or mark to be used consistently with all of your products or services. It is your core mark or name that will always be recognized by consumers regardless of how many secondary marks or names you might have. Eventually, your core mark or name could gain status internationally as being famous, which increases the legal protection available for it.

- QUERY: IS YOUR COMPANY USING INVENTIONS, PRODUCTS, WORKS, OR SERVICES DEVELOPED AND MADE BY OTHERS AS PART OF YOUR OWN BUSINESS?

- SIGNIFICANCE: You must respect the IP rights of others by obtaining appropriate licenses or other permission. You need to be aware of what would be an infringement and how to avoid infringing on another's rights. If you do approach other business owners or competitors for purposes of joining forces with them, it is also important to understand the laws related to anti-trust, unfair competition, and illegal business combinations.

- QUERY: DOES YOUR COMPANY HAVE A SINGLE OUTLET OR MULTIPLE OUTLETS?

- SIGNIFICANCE: You should protect your IP rights in every jurisdiction where you use or might use them. You will need to set up a structure and system to educate the persons in your sale, marketing, licensing, or franchising chains about your IP rights and to enlist their aid in protecting those rights. You will also need to institute measures that keep your brand image consistent among the various outlets.

- QUERY: WILL YOU SELL THROUGH OR JOINTLY WITH OTHER BUSINESSES? WILL OTHER BUSINESSES BE HIRED TO MANUFACTURE YOUR PRODUCTS OR TO PROVIDE YOUR SERVICES?

- SIGNIFICANCE: If consumers become confused as to the origin of products or services, exclusive IP rights will become diluted and loose value. Eventually, ownership rights in IP may even be lost unless there is a clear indication that the rights are protected. You will need to protect your IP immediately at creation, require other businesses to sign agreements strictly recognizing your IP rights, and set up a monitoring system. As the creator and owner of IP rights, your company should never pass on its protective responsibilities to its manufacturer, franchisee, or licensee because if the ownership of the rights becomes blurred or unclear, exclusivity of those rights can be lost.

WHAT IS THE NATURE OF YOUR CORE MARKET?

- QUERY: DO YOU SELL TO MANUFACTURERS, PRODUCERS, OTHER TRADERS OR SERVICE PROVIDERS, END-USER CONSUMERS, OR A COMBINATION OF THESE?

- SIGNIFICANCE: The nature of your IP will depend in part on who is buying your products or services. For example, you will likely need a catchy trademark and trade dress to attract consistent and repeat business from end-user consumers, but manufacturers and producers would be less impressed with your product packaging and more interested in the quality and efficiency of production. Patents become extremely important for protection of inventions that could otherwise be copied by other producers and manufacturers, while end-user consumers are less likely to have the resources or desire to copy and distribute another's invention. In many countries, copyright arises automatically and need not be registered, but if registration is available, additional remedies become available against infringers.

- QUERY: WHAT ARE THE GEOGRAPHICAL BOUNDARIES OF YOUR BUSINESS? A NEIGHBORHOOD? A CITY? A STATE? THE WORLD?

- SIGNIFICANCE: As you move out from your local market to the world, your IP rights will become more and more valuable as an indicator to consumers about the origin and quality of your products or services. For example, if your business is a small neighborhood bakery or auto repair shop, your business will be known to your clients—your friends and neighbors—and you need not spend much time or money on trademarks, patents, or the like. Even if another businessman opens a shop down the street with a name similar to yours, your friends and neighbors will know the difference. If your cake recipe is so fantastically delicious or your oil change system is so efficient and cost-effective that you decide to expand your business geographically, you will be marketing to consumers who have no clue as to your identity. Your IP will then become a major factor in representing the goodwill and reputation of your company, in acquiring consumer recognition and repeat business, and in bringing about the success of your company.

TIP: Given the trend toward electronic commerce today, the geographical limits to your business are likely to become less and less significant. If a business that sells only to local customers decides to create a website, that business has just crossed the line into international geography. Thus, it is essential to recognize that your IP is more than likely to take on a life of its own and to become valuable beyond the 100-mile square mile radius of your current lifestyle.

- QUERY: HOW LARGE IS YOUR POTENTIAL MARKET?

- SIGNIFICANCE: Your IP strategy should reflect the size of your market. Do you intend to attract thousands of consumers or are you selling to a small, niche market? An attractive, inventive, and culturally neutral trademark may be required to capture a sufficient market share of a multi-faceted, international audience. For a large market, you will probably also need an entire IP package, whereas for a niche market, your company's IP strategy is likely to be highly specialized to meet the particular preferences of your customers.

- QUERY: HAVE YOU IDENTIFIED AND STUDIED YOUR MAJOR COMPETITORS?

- SIGNIFICANCE: Knowledge of your competitors and their market share can be of assistance in planning your own IP strategy. Inadvertent infringement, if not actionable, is at least bad publicity and therefore you should develop your own, distinctive IP. With a bit of study as to what makes your competitors successful, you can use a different but equally attractive concept to enter into direct competition, or you can set your own IP to attract a different market with the potential of legally eroding around the edges of your competitor's market but without unfairly competing.

DO IP RIGHTS HAVE SUBSTANTIAL VALUE FOR YOUR BUSINESS?

- QUERY: WHAT PERCENTAGE OF YOUR BUSINESS WILL BE INVESTED IN RESEARCH AND DEVELOPMENT OF ITS PRODUCTS OR SERVICES? OF ITS MARKETING? OF ITS IP?

- SIGNIFICANCE: Your IP strategy should reflect the investment you are making in R&D, marketing, and consumer goodwill. If you make a substantial investment in market research, development, design, tracking of competitors, advertising, promotion, manufacture, transport, and so forth, you should make adequate provision for the protection of your IP rights as well. Adoption of a strong IP policy and practice will protect your total investment and realize the potential of your business.

- QUERY: DO YOU INTEND FOR CONSUMERS TO BE ATTRACTED TO YOUR BUSINESS BY YOUR NAME, TRADEMARK, OR TRADE DRESS?

- SIGNIFICANCE: If your company's name, mark, or trade dress will take a significant role in the promotion and image of your business, you should protect it through all available means. Moreover, it is important to protect each element that will be attractive to competitors. If consumers are attracted, infringers are also likely to target your IP.

NOTE: If you have created a design or logo as your mark or as part of your mark, you should obtain mark registrations for the design separate from any words or names. Copyright registrations can be used to protect your mark as used in a variety of patterns and pictorials. This protection will increase your available statutory remedies against infringers not only in your own jurisdiction but also potentially in foreign countries that adhere to the Berne Convention on copyrights. More countries are members of the Berne Convention than of the international treaties that provide for cross-border trademark protection.

- QUERY: DOES YOUR BUSINESS INCOME DEPEND ON YOUR RIGHT TO THE EXCLUSIVE USE OF INVENTIONS OR DESIGNS?

- SIGNIFICANCE: If exclusive use rights in inventions or designs are a concern, you will need to obtain patent and design registrations wherever you intend to use your IP. Prior to filing for such registrations, you will need to institute strict procedures to avoid public disclosure. In most countries, patents can only be filed within a limited time, generally before the invention is made public or within a short time thereafter. If the registration application is not timely filed, the invention is considered public property.

- QUERY: DOES YOUR BUSINESS INCOME DEPEND ON YOUR RIGHT TO THE EXCLUSIVE DISTRIBUTION OF COPIES OF YOUR WORKS?

- SIGNIFICANCE: In most countries, your works will be protected by copyright from the time they are presented in tangible media. However, statutory remedies may not be available unless you officially register the copyright.

- QUERY: DOES YOUR BUSINESS HAVE A UNIQUE PRESENTATION, SYSTEM, PROGRAM, OR OTHER FEATURE?

- SIGNIFICANCE: To preserve your IP rights, you should carefully identify all IP and treat it as secrets of your business. Confidentiality statements and agreements should be signed by all of your employees, former employees, officers, and others who are given knowledge of the IP. To the extent possible, noncompetition clauses should also be signed. Although these will not prevent the release of your IP to the public or its use by former associates, you will have grounds for damages for disclosure or unfair competition. You should institute security procedures to protect your investment.

WHAT IDEAS AND PLANS DO YOU HAVE FOR EXPANSION OF YOUR BUSINESS AND/OR MARKETS?

- QUERY: ARE YOU CONSIDERING OPENING NEW OFFICES?

- SIGNIFICANCE: You will need to decide what arrangement you will have with the operators of new offices, whether you will oversee them personally, and how you will monitor the quality of their operations and quantity of their sales. You will also need a very specific agreement to protect your IP rights while others are authorized to use them, and an IP monitoring system independent of your contractors.

- QUERY: ARE YOU CONSIDERING OFFERING NEW PRODUCT LINES OR SERVICES?

- SIGNIFICANCE: You will need to decide whether to expand by your own R&D or by acquisition of other companies, including their IP rights. As part of that decision, you will need to consider use of your IP in connection with the new goods or services. Will you use your primary mark? Create a new set of marks? File new copyrights? File new patents? Your company's expansion should be in line with the brand image that you have established.

- QUERY: WILL YOU CONTRACT WITH OTHER BUSINESS OWNERS TO MANUFACTURE PRODUCTS OR TO OFFER SERVICES?

- SIGNIFICANCE: Expansion of your own facilities usually requires a capital investment to acquire or build larger plants or service outlets, to staff and supply them, and to publicize them. Often, a license or similar arrangement is more effective in terms of cost and labor. Although you will be splitting the returns with other business owners, your business can expand with minimal delay as other business owners take on the burden of providing the facilities. As the IP of companies becomes well known internationally, the companies often set up merchandising arrangements by which they license their IP to other business owners to produce goods or services of a different type. In this way, IP owners gain protection of their IP across different classifications of goods and services, allowing them to fight IP infringers more effectively. In any event, all of these arrangements must be carefully considered and drafted to ensure protection of IP rights.

- QUERY: ARE YOU CONSIDERING ATTRACTING DIFFERENT MARKETS OR BROADENING YOUR MARKET APPEAL?
- SIGNIFICANCE: It is not uncommon for companies to begin in one market and expand into a related market. For example, authors of books, clothes manufacturers, and toy makers often create one product line that attracts children and another that is aimed at adults. If cross-market appeal is important, your primary IP should be fairly neutral and generally attractive, and you should consider developing derivative IP that is connected with each product line or service and that can be modified as you change your cross-market strategies.

WHAT ARE THE PARAMETERS IN TERMS OF TIME, FINANCES, MARKET AND CULTURAL PREFERENCES, TRADE OR INDUSTRY TRADITIONS, AND SO FORTH?

- QUERY: WHAT IS THE TIME FRAME FOR YOUR BUSINESS OPERATIONS?
- SIGNIFICANCE: Creation of IP will require time, and protection of it will involve an additional delay before public disclosure. It is essential to establish realistic interim and final deadlines so that your business can commence using its IP as quickly as possible. Otherwise, you will sink so much money and time into R&D and IP protection that you may miss your chance at the market.

TIP: Carefully evaluate each element of your proposal, including the time needed for IP protection, to determine the length of time required to make the entire project a viable business. If the total time to market is not feasible, you should consider whether a large project might be broken into smaller ones. The creation of a core brand image may be of first importance, with an offering of several products or services that are developed as part of the core. While IP protection is perfected and marketing begins, you can then set to work on other aspects of your initial plan and continue to expand and fill out the lines of your business. This strategy will also allow you to evaluate public reaction to your initial presentation and to make changes if needed before further investment.

- QUERY: HOW IS YOUR COMPANY'S BUSINESS LIMITED BY ITS MARKETS?
- SIGNIFICANCE: You should anticipate the difficulties that might arise in selling to the markets that you have targeted. Have you considered all aspects of marketing there, including cultural acceptance, government regulatory requirements, product or service restrictions, transport and infrastructure problems, and so forth? Your business plan should include a list of the potential hardships that you are likely to encounter, ideas for overcoming them, and interim deadlines to monitor implementation of the solutions.
- QUERY: WHAT ARE THE TRADITIONS WITHIN YOUR OWN BUSINESS? WITHIN YOUR INDUSTRY OR TRADE?
- SIGNIFICANCE: It is important to identify traditional practices within your own business and within the industry or trade at large because these will tend to flavor your ideas and policies. Although important, traditions should not control your business decisions all the time. New concepts can often give your company that extra edge above the competition.

- QUERY: WHAT ARE YOUR FINANCIAL LIMITATIONS AND WHERE ARE YOU SPENDING YOUR MONEY IN TERMS OF PERCENTAGES?

- SIGNIFICANCE: Any investment in IP protection, even a small amount, will be completely inadequate if you lose your IP to your competitors. On the other hand, an investment in IP protection that chews away all of your company's profits is not reasonable, either. Your IP strategy should include a considered budget, with some flexibility built in to allow for unexpected items.

TIP: A strict IP policy does not necessarily mean an expensive IP strategy. Rather, your IP strategy should be to save money by inventive IP creation and protection. For example, if you stick to a core brand image without extending yourself into a myriad of unrelated business lines, you will save time and labor because you will not be constantly creating and protecting new IP. If you adopt IP that is very clearly distinctive and inventive, you will spend less time and money arguing over its registration. If you develop protective devices that prevent others from easily copying your IP and that allow you to track the source of unauthorized products illegally made by your authorized manufacturers, you will be able to cut down on the cost of enforcement. These ideas are explored further in the text that follows.

Marrying Your IP Strategy to Your Budget

Presumably one of the reasons that you are reading this book is that you are looking to implement or commence an IP strategy for your business, but at this point you are thinking: "What's the bottom line here?"

The tendency when starting a business is to fail to capitalize it sufficiently to ensure its success, and this same tendency commonly spills over into the development of an IP strategy. While a budget is important, skimping on IP protection and enforcement initially can become more and more expensive as time passes. The budget must therefore be adequate to protect the investment that you are making—your reputation and success hinges on it.

Before determining your budget and the extent to which it will limit your IP strategy, you should carefully consider the following:

1. In the US, the average cost of a single court action to enforce trademark rights tops $130,000, and litigation to enforce patents, copyrights, and trade secrets is often more complex and, accordingly, more expensive.

2. The registration of a worldwide trademark portfolio might cost about US$400,000 over a two to three year period. Initial copyright filings in 30 countries might cost US$30,000 to US$40,000, and initial patent filings in 10 countries might cost US$50,000 to US$70,000, depending of course on the countries and the complexity of the filings. On the other hand, buying your IP from infringers in several countries often costs upwards of US$10,000 per country per infringer, and fighting legal actions to take back your exclusive rights in overseas jurisdictions can cost upwards of US$40,000 per action. Even filing an administrative petition to cancel another's registration can be expensive at upwards of US$5,000. Remember, too, that in any of these court or administrative actions there are substantial time delays during which ownership and protection of your rights will be in limbo.

3. Battling others for your IP rights can result in negative publicity against your company. Instead of being seen as a strong protector of the public interest, your company may be put into a defensive posture of having to take back its rights from smaller, national individuals and local businesses. Moreover, if you lose your rights in any particular country, you may have to revise your IP strategy, develop new or altered IP, and invest even more money in publicizing the modified IP.

The protection of your investment in IP assets does not mean that you have to bankrupt your budget. The amount of money that you should spend on your IP rights depends on two overall factors. First, the amount spent should reflect the value of your IP rights to your business. If you do not ever plan to operate outside a ten-mile radius from your storefront, it is probably not worth your while to protect your IP. Second, wise management can reduce your IP costs. You should plan from the start for your IP portfolio to grow with your business, initiate protective measures from the very beginning, and consistently enforce your IP rights using innovative methods. Thus, if you create and apply an efficient and effective program of IP protection, your IP will be an asset to your company, not a liability.

Be certain to do a sound cost/benefit analysis. In this analysis, consider the cost for the short and long term and consider how to best spend your money for the greatest protection. There are ways to protect IP rights without substantial cash outlays. A good IP strategy will generally combine various methods to maximize both the protection of the IP rights and the potential income of the business.

Implementing the Strategy: Connecting your IP and Business Strategies

Before concentrating on the development of your company's IP and means of protecting it, you should ensure that your IP and business strategies are strongly integrated. Your IP strategy should become one of the cornerstones of your business, and its importance should be given weight equal to the other aspects of your business. You should consider the following as they might apply to your particular business situation:

- Your IP strategy should support and be supported by your marketing plans. The protection of IP rights should be a prime factor when selecting and releasing new promotions and moving into new markets, and the risk of infringement should be limited by clearing all new products and promotions through an IP research and search process.
- Your company's efforts to develop and maintain its goodwill—your reputation and the public's conception of your business—should be closely tied to your IP strategy. Exploitation of your IP will in turn enhance your goodwill.
- Management should be responsive to and responsible for your company's IP needs. No department or employee should be exempt from training and regular review on the company's IP policies.
- Offensive and defensive measures for the protection of IP rights should be viewed as vital to the success of your company's business as a whole, and these measures should be pursued actively as part of your overall business strategy.

- The timeline for production and development of your business products should take into account the protection of your IP, and likewise your IP strategy should reflect realistically the rapid pace of technology and tendency toward quick turnover of products and services in the marketplace.
- Registered and unregistered IP should be given a dollar value, which in turn should be added to the value of your company's assets in its property register and on its balance sheet.
- Periodic inventory of your company's assets should include an assessment of your registered and unregistered IP and its value.
- The potential that your IP may quickly appreciate in value should be considered within your business financial planning, particularly as this value will make your business more attractive in investment and finance circles.
- Regular review and adjustments of your IP strategy should be made as part of your annual business strategy meetings when you consider past performance and future goals.

Failure to connect your company's IP and business strategies can result in the loss of sales and goodwill, reduction of market share, and eventual downfall of the business. A modern day example of a company that was forced out of a major market share in this way is Sony Electronics, Inc. Originally the sole manufacturer of videotapes in beta format, Sony held a competitive edge in the market because the quality of the beta tapes was better than the tapes produced by its competitors in VHS format. However, Sony failed to market and support its products diligently in the home consumer market at a time when its competitors began aggressively marketing the VHS tapes. Retailers and consumers began to perceive beta as outmoded because VHS tapes were flooding the market. With the addition of several other contributing factors, beta tapes disappeared from the consumer market, even though the superior quality of the beta format still makes it the one favored by professional film crews.

Implementing the Strategy: Preventative Measures

SELECTING YOUR IP

The best defense is always a good offense. A strong IP portfolio will facilitate the registration and protection process, deter infringement, provide a secure platform from which to fight and halt infringement, and support a solid claim for damages. The initial strength of your IP portfolio depends on the IP that you select to use in your business. When selecting IP, you should take into account the following considerations.

- THE CREATIVE PROCESS You can create IP in any number of ways. How and where you choose to create is entirely up to you. Whenever you create any type of IP, however, you should keep in focus two essential concepts:

1. What will be marketable? What will attract buyers or investors?
2. What can be protected easily?

The answers to these questions differ depending on the type of IP. Some of the factors you will need to consider for various IP are as follows:

PATENTS

- DO make certain that your invention will work, at least in theory, because it cannot be patented unless it is useful in some commercial sense.
- DO focus on an invention that is generally acceptable for registration worldwide to ensure that you can protect it in your expanding markets.

TIP: You will not be able to register for protection if the invention is not considered patentable. For example, the discovery of a law of nature cannot be patented, and neither can a mathematical algorithm. Patent protection in the US is fairly broad and covers categories that are not within the patent laws of other countries. For example, the US will accept business method patents, which have not yet been considered patentable in most other countries. On the other hand, you may be able to develop an invention in connection with a business method, in which event your IP protection will be strengthened by obtaining utility patents in all relevant markets and protecting your business method by patent in the US and as a trade secret elsewhere. For registration considerations, see Chapter 6.

- DO carefully consider whether your invention is new or novel, and if you find any already existing or published inventions, documents, or other materials that are the same or similar to your invention ("prior art"), consider whether your invention is an improvement or is distinguishable from that prior art.

TIP: Even if you find prior art, if it does not describe all of the elements of your invention, you should be able to distinguish it in order to secure your own patent.

- DO make certain that your invention is in fact innovative, meaning that it yields an unexpected or surprising result.

TIP: An invention is not patentable if it is merely an obvious idea in the sense that any person who has ordinary skill in the art or industry would have expected the same result from the existing, prior art.

- DON'T stop with the discovery of a naturally occurring substance or a general law of nature, which cannot be patented, but instead find an innovative way by which that substance can be used, processed, or otherwise connected to a useful invention.

COPYRIGHTS

- DO derive your work independently of the works of others, meaning that, regardless of whether the idea is new, make certain that your expression of the idea is originally conceived by you.

TIP: Copyright protection is available for original works only, meaning works that are independently conceived by the creator. The term "original" does not refer to the idea on which the work is based, but rather on the expression—the work of authorship. Thus, a work that is independently conceived is protected by copyright even if it is based on an idea that has been around for many years. For example, a cartoonist who independently designs a talking mouse has a right to seek copyright protection, despite the fact that the idea of a cartoon talking mouse—the character of "MICKEY MOUSE," to name one example—has been used in various creations for many years.

- DO add an expressive design to what otherwise would be a merely functional product.

TIP: A work that is purely functional cannot be protected by copyright. However, the work can be copyrighted if it is created for expressive purposes. For example, the design of a coffee mug that is shaped and decorated like a lion may be subject to copyright because the design does not determine how the mug is used.

- DO compile a work from preexisting data or other works and organize and arrange it in a novel way, provided the materials are in the public domain or you have obtained authorization from the copyright holders.
- DON'T copy another's work that is subject to copyright, unless you credit the work to that other person and obtain permission to use the work from the other person.
- DON'T create a work that might be considered indecent, immoral, or otherwise unacceptable or disparaging to society.

TIP: In some countries, such works cannot be protected by copyright, and in some places, the sale of such works may be restricted or banned. Most countries have a procedure by which third parties can contest the protection of such works, usually involving the expense of a court action.

- DON'T create merely a set of printed forms, but instead add originality to your work through innovative explanatory text and presentation so that you can copyright your work.
- DON'T compose your work by merely listing or reciting facts without any innovative expression or presentation.

TIP: Facts are part of the public domain and therefore a work that consists solely of facts is not subject to copyright, but it is possible to acquire a copyright over the expression of those facts.

TRADEMARKS

- DO invent or coin a mark that has no other meaning in any language except to identify your product or service.

TIP: Invented terms are the strongest trademarks in terms of protection. They are considered to be distinctive in and of themselves ("inherently distinctive") because they are the product of one person's imagination and therefore identical or similar copies are presumed to be infringements. Examples of famous invented marks include "KODAK" for cameras, "TYLENOL" for medicine, "MICROSOFT" for software, and "INTEL" for computer chips.

- DO choose a mark that is short and has visual impact.

TIP: Many companies register slogans as well as trademarks, but their focus remains on their primary mark. The protection of slogans by trademark registration can be useful, but the expense must be weighed against the permanency of the slogan. If your slogan is likely to change with the time and market, you might consider protecting it as part of your trade dress or by means of copyright registration.

- DO consider a mark that has a catchy rhyme (such as the famous mark "Ronald McDonald").
- DO select a mark with strong consonants and vowel sounds and a design with strong, uncomplicated elements.
- DO choose a mark that is unexpectedly suggestive of the product or service.

TIP: Care should be taken to avoid being descriptive when you choose a suggestive mark because substantial time and money will need to be spent in trying to get the mark registered over the objections of many trademark registries. For example, the choice of the mark "ENCORE" for a broadcast company that shows re-run movies seems to be suggestive, but one of the dictionary meanings of "encore" is the repetition of a performance in response to a demand. Thus, this mark is arguably descriptive and will be difficult to register in countries with strict examination policies.

- DO consider whether the mark creates a suitable image for your company to achieve its desired position in the market.
- DO chose a mark that can be transferred into any media, and be certain to consider new technologies including domain names, holographic product labels, light signs, and computer games.
- DO check to see whether your proposed mark has any linguistic meaning (in sound or spelling) in any of the major languages used today, particularly English (including derivative forms of English in Canada, America, India, South Africa, Australia, and their possessions), Chinese (Mandarin and Cantonese), Japanese, Korean, Hebrew, French, German, Spanish, Italian, Hindi, Russian, and Arabic.
- DO consider the potential longevity of the proposed mark, and potential spin-offs.

TIP: Marks that reflect fads or short-term trends are usually not good investments. Such marks can be secondary marks that are filed once and then not renewed, but your core image marks should have long-term appeal.

- DON'T choose a descriptive or generic term that has any direct reference to your product or service whatsoever.

TIP: A mark that consists of a word or design that is generic or directly descriptive of the product or service is very difficult, if not impossible, to register in most countries because all businesses have a legitimate interest in using it. Moreover, from the consumer viewpoint, such marks are weak because they lack identifying features that stick in a buyer's memory. It might be possible to register such a mark if it is supported by evidence that it has attained through commercial use a secondary meaning and is recognized by consumers as referring to the products or services of the mark owner. For example, the mark "BANK OF AMERICA" can be supported by significant evidence of use and secondary meaning. But why should you go through the hassle and expense of justifying your mark when you can initially choose a nondescriptive mark?

- DON'T choose a mark that might be similar or suggestive of your competitor's mark, because you might be accused of infringing or unfairly competing.

TIP: Be careful of using descriptive words in your product labels, also. Your choice of descriptive words must not infringe on the IP rights of your competitors, particularly when you might select other words for the same purpose. For example, a potato chip company that used the trademark "KETTLE" won an infringement suit against another potato chip company that described its products as KETTLE CHIPS. In finding infringement, the court noted that although the chips might have been cooked in a kettle, the cooking vessel could just as easily have been called something else.

- DON'T use a mark that has barely been altered from a common word, such as by merely changing a "c" to a "k."
- DON'T use a mark that has a meaning or sound in any language that might be considered immoral, scandalous, deceptive, vulgar, derogatory, or negative.
- DON'T choose a name that contains or consists of highly diluted or over used words or abbreviations, such as micro, café, e-, .com, sport, or blast.
- DON'T use a mark or name that has a reference to a historic, heroic, or famous figure or place.

TIP: Famous people are protected from unauthorized use of their names and performance styles by a theory called "right of publicity" and they can recover damages if you exploit their name or style without their consent. No trader can claim exclusive use of historic or heroic names, and these might be considered misleading to the public as well. For example, the mark "BUFFALO BILL," referring to a once famous performer in a traveling show about the US frontier, has been used for all sorts of goods and services—potato chips, beverages, football teams, real estate companies, insurance companies, just to name just a few—and therefore has little distinctive effect in the minds of consumers.

- DON'T include any reference to a country, flag, coat of arms, red or blue cross, religion, head of government, or any other symbol of international or national repute that would suggest an official connection with a government or international agency or association (such as the Red Cross or the Olympic Committee).
- DON'T select a mark or name that constitutes an arbitrary word, meaning a common word that is completely unrelated to the product or service.

TIP: Many arbitrary words have been used with success (for example the mark "APPLE" for computers and "TIDE" for detergent). However, the success of these marks and names has often been won through ingenious and lengthy marketing promotions and arduous legal battles. You are likely to find difficulty in protecting an arbitrary word against use by other traders in relation to unrelated products because an arbitrary word is common in the language and cannot be claimed by any single trader. It is neither invented nor coined, and therefore very little creativity has been used to produce it. As a result, enforcement tends to be expensive and difficult, and there is a higher risk of customer confusion and bad publicity.

- DON'T use a mark that consists only of a word having as its primary meaning a personal name or surname, unless the name has attained a secondary meaning through your company's commercial usage of it.

TIP: Although there are exceptions, names are generally not good choices for trademarks because other people with the same name have a legitimate reason to use it, too. To obtain protection, you may have to agree to co-existence of your mark with features that minimize customer confusion. If the name acquires a secondary meaning—examples include the trademarks "DISNEY," "JOHNSON & JOHNSON," "GUCCI,"

"HEINZ," and "FORD"—then protection is available. However, the owner of the mark must have substantial proof of the secondary meaning, and the owner is likely to have to fight consistently and frequently to keep exclusive use of the mark. If you are determined to use a person's name, consider a mark derived from the name instead—examples include "ADIDAS" and "ALMAY."

- **MARKET AND INDUSTRY RESEARCH** When selecting IP, it is important to know what IP is presently in use in your company's market or industry. Your invention, mark, trade dress, copyright, trade secrets, and other IP need to be different from those of your competitors. You can distinguish yourself from your competition only if you know your competition. If you infringe on another's IP, even inadvertently, the result could be costly, not only in terms of money, but also in the time, labor, and public relations that will be required to put the matter right.

  Market and industry research can also provide you with important information about consumer and investor preferences. Take a little time to track your major competitors to understand why they have succeeded. Review the market share of your competitors in comparison to the entire market to discover what segment of the market has not been reached by your competitors. Analyze the market to see whether it tends to be brand-conscious, quality-conscious, price-conscious, and so forth.

  In your research, you should seek to discover apparent IP policies and strategies that your competitors have implemented. How well have they protected their IP rights? Do they appear to strictly enforce their IP rights? Have they formed any centralized enforcement associations with members from within the industry? What inventive means have they used to protect their IP rights?

  Finally, you should review information available from within the industry of IP protection. An entire trade has arisen based on the need of companies for enforcement of their IP rights. Many of the major players—investigators, attorneys, IP agents, brand and advertising firms, Internet and domain name registration companies, and encrypting consultants—offer tips about the selection of IP, as well as information on how to protect it after creation.

- **PRIOR IP RESEARCH** In most countries, IP rights can be registered only if there is no prior registration of identical or similar IP rights. For a patent, an invention must be "novel" or "new," meaning that it must not be identical to "prior art," which is the publication (whether by journal, patent application, news article, papers presented at meetings, etc.) of the same invention anywhere in the world prior to the date of current application. For a trademark, a mark must not be similar or identical to any other mark in an earlier pending application or an issued registration at least within the same country. In some places marks that have previously become famous in the world cannot be copied or imitated. For a copyright, the work must be a new presentation.

  For IP that can be registered, it is important to determine whether any other person claims a prior right in identical or similar IP. A search can be done at most IP registries. In addition, you can review other sources and indices for possible conflict with your proposed IP. For similar or identical trademarks, you should search through industry and trade periodicals and journals, Internet sites, telephone directories for your major markets, business directories, and brand and trademark indices. For patents, you should check technology, scientific, and industry journals and periodicals, newspaper and magazine articles, and published college and other school thesis indices.

Search services are provided by attorneys and professional search agencies. A number of organizations are available that can conduct searches for you through worldwide databases. However, before you contract with them, be certain to assess exactly what their coverage is in terms of geography, time, and topic before agreeing to pay for a search. Also, searching can be expensive, and therefore you should take care to narrow your search instructions to the primary countries where competing IP is most likely to have been registered or used.

There are some side advantages to conducting searches of IP registries on a regular basis. Searches allow you to monitor the IP activities of your competitors, watch trends in emerging technology, and spot start-up companies just entering your industry or trade. The mere fact that IP has been registered does not mean that it has also been used, and if it has not been used by the owner, you might be able to challenge the IP rights or acquire a compulsory license.

- VERIFICATION OF ACCEPTABILITY You should ask your attorney for an opinion about the acceptability of your IP in terms of ease of protection within IP laws. Also, test marketing, opinions from industry or trade contacts, and consumer surveys are all means of verifying whether IP is attractive enough to be profitable. If you are creating a patentable invention, you may want to perfect a working model of it. But don't forget to keep your IP confidential until it is fully protected. Any disclosure should be made only after you have consulted an attorney regarding the consequences and only after you have protection in place.

BUILDING WALLS OF DETERRENCE

Careful selection of your company's IP is one means of going on the offensive against potential infringement, and adding preventative measures to your products or services is another. Like preventative health care or maintenance, preventative measures against infringement involve the investment of time and money in advance and in anticipation of later problems that might possibly arise. The cost of preventative measures is usually substantially less than the expense likely to be incurred in trying to stomp out infringement after it is in progress. The media are likely to be friendlier, too, if your company takes a less aggressive stance against competitors than if your company is always in a fight for its IP rights.

Preventative measures are inventive means of deterring infringement. These might take the form of certain elements added to your product at the manufacturing stage to make duplication so difficult and expensive that infringers will not bother. It might include specific encryption, coding, or passwords within your products or on your labels that cannot be copied and that will allow you to track infringements, illegal imports, and unauthorized products. Extra touches, such as product promotions or license certificates that cannot be duplicated, can also be added to the performance of services to ensure that consumers will recognize the real thing. Holographic art, special fibers, special color dyes, and any number of preventative measures can be used on your products.

Education of the public is an important and often overlooked preventative measure. Advertising and promotional programs can emphasize why a consumer would want the real thing and how to recognize the real thing in a sea of fakes. You might consider offering articles and testimonials about the importance of respecting IP rights to various forms of media that will be circulated within your markets. You could also become involved with international and governmental groups where IP laws, regulations, and policies are made. In many countries, trade officials will personally welcome your business, and you will have the opportunity to educate them on the importance of preventing infringement before it starts.

ENSURING CLEAR TITLE

The ownership rights in your company's IP should be clear to every person who has any contact whatsoever with that IP. Joint creators should have an agreement prior to making the creation. Employees should be instructed and periodically reminded about all of the company's IP rights. You should have clear and solid agreements by which all employees and contractors acknowledge that the creations are works for hire or commission and further waive and assign their ownership rights to the company.

For inventions, the creator-employee will be considered the patent owner and will have the right to assign or license the invention to third persons unless the employment agreement makes an express assignment of all inventions to the employer. Without such an express assignment, the employer has only an implied royalty-free license. To ensure clear ownership title, most companies also require their inventor-employees to sign assignment agreements for each specific invention, as well.

The responsibility for securing and enforcing IP rights should always remain with your company. Do not authorize a licensee, franchisee, or other indirect representative to obtain registrations or to fight your legal battles against infringers. Prohibit others from making any changes, copies, or spin-offs of your IP, and require strict adherence to the agreement terms for use and commercial exploitation of the IP. Make it clear that ownership of the IP rights remains with your company and that if the agreement terminates, so do all rights to the use and possession of the IP and all materials connected with the IP. Ownership rights can become fuzzy, and may be lost if you allow others to exercise and alter them on your behalf.

Products licensed to consumers, such as software, should carry strict agreements that require consumer acceptance on implementation of the product. License agreements with manufacturers, franchise agreements with service providers, and all other contracts by which use but not ownership rights are transferred must contain strict provisions for ownership and protection of the IP rights. These terms should be clearly explained and emphasized. All such licenses must be registered if required to ensure validity in local jurisdictions.

When IP rights are transferred, the assignment contract will be judged as if it were a transfer of tangible property. Thus, it should provide for consideration, mutual obligations, and conveyance of property rights. There must be mutual agreement and understanding of the terms. To be valid against third parties, it must be recorded against any registered IP rights to which it relates.

Implementing the Strategy: Avoiding the Pitfalls

PRESERVING EVIDENCE OF CREATION AND USE

Proof of creation—the time, date, ideas, and expression—is the responsibility (or burden) of the creator who claims to own the IP rights. This proof can be essential when claiming that a third party has infringed your rights or when contesting or seeking cancellation of a third party's IP registration. Proof of use is needed in countries that recognize ownership rights in the first person to use the IP, and it can even be used sometimes to overcome a third party's registration in countries that recognize ownership rights in the first to file. The key to winning a claim of ownership is in the quality, quantity, and methodicalness of your records of creation.

Be certain to keep all of your notes, sketches and drawings, outlines, advertising layouts, draft and final press releases, and lists of potential products and ideas. Each should be marked with a date and time. If your IP consists of an invention, retain the laboratory notebooks with dates and times related to the theories under consideration, the research undertaken, and the results reported.

When you begin commercial use or public disclosure of your IP, retain a file of dated evidence of such use. In this file, it is important to preserve samples of first use of your IP in any commercial setting whatsoever, first use with each product or service subsequently introduced, and first use in any particular country or region. Regular additions should be constantly made to the file to compile thick documentation of the widespread and continuous use of your IP. This file should also be expanded to include copies of registrations, press releases, articles, financial indices, and all other materials that show the status and public recognition of your company and the implementation of your IP policy and strategy as you protect, encourage, and enforce your rights worldwide.

Why collect all of this paperwork? Proof of first use is necessary in many forums, and it is the burden of the owner to provide such proof. In many countries, the first user of IP will be recognized as the owner of IP, even if another person managed to file a registration first, but the first user must be able to provide sufficient proof. If you are sued for infringement of a trade secret, your evidence showing that you were first to create the IP will negate such a claim. Unregistered IP can often be protected against infringers if the person claiming ownership can prove first creation and use. Evidence of substantial, long-term, worldwide continuing use in addition to first use frequently preserves an owner's rights in what has become a famous trademark, even if that trademark has not yet been registered in the particular country from which an infringer hails.

It is absolutely essential that you take a long-term view of your IP rights. Many companies ship their records off to musty storehouses after a few years, and others destroy them. The significance of all of your documents, records, notes, drafts, sketches, invoices, catalogues, magazine spreads, and so forth, that feature your IP is often lost on those who have created the IP. Companies fail to allow sufficient time or space for accurate record-keeping, fail to educate their employees as to what constitutes legal evidence and its significance, and fail to institute efficient systems of collection and cataloguing.

TIP: Do not fall into this trap. Your IP strategy must include evidence collection, indexing, and education. Your IP policy should be strict with regard to the preservation of such evidence. Ask your attorney to advise you with regard to the evidence that might be required to support claims of ownership, use, and reputation. Once you have set up a system, you should periodically review the collection process and retention facilities to ensure that the materials being kept are relevant and complete, that a standard procedure is being consistently applied, and that retrieval will be efficient and organized.

If your attorney comes calling for evidence to prove ownership and worldwide use but you have not kept a strict collection policy, your employees will have to spend many hours scrambling about in stacks and rows of boxes, fishing in libraries, interviewing retirees, and gleaning whatever tidbits can be found from regional sales representatives spread about the globe. Often, sales and advertising figures are compiled in totals without breakdown for particular products, regions, or countries and it is impossible to obtain these breakdowns in later years. If your company has operated for more than a few years, most likely much of the evidence will no longer be available. Even if you can find it, the pressure of meeting administrative and court deadlines is likely to mean that your collection becomes whatever can be hastily brought together, and you may be hard-pressed to justify the gaps.

DEALING WITH UNSOLICITED IDEAS

There are hundreds of would-be creators in the world who would like to see their creations come to fruition through your company—for money, of course. Unsolicited ideas can be a tremendous cause of anxiety to a company because of the potential that the company is already developing an identical or similar idea independently. If the company releases its own IP independently, it may nevertheless be vulnerable to an infringement claim from the person who submitted the unsolicited idea. Such suits, even if unfounded, will cost the company in terms of time, money, and adverse public relations.

As part of your company's overall IP policy, it is essential to develop a specific written policy and practice for dealing with unsolicited ideas. The most important feature of this policy should be to screen all of the persons in your company who are responsible for generating ideas from unsolicited ideas. This screening process should consist of two parts. First, your company personnel must be educated about the potential risk and trained to deal with it. Second, you should appoint and train a specific person in your company to handle all unsolicited ideas, and that person should be kept separate from the idea-generating team.

A common strategy employed by leading companies today is to train every employee to stop reading or conversing immediately on becoming aware that an unsolicited idea is being presented. That employee is instructed to forward the correspondence (letter, electronic, or otherwise) or refer the oral inquiry or discussion about an unsolicited idea to a designated person in the company. The designee is instructed to reject the idea without reading or hearing it and to send the would-be creator a written explanation of the company's policy, plus a statement confirming that all correspondence or other materials related to the unsolicited idea have been expunged from the corporate records.

TIP: You might consider using a cautionary notice in your publications, newsletters, websites, and other public relations materials to warn potential would-be creators about your strict policy against accepting unsolicited ideas. Such a warning may serve to deter all but the most determined, whose correspondence can then be shunted through the recommended procedure.

USING YOUR IP BEFORE PERFECTING PROTECTION

Publication or public disclosure of your IP can result in the loss of valuable property rights. Whether you are inventing, crafting a trademark, writing a novel or play, creating a musical score, you must be careful to protect your creation from public exposure until you know that your ownership rights are protected.

As you are creating your IP, you should already have in place a means of protecting it. After you have finished your creation, you will need to strengthen the protection of your rights. Keep the following cautionary notes in mind to ensure that you protect the value of your IP:

- Most countries follow the rule that ownership of a patent or trademark is granted to the first person to file for registration. Thus, if you have disclosed your ideas to a third person before filing for registration, it is possible for that third person to file first and claim ownership.
- Some countries will recognize ownership in the first person to invent or use the IP in question, but proof of use is essential to support the claim of ownership. In these countries, you need not rush straight to the registry before beginning to use your IP, but be certain your proof of invention or use is in order and act diligently and timely to secure registrations. The wise course of action is to file an application based on intent to use the IP and then later provide the proof of use to finalize the registration if necessary.
- A long list can be compiled of individuals and companies that in hindsight have recognized the value of IP too late and have lost significant sums because of failure to protect the IP before public disclosure. One example is the creator of the term "Magic Marker," which was released into the public domain and could not be reclaimed. Similarly, the marks "286" and "386" (for computer chips) were ruled to have entered the public domain and become generic before protection was sought, and therefore use by competing traders was not infringement.
- Inventors commonly like to reduce their ideas to practice, but this is not necessary prior to filing a patent application. If an inventor does want to build a working model for purposes of testing the invention and obtaining financing, caution should be taken to avoid public disclosure. Experimental use will not constitute prior art, provided the intent of the use is clear and that unlimited public access is not permitted.
- For inventions, the existence of prior art will prohibit you from obtaining a patent in nearly all countries. Any public disclosure or use, even inadvertent, will trigger a very short deadline for filing a patent in most countries. Your own patent application in one country will be considered prior art in other countries, as it is a published disclosure of your invention. Therefore, you must be prepared to move quickly and take advantage of treaties that allow recognition of filing dates across international borders.

- Trade secrets must be protected from public disclosure all the time. To qualify for protection, a trade secret must give your company a competitive advantage. It need not be new or novel, but it must always be kept in confidence. You should alert your employees to the presence of trade secrets, obtain written confidentiality agreements from them, and train them on how to handle trade secret materials.

SEEKING LEGAL ADVICE

The importance of seeking advice from a legal counselor who is knowledgeable in IP issues cannot be over emphasized. Your attorney can point out flaws in your IP policy and strategy, advise on your proposed IP, and recommend preventative measures. To offer advice relevant to your specific situation, your attorney must be familiar with your trade or industry, your markets, your current IP portfolio, and your business goals, and it is your job to prepare and provide sufficient material for your attorney to gain a clear picture.

TIP: It is unwise to brief your attorney quickly and then leave the creation and implementation of an IP strategy solely to the attorney. Your attorney cannot know all of the parameters of your situation. While your attorney can suggest and advise you on the various options and the legal effects of your actions, your attorney will not make your business decisions for you.

Be prepared to meet with your attorney at regular intervals to ensure that your IP rights continue to be maintained and protection is expanded as your business grows and changes. If your company is serious about its IP, your policy should be to spend the time understanding the legalities of IP rights and protection. You might also consider asking your attorney to be part of the educational program that you implement for your employees, or at a minimum to meet with upper management of your marketing, financial, R&D, and administrative departments.

CHAPTER 6

Ensuring the Value of Your IP Rights: Protection After Creation

AS A TRADER AND CONSUMER, you must always remember one simple thing: IP rights are affirmative, not defensive. Creation gives you ownership rights. Registration confirms your ownership rights. However, merely creating and registering IP will not prevent someone else from using, and even registering, similar or the same IP in global markets. This means that you must make the effort to assert the rights that you claim against others who infringe them, and in turn you are responsible for respecting the IP rights of others. If you fail to assert your rights, the infringer will not be stopped. Wherever civil, criminal, or customs sanctions are available, you must be ready to press them. The IP laws of a country may provide you a remedy, but it is you who must exercise *affirmatively* your right to the remedy.

Registering Your IP

WHY REGISTER?

The reasons to register IP are numerous:

- Registration of your IP is the least expensive means of establishing ownership and deterring infringement, provided you carefully develop and implement your IP strategy.
- A registration serves as a public notice to other traders that you have a claim of exclusive rights.
- In most countries, registration entitles you to use an actual notice of registration.
- If you intend to license or sell your ideas or works to other companies, an IP registration is likely to open the door more quickly because most companies refuse to look at unsolicited ideas and works.
- Perhaps most importantly, registration in compliance with a statutory system usually affords you remedies against infringers that are available only by statute and only for registered IP. In fact, in some countries, no remedies are available for infringing activities taken against unregistered IP.

A note of caution, however. You should not just blindly whip about registering all of your IP wherever possible. There are two absolutely essential considerations that you must take into account. First, always make a careful cost evaluation a part of your IP strategy and continue to regularly revise the value of your IP in relationship to registration and enforcement costs. Second, always remember that registrations are in effect public records. While they will serve as public notice of your claim to exclusive rights, they will also make your rights visible to the public.

For trademarks, which will be released and even promoted to the public, disclosure through registration is not a problem. For some ideas and works, a patent is the best means of ensuring your competitive edge and the value of your invention, particularly if you plan to license it (in other words release it to the industry). However, for other ideas and works—for example, your secret formula, recipe, or method—disclosure in a patent may not be what you really want to do. It might be preferable to keep them as trade secrets locked within the halls of your business.

TIP: Trade secret protection is not always the best. Another trader may legitimately perform "reverse engineering" on any product that you have placed into the public domain. You can then no longer claim exclusive trade secret rights, but if you have registered a patent for the product, your exclusive rights are protected at least for some years. Also, trade secrets are not necessarily protected in every country, and even if there is protection, it is more frequently addressed through court systems, which may or may not be familiar or sophisticated. Finally, remember that if you have to seek enforcement of a trade secret, it has already probably been publicly exposed and will have lost at least some value.

Therefore, before you reveal your deepest business secrets in a registration application, you should consider the effect of registration, carefully select the IP to be registered and to be left unregistered, and definitely seek legal advice to try to sort out the complexities in terms of your own business situation.

If you decide not to register some of your company's IP, be certain that you have nevertheless implemented a protection system for it as part of your IP strategy. This system should include confidentiality and nondisclosure agreements, obvious and clear notices of IP rights, strict management and monitoring procedures, and training of employees, franchisees, and others who are authorized to use the IP. Do not stop reading this chapter at the registration section. Be certain to follow through on the remainder of the recommendations because your IP will have value to your company only if you take the necessary actions to promote and preserve that value.

WHAT SHOULD YOU REGISTER?

- PATENTS, COPYRIGHTS, TRADEMARKS The most common registries available internationally, regionally, and nationally accept registrations for the traditional types of IP: patents, copyrights, and trademarks. Historically, these rights have developed through different paths with the result that a patent can be obtained only by registration, while a copyright arises automatically at the time a work of expression is fixed in a tangible form. In a few countries, copyright registries have actually been eliminated (for example, the United Kingdom). In many countries, trademarks and copyrights can be protected by court actions even if they have not been registered, although registration makes additional statutory remedies available.

- DOMAIN NAMES Registration of domain names has become increasingly significant in the past decade, and today it is essential. However, it is also fairly confusing because of the technological explosion in available domains, companies, servers, and so forth. Domains are being set up in countries as diverse as Australia and Tuvalu. The number of users and websites is multiplying every day. Domain names are commonly treated like trademarks in both practice and in the law. The best strategy is to register all of your primary marks as domain names, plus your company or trade name if that is different.

- APPELLATIONS OF ORIGIN It is a common practice to include a geographical indicator on the labeling of products or services. The food industry in particular is famous for adding geographical source names to their products, one of the most well known being the name "Champagne." Although not IP in the technical sense since they are not a work of creative intellect and a single trader cannot claim exclusive rights in them, appellations of origin can function in a fashion similar to trademarks by serving to distinguish your products or services from those of other traders who are not located in the same place. If you use an appellation of origin in connection with your product or service, you should consider whether to register it.

  To register an appellation, you must first find out if the country of origin has a registry or another listing or agency by which the names can be recognized. Assuming there is a registry, you must also determine whether the name qualifies for registration. An appellation of origin (1) must be the geographical name of a country, region, or locality from which the product originates, and (2) must serve to indicate particular qualities and characteristics that result exclusively or essentially because of natural and human features present in that geographical area.

  Once registered in the country of origin, the appellation of origin can be registered internationally with the World Intellectual Property Organization (WIPO), provided the country of origin is a member of the Lisbon Agreement. This registration is available through the following signatory countries: Algeria, Bulgaria, Burkina Faso, Congo, Costa Rica, Cuba, Czech Republic, France, Gabon, Haiti, Hungary, Israel, Italy Mexico, Portugal, Slovakia, Togo, Tunisia, and Yugoslavia.

- CROSS-OVER REGISTRATIONS The best IP strategy will take into account the advantages of protecting different aspects of IP through different registrations. For example, the trade names and slogans used in an advertisement might be protected by trademark registration, while the artwork or the text and tune of a promotional jingle can be protected by copyright. A trademark logo can be developed into a fabric pattern, and the design can in turn can be protected by copyright. Characters in a software game are protected by copyright, the name of the game might be registered as a trademark, and the program itself can be protected by a separate copyright. As more and more elements go into making a product, more and more IP rights will need protection: a company's new type of compact disc (CD) box is patented, the advertising text, label design, song words, and musical scores are all copyrighted, the mark and logo used on the labels and imprinted on the CDs are registered as separate trademarks, and the formulas for the unique iridescent colors used on the CD and the long-lasting scent emanating from the labels are protected as trade secrets.

TIP: When evaluating your company's IP, identification is only the first step. It is essential to break out each product or service into the different types of IP rights that can be protected. The second step should be taken with the assistance of legal counsel. It involves reviewing the effect of the different registrations and the extent to which the protection and remedies they offer will be beneficial and practical within the particular circumstances of your business and markets. You should then be sufficiently informed to consider whether you need to cross-register your IP.

WHERE SHOULD YOU REGISTER?

Registrations of IP rights are primarily national. This means that if you secure a registration in one country, it will not give your IP rights protection worldwide. Of course, national registrations in every country means advance costs before you realize the value and profit from your IP, which may not match your immediate budget and may not be satisfactory under your risk-cost analysis.

Most companies build their IP strategies on a geographical step-up program. That is, they identify the countries of highest priority, second priority, third priority, and so forth. As each geographical level is achieved, an intermediate review is made, plans are altered to accommodate market, political, industry, and company policy changes, and the registrations are then filed at the next level. This procedure allows the company's reputation and markets to increase commensurate with the expansion of registrations into more and more countries.

When selecting the countries of highest priority for the registration of your company's IP, you should consider the following places:

1. Countries where you plan to market or use your IP within the next five years.
2. Countries where there are substantial markets for your industry, even if you may not expand there for several years. This factor is particularly important if your business is targeted at a niche market. For example, if you sell surf and scuba gear, you should register your IP in the countries where these sports are popular.
3. Countries where your IP might become known through mediums that cause reputation to spill over the boundaries and create a new market demand. In particular, consider countries with significant tourist and travel trades, regional trade pacts, and well known clearing centers for imports and exports.
4. Countries where your IP is likely to be infringed, especially if products are likely to be exported or imported in those countries with minimal customs regulation.

At the second and third geographical levels, you might place countries where you have secondary markets, where IP can be easily and inexpensively registered, and where applications must be made within a certain time after your initial IP applications have been filed. These intermediate levels typically include countries where registrations can be obtained on the basis of international and regional treaties. Countries that would be of even less priority might include those with substantial political unrest (unless you are selling weapons), undeveloped infrastructures (unless you are in an infrastructure industry), and significant poverty (unless you have markets there).

HOW DO YOU REGISTER IP RIGHTS?

In many countries, applications for IP registrations can be filed directly by the IP owner, although sometimes agents within the country must be used unless the IP owner has established a residence or branch office there. Nevertheless, employing legal professionals to carry out your company's program of IP registrations is highly recommended because the task of multiple worldwide filings is quite complex and time-consuming for the uninitiated. It involves different national laws and agencies plus distinct procedures, practices, deadlines, and filing requirements. Even within a single country, different types of IP are subject to completely different registration requirements and may be registered at different agencies or departments within agencies. For most companies, there are simply too many differences, making direct filings less cost-effective than instructing an IP attorney or agent to secure the registrations.

A general familiarity with the registration process is advisable so that you can ask the right questions, feel satisfied with your instructions, and monitor the progress of your IP registrations. In the most basic format, registration involves the steps described here for each traditional type of IP:

- COPYRIGHT Works of expression are protected by copyright from the moment they are placed into a tangible medium. No registration formality is required to secure protection. In many countries, registration will enhance the remedies available for infringement, and therefore it is advisable.

  Registration is made by filing an application together with a fee, a description of the work, and if required by national law, a copy of the work. The application process can be somewhat tricky if the work was made for hire, a prior work was registered, or the work contains materials subject to the copyrights of others. A copyright registry official usually makes a formal examination of the application, which involves a review of the application for compliance with the formalities required. The examiner may ask the applicant to correct or make further disclosures in the application before it is approved. Once accepted, the registration is placed on file and a notice or certificate is issued to the copyright owner.

  The term of validity for a copyright varies depending on national laws. Most commonly, a copyright held by an individual is valid for the individual's lifetime plus 50 or 70 years. For specific owners (such as companies, anonymous creators, and creators using pseudonyms) and for certain types of works (such as sound recordings and broadcasts), terms of validity often are set as a fixed period from the first date of first creation or publication, sometimes with one or two short renewal periods. At the end of the copyright protection term, the work enters the public domain.

- PATENT An invention is not automatically protected at the time it is made. Exclusive rights come into existence only when a patent is secured.

  To register a patent, a rather complicated document must be prepared that typically consists of an abstract of the invention, a detailed description, claims setting forth the breadth of protection, prior art references, and technical drawings. In some countries, the document must be prepared or translated into an official language. This document together with an application and a prescribed filing fee are submitted to the national patent registry. Additional supporting documentation must be filed if the applicant has filed a patent application elsewhere and is now claiming a priority date based on the earlier filing. Also, many patents are subject to assignment—a transfer of ownership rights from the inventor to a person who will exploit the patent—requiring the filing of additional documentation to prove ownership rights.

  Most national patent registries will first examine applications for compliance with formal requirements (paper size, requisite fee, signatures on documents, and so forth). The examiner may request the applicant to make corrections in the application to comply with formalities. A notice of the patent application will usually be published in an official government journal, although this often happens long after the filing date, even 18 to 24 months later.

A few countries recognize and record patents that have been previously issued in another country, in which case a substantive examination is not made and notice of recordal is simply issued after publication. Most countries do make a substantive examination, which begins after publication with the applicant's Request for Substantive Examination, although the filing of a Request is not required in every country. Failure to timely submit the Request may result in withdrawal of the application. The patent is passed through a fairly rigorous examination for inventiveness, prior art, scope of protection, and so forth, and if changes must be made, the applicant will be notified to make amendments, which must be filed within a specified period to avoid abandonment of the application. Assuming the official examiner is satisfied, the patent will be accepted and granted.

In some countries, there is a procedure by which third parties can oppose the grant of a patent. The opposition period usually starts from the time the patent registry issues an official notice of the grant and runs for several months. The patent applicant is permitted to respond to the third party's opposition and to amend the application to overcome it. The official examiner will then reexamine the patent and, if found acceptable, will grant it.

The term of a patent depends on national law, and there is a lot of variation. In some countries, patents are valid for 20 years without any renewal. Other countries impose terms of 5 or 15 years and allow for renewal periods for a total protection term of up to 20 years. Patents for designs, plants, and other special inventions may have shorter terms—sometimes 10 years with or without a renewal period of 5 years. Most countries impose maintenance or annuity fees (basically property taxes) that must be paid annually or at other periodic intervals to keep the patent in force. An invention will enter the public domain once the patent has elapsed.

■ **TRADEMARKS** National requirements for the registration of trademarks are still quite different, despite the attempt in recent years through international trade treaties to make the systems more uniform. In many countries failure to register will result in no protection whatsoever, although in some countries there is minimal protection available under court-developed doctrines or laws regulating unfair competition and trading practices.

The registration process typically involves the filing of an application with supporting documents, which may include a declaration or sworn document identifying the applicant as the mark owner, a registration certificate from the applicant's own country, plus numerous representations or replicas of the mark in special formats. If the applicant seeks a date of filing that is based on an earlier application in another country, additional documentation must be submitted to support that claim. Evidence of any assignments and license arrangements must also be submitted, although disclosure of the entire contract can usually be avoided by submission of a deed or other similar documentation that references the contract.

In most registries, the application will be examined for compliance with certain formalities before being passed to an examination of its substance. During these examinations, the registry officials may issue any number of notices, requests for clarification or amendment, or objections to the applicant, who is then given a short time to respond. Assuming the applicant eventually satisfies the registry officials, the application is finally accepted. At this point, the application will either be published or registered and then published. The publication in an official journal starts a short period within which the trademark may be opposed by third parties. Absent any opposition, the trademark will be considered registered and registration will be confirmed to the applicant.

Terms of validity for trademarks are becoming more standard as countries join the international treaties. The most common term is 10 years, but the initial term is renewable (also for 10 years at a time) indefinitely. Renewal may be contingent on proof of use in the country. Failure to renew a trademark allows it to enter the public domain.

WHEN SHOULD YOU REGISTER IP RIGHTS?

Time is a significant factor in the registration of IP rights. If you delay too long, you are likely to lose your rights to the public domain. If you begin registration before you are ready to file applications worldwide, you may lose your rights to the public domain. International treaties can be useful for preserving your rights for a short period of time (6 months to 1 year), but only in countries that have signed the treaties. You need to find just the right balance, preferably with the assistance of legal counsel. Keep in mind these rules of thumb:

- COPYRIGHTS In most countries, copyrights automatically attach when a work of expression is recorded in a tangible medium. However, in some countries, additional statutory remedies for infringement are available only after registration has been secured, and the infringement must have occurred after the filing date of the registration.
- PATENTS Patent protection is not available if the invention has been publicly released. Publication of an application is considered prior art. Some but not all countries allow a grace period (6 months to 1 year) for filing after the applicant has published the invention. Therefore, it is essential to file your patents in all of the intended countries within a short period of time before your registrations are barred by prior art.
- TRADEMARKS There are no specific deadlines by which you can lose your mark to the public domain, but many countries follow a first to file or first to use rule, which means you could lose your rights to local companies who file or use before you enter the market. Also, in some countries, statutory remedies for infringement can be claimed only if the trademark has been registered prior to the infringement.

Applying Notices to Your IP

Whenever possible, you should ensure that your IP shows a notice of your rights. If you hold a registration, the notice that you can use is likely to be regulated by the laws of the country where you display it. For patents and trademarks, it is also important not to display a notice claiming that your IP has been registered before the registration has issued, as this may be punishable by fine in some places.

The most commonly accepted notices for IP rights are as follows:

Copyrights: Copyright © [*year*] [*name of holder*]

Patents: ® or Reg. Pat. [*number*]

Trademarks: ™ or ® (*but* ™ *often indicates an unregistered mark*)

Trade Secrets: Confidential Property

Seven Easy-Care Steps To Protect Your Trademark Rights

Protection of your trademark rights begins with you. The manner in which you use your trademark may determine whether you can continue to claim exclusivity or whether you lose your rights to the public domain. Follow these seven simple rules on all business documents, including contracts, memorandums, advertising literature, displays, packaging, labels, correspondence, invoices, flyers, and other similar items. Make it a top priority to ensure that all members of your company know and follow these rules. If you see or hear your trademark used in third party sources, such as in media articles, dictionaries, business reference publications, speeches, and educational materials, ensure that those sources are aware of your rights and are also following these rules.

1. TRADEMARKS ARE LONERS.

Use a trademark in such a manner as to distinguish it from all surrounding text. This may be accomplished by the use of ALL CAPITALS or "Initial Capitals Within Quotes." At a minimum, use Initial Capitals. You could also use italic or bold fonts for the trademark, or if color printing is available, a distinct color. Assuming you follow Rule 3, below, be certain that the trademark stands alone and that any generic product name is NOT given the same treatment as the trademark.

EXAMPLES
FLYREELER fly-attracting ointment
"Flyreeler" fly-attracting ointment
Flyreeler fly-attracting ointment

2. TRADEMARKS ARE STATUS SEEKERS.

Indicate that status of your trademark whenever possible. If the trademark has been registered, use the trademark notice ® or whatever marking is permitted by the country where you are providing your goods or services. Another marking notice that is often used to designate trademark rights is ™, and a third option is to include an asterisk with a footnote reference to your ownership rights. The notice you use, or whether you may use a notice at all, is dependent on the local laws of the country where you are providing your goods or services. The marking notice should appear at least once in all printed matter, preferably when the trademark first appears.

EXAMPLES
FLYREELER® fly-attracting ointment
FLYREELER™
FLYREELER* *A trademark of BugGone, Inc.

3. TRADEMARKS LIKE GOOD COMPANY.

A trademark is a proper adjective. It should therefore be followed by, and not used as, the noun that is the common name of the product or service. It is preferable to follow this rule wherever the trademark appears in literature, but at the least it should be used properly the first time. If the trademark is used in connection with many types of products, and therefore a single descriptive noun will not apply, a term with broader meaning, such as "products" or "product line," may be used instead. Also, the word "brand" may be used to reduce the possibility that the public may begin to use the trademark as a generic name for the product.

EXAMPLES
FLYREELER® fly-attracting ointment
FLYREELER® brand fly-attracting ointment
"Flyreeler" brand products
the FLYREELER® brand product line

4. TRADEMARKS DO NOT LIKE CLINGING VINES.

A trademark is not a noun. It cannot posses something else. Never use it in the possessive form, unless of course the trademark is possessive (e.g., MIMI'S® restaurant).

EXAMPLES	
Incorrect	Correct
FLYREELER's banana-like odor will catch flies every time	The banana-like odor of the FLYREELER® ointment will catch flies every time.

5. TRADEMARKS ARE SINGULAR.

A trademark is a proper adjective and therefore should never be used in plural form, unless of course the trademark itself is plural (e.g., J.C. Penneys® or Mervins®).

EXAMPLES	
Incorrect	Correct
For a large area, use two FLYREELERS.	For a large area, two bottles of FLYREELER ointment will be needed.

6. TRADEMARKS ARE ALWAYS PROPER, NEVER COMMON.

As proper adjectives, trademarks must never be used as common descriptive adjectives or as verbs. A trademark must be reserved to identify your company as the source of the product or service. It should not describe the materials or characteristics of the product or service, nor should it be used to refer to an action taken in connection with the product or service.

EXAMPLES	
Incorrect	Correct
The FLYREELER® electronic flycatcher hangs easily from a porch light or kitchen curtain rod.	The electronic fly-catcher spread with the FLYREELER® ointment will hang easily from a porch light or kitchen curtain rod.
FLYREELER® those pesky pests.	Use FLYREELER® brand ointment in your flycatcher and your house will be fly-free today.

7. TRADEMARKS ARE PROUD OF THEIR OWNERS.

If the name of the trademark owner is not apparent from the literature, label, or other documentation, include a notice of ownership. This rule is of particular importance if a company's trademark is not the same as the company's name.

EXAMPLES
FLYREELER* *A registered trademark for fly-attracting ointment made by BugGone, Inc.

(Used with permission of Stephen L. Anderson, Anderson & Shippey, Irvine, CA. ©1997 Stephen L. Anderson.)

Using Your IP

The creation of IP is a wasteful exercise unless you also put your IP to use. The value of your IP will increase as you use it, and you will reap the rewards of a growing, international clientele. Many countries, including the US, Canada, Mexico, Turkey, and the United Kingdom, have use requirements for registered IP to remain registered. In addition, many countries will impose compulsory licenses on your registered inventions if you fail to use them within a reasonable time.

Use of IP can take many forms other than direct sales or performances, and whether an activity qualifies as use in a particular country is dependent on national laws. Use might include advertising without sales, supplying a product to an organization in a country at no charge, spill-over broadcasts and movies through media that reach across the border, and sales on international transport carriers (trains, planes, and the like). The manufacture and export of products is a form of use, as are indirect sales through a licensed manufacturer or producer.

TIP: Always remember to ensure that you keep evidence of your use in the event that you need to prove your ownership rights, the geographical extent of your reputation, and the fame of your name. If you have authorized another person to use your IP, be certain to record that agreement against your registered IP so that person's use is considered to be your own company's use.

If you authorize another person to use your IP, you must ensure that you have retained your IP rights by using a strict license or franchise contract. In addition, you should investigate the other person thoroughly before making any agreement and monitor the arrangement through independent means thereafter. Failure to take a strong stance in your licensing and franchising arrangements can result in loss of value in your IP, and even in loss of the IP itself. If you are selling licenses to the consumer market or performances to the public, you must take additional precautions—such as copy-disabling features, strict taping and photograph policies, and an educational spin on promotion—because of the nearly impossible task of catching every infringement once the IP rights are let loose in public.

When Diligence is Due: Preventive Maintenance

WHAT IS DUE DILIGENCE?

Due diligence is a process for the independent review and verification of information about a potential business transaction and the parties related or connected to the transaction. The process typically begins with disclosure and review of public documents such as company, tax, name, and mark registrations, ownership and tax records, and profit-loss and financial statements. A more in-depth study is then undertaken to ferret out the accounting procedures, the accuracy of information provided, and the relationships, backgrounds, and political connections of the proposed business owners.

DO YOUR DUE DILIGENCE BEFORE YOU SIGN

Before putting your IP rights at risk—whether through licensing, signing up a distributor or manufacturer, or entering a joint venture or other business relationship—due diligence is a "must-do" task. Even in countries where IP rights appear to be protected by law and enforced by strict governmental controls, you can get into trouble if you do not seek out the truth before you sign the contract.

WHY IS DUE DILIGENCE IMPORTANT?

Due diligence is significant to the discovery and evaluation of the risks involved and the potential for success of your business venture. When you build any business relationship with another party, an independent evaluation will reveal whether your proposed counterpart is in fact worthy of your trust. Your name, property, good will, reputation, and livelihood are on the line.

Of course, your contractual clauses may require disclosures of questionable liabilities, transactions, and connections, but most likely you will not be informed that your potential partner has been involved in fraudulent or criminal activities, has contacts with organized crime, or uses influential links with government officials. You may demand quality control and compliance with certain safety and health standards, labor protections, and discrimination laws, but you cannot know whether these conditions can or will be met without independent verification.

The initial cost of due diligence can avoid a disaster, as in the following cases:

- An international bank requested due diligence on a company that was filing for liquidation. The background check revealed that the company was still operating, business was booming, plans for expansion were being implemented, company assets had been transferred to friends and relatives, and the liquidation was intended as a means of deceiving creditors.
- A corporation seeking a joint venture with a clothing manufacturer requested due diligence. During an undercover inspection of the premises, the manufacturer was found to be making jeans and shirts displaying the trademarks of several famous companies, but he could not produce any license, contract, registration, or other document authorizing his use of those marks. A further check revealed that the owner of the business had a criminal record for trademark infringement.
- Based on books and legal documents disclosed, a company was about to sign a license agreement for the manufacture of its goods. It first requested due diligence in the form of undercover interviews with neighbors and employees of the factory. The investigation revealed that the factory equipment was temporary and portable and that the factory was not producing any goods. Rather, whenever the owner was alerted that a potential partner or buyer would be arriving for an inspection, he simply set up the equipment and hired workers into a vacant facility to make it look like it was in operation.
- A manufacturer of hydraulic lifts for auto repair shops entered into an exclusive distributorship with a company. In the first year, substantial profits were realized, but sales in the second and third years decreased substantially until a mere trickle of income was being realized. An investigation showed that the distributor had set up another competing company. The manufacturer had not realized that the local distributor was able to make quality equipment. By the time he found out, significant market share was lost to the domestic company.

HOW IS DUE DILIGENCE CONDUCTED?

In general, due diligence is conducted in several phases, during which you should employ a team of professionals to assist you in evaluating the risks and promised potential of the proposed transaction. Your first decision must be to set the scope and depth of due diligence to account for the circumstances of the transaction. You will need to consider such factors as whether you are establishing a long term relationship or a single, short term transaction, whether the business partner's country has a stable government and reliable legal system, and whether the goods or services are of such a nature as to be attractive to questionable influences.

In general, these steps are recommended:

- You should insist that the other party adhere to disclosure schedules required by contract, provide detailed business data and audited accounts, and permit you to interview senior management personnel.
- You should employ your own legal and financial advisors to review the information you collect on the business operation.
- You should request an opinion from legal and financial advisors about the local laws, customs, and practices of doing businesses in the country, both for purposes of alerting you to the need for in-depth due diligence and also for purposes of

evaluating the information you receive about the particular business within the context of a country and culture that differs from your own.

- You should hire an investigator, accountant, or law firm to provide you with whatever information and documents are available in public database files and record registries for the business and for its owners and key personnel, including documents that must be filed with official authorities for taxation, business formation, financial registration, company name registration, and brand or mark registration.
- You should instruct an investigator to check into and observe the following:
  - Political and social standing, power, and influence of the business owner and key personnel.
  - Credit standing of the business owner and key personnel.
  - History of the business in terms of meeting its liabilities, meeting its production requirements, and maintaining its financial stability.
  - Reputation of the company among the local trade and industry for quality, fair trade, and ethical business practices.
  - Quality of products or services offered.
  - Working conditions and treatment of employees.
  - Management style and effectiveness.
  - Conflicts of interest, such as affiliation with another business that is directly competitive with your own business.
  - Previous or pending litigation, criminal convictions, or bankruptcies against the business or its owner or key personnel.
  - Evidence of corruption, counterfeiting, unfair trading, or other illegal activities.
  - Motivation of the business owner for entering the transaction with you.

IS YOUR DUE DILIGENCE EFFECTIVE?

You cannot be absolutely certain about whether your due diligence has been effective. Even ties to influential relatives or organized crime can be so well hidden that a thorough investigation will not reveal them. There are some precautions you can and should take, however, to make your best effort at due diligence.

- Use attorneys and accountants who have a reputation for integrity and who are knowledgeable about the country, practices, and political relationships within the country.
- Use an investigative service with a reputation for honesty and with the right contacts within local law enforcement to get in-depth information. Your investigator must know what information is available, how to obtain it, who to approach, and how to maneuver within the cultural and business traditions of the particular country and industry.
- Insist on a "deep probe" by an investigator who will conduct personal interviews with key personnel and who is familiar with what to look for when making personal observations of company premises and practices.

- Proceed with caution by creating a relationship that is limited in the beginning and that can mature over time through incentives for expansion.

Watching for Infringements

Your company must take assertive steps to monitor your IP rights in order to ensure that the value of your IP is maintained. The following actions should be implemented as part of your IP strategy:

- Schedule regular educational updates of your company's employees with regard to the confidentiality of trade secrets.
- Implement a system for the review of industry, trade, business, popular journals, and other media for potential infringements.
- Hire a trademark and patent watch service to periodically review government publications worldwide for filings that infringe on your own IP rights.
- Hire a private investigation firm to periodically survey the markets where infringements are most likely to be found.
- Contract with an independent agency to audit the production of your licenses at regular intervals.
- Set up a system of incentives for consumers, licensees, franchisees, sales representatives, retailers, and others who come in contact with your IP to report possible infringements, and act quickly and decisively on such reports.
- Keep a watchful eye on your established competition and on rising companies.

Stopping Infringements of Your IP

Although some problems, particularly minor ones, can be dealt with in face to face negotiation with an infringer, in most situations you will probably need to call in the legal professionals to put an absolute halt to infringing activities. Stopping infringements is a complicated business because the facts, parties, procedures, practices, and laws involved in each situation will vary. There are no international mechanisms, and therefore fighting infringement must be done on a national level.

With the assistance and involvement of your legal counsel, you should devise a plan of action to attack infringements immediately and quickly whenever they are found. You should ask your attorney to explain what remedies you might have in the locality of the infringement. These might include (1) judicial remedies, such as temporary injunctions, permanent injunctions, court actions for damages based on passing off, infringement, unfair trade practices, breach of contract, and anti-trust; (2) administrative remedies, such as for cancellation of or opposition to an illegal registration; and (3) criminal actions, such as for illegal manufacture and sale of infringing products, unfair business practices, and anti-trust activities.

Your attorney will also make you aware of possible defenses that might be raised against your claim of infringement. For example, the other party may claim that an idea was conceived independently through parallel research, that use was believed to be within the exception of "fair use" as permitted by law, that the IP owner has not used the IP within a reasonable time, or that the suit is barred because it was not filed within a time limit set by statute. Any evidence that might indicate the presence of one of these defenses should be immediately brought to your attorney's attention so that a strategy can be devised in advance to overcome the defense, thereby avoiding a later, fatal surprise.

Enforcement of IP rights may seem expensive, but taking an aggressive stance against an infringer will usually pay off in the end. In some countries, treble damage awards can be made against an infringer who acted in bad faith. When settling, it is possible to insist on payment of your legal costs, particularly if you have a strong case of bad faith infringement. Most importantly, if your company gains a reputation in the industry for strict and quick enforcement, that reputation will help to deter infringers, who are more likely to pick on easier targets.

Contracting with Professional IP Development or Management Companies

As important as it is to monitor, maintain, and enforce your company's IP rights, it can become virtually impossible to do so effectively, for the practical reasons that these activities are not the primary function of your company and the world is just too big a place. In today's world, there are companies that specialize in the development and management of IP rights, and often it makes sense to leave the work to them, provided you instruct and monitor them carefully.

- INVENTION DEVELOPMENT COMPANIES There are quite a number of companies available that offer patent filing, developing, and marketing services. These companies specialize in assisting inventors to evaluate, perfect, broker, and promote an invention. They may prepare and file patent applications, and advise on other licenses or compliance requirements that must be met prior to manufacturing or selling an invented product. Extreme care and due diligence must be exercised in choosing one of these companies, including a check with business registries and consumer bureaus. Beware of companies that agree to draft and file your patent for you but do not tell you whether this service is performed by an attorney.
- COLLECTIVE MANAGEMENT ORGANIZATIONS (CMO) For works protected by copyright, there are various industry-specific organizations that have systems through which the copyright owners receive payment for use of their works. These organizations are especially useful for owners who would otherwise have to monitor and negotiate with hundreds and thousands of users of the works worldwide, and for users who would otherwise have to seek licenses or permission from hundreds and thousands of owners each time a work is used. A CMO will typically manage rights of public performance, broadcasting, mechanical reproduction, and photocopying, and it may negotiate licenses and collect and distribute royalties. Foreign IP portfolios are managed through reciprocal representation agreements with CMOs in other countries. Examples of CMOs include the Confederation of Societies of Authors and Composers (CISAC), International Federation of Reprographic Reproduction Organisations (IFRRO), the Association of European Performers Organizations (AEPO), International Federation of Actors (FIA), International Federation of Musicians (FIM), International Federation of the Phonographic Industry (IFPI), and the Software Publishers Association (SPA).

CHAPTER 7

Parties to IP Rights, Part II: Protection of the Weak and Strong

AS THE PRODUCTS, SERVICES, CREATIONS AND PROCESSES to which IP rights attach move from owner to user to consumer, the various parties that touch on those rights will tend to change position in their bargaining power, from strong to weak to strong and then weak again. The ownership of IP rights is complicated by the fact that, although the tangible properties may be transferred from hand to hand, the intangible IP rights remain with the owner. To a large extent, the owner must count on the integrity of consumers to respect the owner's IP rights, because of the expense of fighting all but the most flagrant infringements.

Creator

KNOW WHO OWNS IT

Your company's employees create IP—perhaps clothing designs, trademarks, logos, and inventions for the transference of designs onto fabric. You decide to license the IP rights to another company to manufacture your clothing. Your license agreement states that the licensee must protect the mark within its own country on your behalf, and based on that authority, your licensee files twelve trademark applications for your marks in his name to ensure coverage of stickers, paper, jewelry, luggage, and other clothing accessories. If your licensee is allowed to retain the trademarks, he will also have a right to use them on his own goods and your own marks are liable to be diluted. You will have to negotiate with your licensee for the ownership rights to the trademarks, if possible, paying only the filing costs.

Meanwhile, your employee who invented the design transference process itself licenses it to his friend who wants to use it in the production of canvas bags. With regard to your own employee, if you do not have an express agreement assigning his rights to the company, you will have some tricky negotiations with him and his licensee, because a patent belongs to the inventor in the absence of an assignment to the employer.

THE MORAL: Your ownership rights in your IP must be clearly stated in agreements and understood by all parties, and you should be the only person responsible for asserting your IP rights.

SECURE OWNERSHIP RIGHTS BEFORE REVEALING THE IP

A lot of time and labor has been spent in developing your company's database program. Now that it is perfected, your company's management is considering whether to license it to a software publisher or otherwise to sell rights to use it to other companies within your industry. Before you label the supporting documentation as confidential and identify the software as a trade secret of your company, one of the programmers discusses it with a software publisher, who realizes the potential and begins to develop a similar system. Finally, you decide to file a copyright registration, but you find that the software publisher has already begun distribution of a very similar program. You may not be able to retrieve your rights because you failed to diligently protect your trade secret and it has now entered the public domain.

THE MORAL: Valuable rights can be lost through inadvertence or neglect of your IP strategy. It is important to train your employees, secure registrations, and place ownership notices on your IP.

CHECK OUT THE OTHER PARTY

A manufacturer approaches your company's representative at a trade show and suggests a license agreement for country X. Your representative provides some literature and a few product samples to the manufacturer and refers the name and address of the manufacturer to the licensing department. The concept is passed about from desk to desk for a time, and then finally someone tries to contact the manufacturer but gets no response. Two years later, your company decides to file a trademark and expand your sales into country X, at which time you learn that the manufacturer has already registered an identical mark, has been producing and selling similar goods locally for several years, and has begun exporting to two neighboring countries. You will now have an expensive infringement action in more than one jurisdiction, whereas you could have been receiving royalties from a licensee if you had made the original deal. It is also probable that you will receive bad press from the local media for crushing a native business. On the other hand, if you had done due diligence on the manufacturer, you might have found out about his propensities for infringing prior to handing over your merchandise, in which case you could have kept a closer watch on that market.

THE MORAL: If you pay attention to due diligence, you are more likely to gain the right partners and profit from your IP rights, and less likely to have to fight against infringement.

LIMIT YOUR RISK FROM FACTORS BEYOND YOUR CONTROL

Your company designs, manufactures, and sells high quality designer clothing for teenagers, and your logo is considered one of the most attractive in that market. All the trademarks, copyrights, and designs have been filed, and trade secrets have been carefully protected. Nevertheless, your company has to fight more and more infringements to protect your trademark and products, and you have just found goods being imported into a country without your authorization and undermining your exclusive country distributor there. Given the growing attractiveness of your mark, your IP strategy needs to be adjusted to ensure that you can track your products, audit your licensed manufacturers and distributors, and deter infringements through innovative protective devices.

THE MORAL: By managing factors within your control, you can anticipate and take the offensive against infringers.

TREASURE YOUR IP RIGHTS

Based on your business plan, you start up your company, and soon your markets are multiplying and your profits are flowing. You are keeping close watch on the quality of your products, and your reputation is spreading quickly worldwide, but your IP rights are not as important as keeping a fast turnover among your designers. You have been sent infringing products from various markets, but you have not bothered to follow up because of the expense. Then your market share starts to slide and your products stop selling. An investigation reveals that your trademark has been registered by other companies in 15 countries where you have major markets, a number of companies have registered designs that are similar to the ones you have been using, and local markets are being flooded with less expensive infringing copies of goods similar to yours and of similar quality. It will cost you dearly to sort out all these infringements and retrieve your IP rights.

THE MORAL: Your company's IP can become one of its most valuable assets if you treat it as a treasure, but if you fail to polish it, perfect it, and protect it, your company's IP will tarnish and become a liability.

Licensee, Assignee, or Franchisee

VERIFY THE CREATOR'S OWNERSHIP RIGHTS

You have been offered rights to use or own another's IP. You complete all of the paperwork, accept transfer of the rights, and start producing and selling within the terms of the agreement. A few months later, you receive a notice to stop infringing on the IP rights of a third person and you become embroiled in a passing off and infringement action. The party who offered you the rights has since vanished. Proof of what you believed were your own rights may save you from penalties for bad faith use of the IP, but because you failed to do due diligence, you could lose your initial payment price for the rights, your investment in the new business and in building goodwill, plus profits gained from your infringing use. In some countries, you may even be held criminally liable, ruining your reputation even if the charges are dropped because you had no intent to infringe. You might be able to negotiate a license or franchise, thereby saving some of your investment, but the terms are likely to be strictly against you at least for a time, until you prove yourself to be a trustworthy advocate for the rightful owner.

THE MORAL: Due diligence is just as important for the licensee or assignee, and if you take the other party at face value, you could find that the rights you have just purchased are not worth the paper on which they are written.

KNOW WHAT YOU ARE GETTING

Your understanding of the license, franchise, or assignment contract is that the rights being offered are of great value in the market. There is a promise of high profits and an assurance that the IP comes with a solid reputation and valuable goodwill. You sign the contract and make your investment, only to find that the IP has little or no value in your own markets. The IP owner does not permit any alterations. You cannot succeed under the restrictions placed on your use or ownership rights, and you will be liable for a strict termination penalty or for damages for breach of contract if you do not perform your end of the bargain.

THE MORAL: Before signing a contract, be certain that you understand all of its terms and that you have done due diligence in terms of the marketability and reputation of the rights that you are receiving.

RESPECT THE CREATOR'S OWNERSHIP RIGHTS

An exclusive license or franchise agreement is on the table giving you authority to protect the IP creator's ownership rights in your own country. It also requires you establish a system to monitor use of the IP in your own country and to report infringements to the IP owner. The system is completely within your discretion. After signing the agreement, you review the IP registrations in your country and find that the owner has not registered trademarks for goods that could easily be sold in connection with the products currently authorized. You also find that the owner could have registered patent or design rights but has not done so. You file registrations without informing the owner. Finally, you decide that monitoring and reporting infringements is fairly expensive, and therefore you take the most minimal steps to avoid breach of the contract. Unauthorized products begin to appear at below-market prices and start to cut into your market share. At the same time, the IP owner discovers your extra registrations through a routine check. You complain about the unauthorized products, but the IP owner is unwilling to assist you because you have gone beyond the spirit of your agreement, if not the terms, by failing to respect the ownership rights in the IP.

THE MORAL: Do not take a mile when you are offered an inch. The protection of IP rights is in everyone's best interest because any undermining of those rights will dilute them, reduce their value, and ultimately affect everyone's profits.

Attorney for Creator

The complexity of negotiating and formulating a license, assignment, or franchise involving IP rights means that you have most probably sought legal assistance. You should know that your attorney can provide you with services related to the following issues.

- **CHECK OUT THE OTHER PARTY**

Your attorney can:

- Review the other party's business standing and qualifications.
- Obtain a financial and operational background check.
- Assist you to analyze the reports for unusual or conflicting information.

- **CHECK OUT A COUNTRY'S POLITICAL AND LEGAL SITUATION**

Your attorney can:

- Advise you on a nation's system of laws, the development of its judicial system, and the policies of its government in relation to your contractual dealings with a national of that country.
- Caution you about your own country's boycott and embargo policies, travel alerts, and trade restrictions with respect to other countries.

- Apprise you of trade and legal incentives for doing business in other countries.

- **REVIEW UNFAMILIAR NATIONAL REQUIREMENTS**

  Your attorney can:

- Explain the effect of import, export, immigration, labor, environmental, consumer, and other regulatory laws that might affect your transaction.
- Review your IP portfolio to establish whether protection is complete under the laws of your own country and the other party's country.
- Identify whether your transaction might have to be recorded to ensure its validity in your country or the other party's country.
- Check whether any documentary, stamp, or other taxes might apply to the transaction.

- **NEGOTIATE AND PREPARE THE AGREEMENT**

  Your attorney can:

- Review the terms of typical agreements and assist you in tailoring your agreement for the particular transaction.
- Inform you of provisions that you need in order to comply with the peculiarities of the national legal system or to cover matters not otherwise encompassed by those laws.

- **REVIEW RISKS INVOLVED**

  Your attorney can:

- Advise you on monitoring and protecting your IP rights against infringement in the other party's country, whether the infringing acts are committed by the other party or by third parties.

Attorney for Licensee, Assignee, or Franchisee

It is most unwise to enter into a contract for the use or ownership of IP rights without legal advice, particularly because that contract is likely to have been framed by the attorneys of the IP owner. You should keep in mind that your attorney can assist you with the following key issues when considering whether to accept or decline the offer being made by the IP owner.

- **CHECK OUT THE IP OWNER**

  Your attorney can:

- Review the IP owner's business standing, qualifications, and registration or other proof of ownership.
- Obtain a financial and operational background check.
- Assist you to analyze the reports for unusual or conflicting information.

- **REVIEW UNFAMILIAR NATIONAL REQUIREMENTS**

  Your attorney can:

- Explain how import, export, immigration, labor, environmental, consumer, and other regulatory laws will affect your business if you agree to the transaction.
- Review the IP portfolio presented by the IP owner to see whether protection is complete under the laws of your country and recommend that you seek additional protection from the IP owner.
- Identify whether your transaction might have to be recorded to ensure its validity in your country.
- Check whether any documentary, stamp, or other taxes might apply to the transaction.

■ ASSURE YOUR UNDERSTANDING OF THE AGREEMENT

Your attorney can:

- Explain the terms of the agreement offered and recommend negotiating points in your favor.
- Clarify the interests that you are purchasing in the IP and your liabilities in the event of breach.

■ REVIEW RISKS INVOLVED

Your attorney can:

- Inform you of the potential effect of infringement by third parties, and the most time and cost efficient means by which you can assist in monitoring infringement.
- Recommend means by which you can reduce the risk you are taking in investing in another's IP, the value of which is dependent factors beyond your control, such as the IP owner's reputation, goodwill, and policies of enforcement.

CHAPTER 8

Ensuring Precise Contractual Protection of IP Rights

TO THE EXTENT POSSIBLE, you should protect your IP rights through clear and concise contract provisions. Regardless of whether you are the IP owner or the IP user (consumer, licensee, assignee, franchisee, or otherwise), the best means of ensuring that your intent is carried out is by specifically stating your intentions within an agreement. Do not rely on statutory or judicial implications and interpretations because these will not necessarily reflect your will.

In any agreement, it is impossible to cover every possible contingency that might arise. Nevertheless, you should try to draft contract provisions that are clear and that anticipate as many situations as possible. The more definitive the terms, the fewer the disputes will arise and the less expense you will incur in resolving conflicts. Use precise language and avoid legalistic terminology whenever possible, particularly if some of the parties do not speak your language fluently.

The following contract clauses are from a software license. They are not intended to fit your particular IP situation, but rather to give you practice in finding ambiguities and tightening up phrases. Many of the concepts mentioned relative to the software publisher (licensor) and the consumer (licensee) can be taken in a more general context. It is essential to prepare a contract within the circumstances of your own IP situation and not to rely on standard forms or clauses. The following clauses should serve to clarify some of the points your attorney may make and to suggest why your attorney has included certain standard provisions in your agreement.

Provisions of License Agreement (Computer Software)

FORMATION OF THE CONTRACT

- POOR PROVISION:

[*Company Name*] is licensing (not selling) [*Software Name*] ("Software") to you.

ANALYSIS: A contract is formed when each party clearly manifests intent to be bound by the terms that are mutually understood. Typically, this intent is shown by both parties signing the contract. However, a license agreement for a consumer product, such as software, is not likely to be signed by both parties because of the nature of the transaction. Instead, the contract is considered formed when one party (the company) offers the product to the other party (the consumer), who accepts by taking unilateral action (opening the software package).

The provision here states the offer by the company, but it leaves the acceptance to implication. Does the mere purchase of the software imply acceptance of the license terms? Is there an acceptance of the contract terms even if the consumer has not read the terms? If a dispute arises, will a court imply acceptance merely because the consumer used the product? To ensure that both parties understand the importance of their actions—one in making an offer to license, and one in opening the envelope—the provision that follows clearly sets forth the results intended by their actions.

■ BETTER PROVISION:

[*COMPANY NAME*] IS WILLING TO LICENSE THE SOFTWARE [*SOFTWARE NAME*] ("SOFTWARE") TO YOU ONLY ON THE CONDITION THAT YOU ACCEPT ALL OF THE TERMS OF THIS LICENSE AGREEMENT. BEFORE YOU OPEN THE ENVELOPE CONTAINING THE SOFTWARE, PLEASE READ CAREFULLY ALL OF THE TERMS OF THIS LICENSE. BY OPENING THE ENVELOPE, YOU ACCEPT THE TERMS AND CONDITIONS OF THIS LICENSE.

IF YOU DO NOT AGREE TO THESE TERMS AND CONDITIONS, [*COMPANY NAME*] IS NOT WILLING TO LICENSE THE SOFTWARE TO YOU AND YOU MUST RETURN THE UNOPENED ENVELOPE TO THE PLACE WHERE YOU PURCHASED IT, IN WHICH CASE YOUR MONEY WILL BE REFUNDED.

EXCHANGE OF MUTUAL CONSIDERATION

■ POOR PROVISION:

[*Company Name*] GRANTS TO YOU A NONEXCLUSIVE RIGHT TO USE THIS COPY OF THE SOFTWARE.

ANALYSIS: A contract is supported by the exchange of consideration—that is something of value—between the parties. This provision suggests that the company's consideration is in the form of a grant of the right to use its property (the software). For purposes of legal interpretation, the consideration given by the consumer need not be expressed. It is assumed that the consumer has paid a price for the software. However, for practical purposes, it may be useful to remind the consumer that a license fee is included in the price of the software. This should underscore to the consumer the fact that the price of the software consists of a minimal amount for the hard medium on which the software is recorded and the written materials are printed plus a license fee for use of the software and written text itself.

■ BETTER PROVISION:

IN CONSIDERATION OF YOUR PAYMENT OF THE LICENSE FEE, WHICH YOU PAID TOGETHER WITH THE SALES PRICE WHEN YOU OBTAINED THIS COPY OF THE SOFTWARE, [*Company Name*] GRANTS TO YOU A NONEXCLUSIVE RIGHT TO USE AND DISPLAY THIS SAME COPY OF THE SOFTWARE WITHIN THE TERMS AND CONDITIONS OF THIS LICENSE.

OWNERSHIP RIGHTS OF THE PARTIES

■ POOR PROVISION:

THE SOFTWARE AND ALL PACKAGING AND WRITTEN MATERIALS PROVIDED WITH IT ARE PROTECTED AS THE INTELLECTUAL PROPERTY OF [*Company Name*], EXCEPT THAT SOME COMPONENTS ARE THE PROTECTED PROPERTY OF OTHER OWNERS AS NOTED SPECIFICALLY IN THE MATERIALS.

ANALYSIS: Clear expression of the ownership rights is extremely important, but this provision is often shortened because of space restrictions. The above provision states only the ownership rights of the company, leaving out what the consumer has purchased. To underscore exactly what the consumer owns, it is probably wise to give an express explanation here. The purpose of this clause is to deter infringement, and it should therefore be emphasized, not reduced.

- BETTER PROVISION:

THE TOTAL PRICE YOU HAVE PAID FOR THIS SOFTWARE PACKAGE CONSISTS IS THE SUM OF THE SALES PRICE AND THE LICENSE FEE. WHEN YOU PAID THE SALES PRICE, YOU BECAME THE OWNER OF THE MAGNETIC OR OTHER PHYSICAL MEDIA (SUCH AS A DISK) ON WHICH THE SOFTWARE IS RECORDED OR OTHERWISE FIXED. WHEN YOU PAID THE LICENSE FEE, YOU BECAME AUTHORIZED TO USE THE SOFTWARE, BUT YOU DID NOT ACQUIRE OWNERSHIP RIGHTS TO IT. THIS LICENSE FOR THE SOFTWARE IS NOT A LICENSE FOR ANY OTHER SOFTWARE PRODUCT MADE BY [*Company Name*], AND THIS LICENSE DOES NOT ENTITLE YOU TO USE ANY OTHER SOFTWARE OWNED BY [*Company Name*]. WITH THE EXCEPTIONS STATED IN THIS PARAGRAPH, [*Company Name*] RETAINS ALL TITLE AND OWNERSHIP RIGHTS TO THE COPYRIGHTS, DESIGNS, PATENTS, TRADEMARKS, AND OTHER INTELLECTUAL PROPERTY RIGHTS OF THE SOFTWARE, ALL COPIES OF THE SOFTWARE, ALL DERIVATIVE WORKS, AND ALL MANUALS AND WRITTEN MATERIALS PROVIDED WITH THE SOFTWARE, REGARDLESS OF THE FORM OR MEDIA IN OR ON WHICH THE ORIGINAL AND OTHER COPIES MAY EXIST. THIS PRODUCT CONTAINS OTHER PROPERTIES THAT ARE OWNED AND LICENSED TO YOU BY THIRD PARTIES. USE OF THESE OTHER PROPERTIES IS SUBJECT TO THE TERMS AND CONDITIONS OF THE ADDITIONAL LICENSE AGREEMENTS ENCLOSED WITH THIS PRODUCT. [*Trademark Name*] IS A TRADEMARK OF [*Another Company Name*], [*Trademark Name*] IS A TRADEMARK OF [*Another Company Name*], AND [*Trademark Name*] IS A TRADEMARK OF [*Another Company Name*].

PERMITTED USE

- POOR PROVISION:

YOU MAY USE AND DISPLAY THE SOFTWARE ON ONE (1) COMPUTER AT ONE (1) LOCATION TO PRODUCE DOCUMENTS FOR YOUR OWN USE, YOUR EMPLOYER'S USE, OR YOUR CLIENT'S USE.

ANALYSIS: If permitted use is too narrow, the consumer will not bother to use the software, but if it is too broad, the value of the license is lost. The above paragraph appears to be limiting use of the software, but it is too vague given the technological practices and advances of the past decade. It is unclear because it is silent with respect to the use of multiple computers by a single user (such as users who have offices at home and work), use of a single computer by multiple users, or use of the software over a network. Although it is impossible to anticipate every situation in which the software might be used, the consumer should be given better parameters by which to judge compliance with the use rights granted.

- BETTER PROVISION:

THE LICENSE GRANTED IN THIS AGREEMENT IS FOR USE AND DISPLAY OF THE SOFTWARE ON A SINGLE COMPUTER HAVING A SINGLE PROCESSING UNIT (CPU) AT A SINGLE LOCATION. IF YOU USE SAID COMPUTER MORE THAN 80 PERCENT OF THE TIME (MEANING YOU ARE THE PRIMARY USER OF THE COMPUTER), YOU MAY ALSO USE THE SOFTWARE ON A LAPTOP OR OTHER PORTABLE COMPUTER AND ON ONE OTHER COMPUTER AT A DIFFERENT LOCATION, SUCH AS AT A HOME OR BUSINESS OFFICE. YOU MAY USE THE SOFTWARE TO PRODUCE A DOCUMENT, A PUBLICATION, OR PRESENTATION MATERIAL FOR YOURSELF, AN

EMPLOYER, OR A SINGLE CLIENT AT A TIME. YOU MAY ACCESS THE SOFTWARE FROM A HARD DISK, OVER A NETWORK, OR ANY OTHER METHOD YOU CHOOSE, SO LONG AS YOU OTHERWISE COMPLY WITH THIS LICENSE. IF A SINGLE COMPUTER IS PART OF A MULTI-USER SYSTEM, THIS LICENSE COVERS ALL USERS ON THE SYSTEM WHO ARE WORKING TOGETHER ON A SINGLE PROJECT.

PROHIBITED USE

- POOR PROVISION:

[*Company Name*] RESERVES ALL RIGHTS NOT EXPRESSLY GRANTED TO YOU IN THIS LICENSE AGREEMENT. YOU ARE NOT PERMITTED TO COPY, MODIFY, MERGE, OR OTHERWISE ALTER THE SOFTWARE. YOU MAY NOT DISASSEMBLE, DECOMPILE OR REVERSE ENGINEER IT. FAILURE TO COMPLY WITH THIS LICENSE WILL VOID ALL WARRANTIES AND TERMINATE THIS LICENSE. VIOLATORS WILL BE PROSECUTED.

ANALYSIS: With a bit more detail, this clause can be strengthened and tightened to ensure that consumers completely understand the consequences of noncompliance with the license terms. It should also recognize the legal concept of "fair use," which allows a consumer to make a copy for purposes of back-up or archive unless expressly prohibited by the License. There is also no express prohibition against using the Software in a public manner, such as for visual support at a seminar. It is important to consider potential public uses of products that have been licensed for personal home or business use. If the software is broadcast or otherwise used in a public presentation, a republication occurs, which is a separate right that belongs to the IP owner and can be exercised only with the IP owner's consent.

- BETTER PROVISION:

[*Company Name*] RESERVES ALL RIGHTS NOT EXPRESSLY GRANTED TO YOU IN THIS LICENSE AGREEMENT. YOU MAY BE HELD LEGALLY RESPONSIBLE FOR ANY COPYRIGHT INFRINGEMENT THAT IS CAUSED OR ENCOURAGED BY YOUR FAILURE TO ABIDE BY THE TERMS OF THIS LICENSE. YOU ARE STRICTLY PROHIBITED FROM EXERCISING ALL SUCH RIGHTS INCLUSIVE OF THE FOLLOWING, ALTHOUGH THIS LIST IS NOT EXCLUSIVE:

1. COPYING THE SOFTWARE, INCLUDING ANY COPY OF THE SOFTWARE THAT HAS BEEN MODIFIED, MERGED, OR INCLUDED WITH OTHER SOFTWARE, WITH THE SINGLE EXCEPTION THAT YOU MAY MAKE AS "FAIR USE" ONE (1) COPY OF THE SOFTWARE SOLELY FOR BACK-UP OR ARCHIVAL PURPOSES, PROVIDED THAT COPY IS MARKED WITH THE SAME PROPRIETARY AND COPYRIGHT NOTICES AS WERE AFFIXED TO THE ORIGINAL.

2. COPYING THE MANUALS AND WRITTEN MATERIALS PROVIDED WITH THE SOFTWARE.

3. SELLING OR DISTRIBUTING THE ORIGINAL OR ANY COPIES OF THE SOFTWARE OR THE ACCOMPANYING MANUAL AND OTHER PRINTED MATERIALS.

4. USING THE SOFTWARE OR ANY OF ITS CONTENTS ENTIRELY OR PARTIALLY FOR THE PRODUCTION OF ANY STOCK FORM DOCUMENTS, PUBLICATIONS, OR PRESENTATION MATERIALS TO BE PROVIDED, SHOWN, OR DISTRIBUTED TO MORE THAN A SINGLE CLIENT OR TO BE TRANSFERRED, SOLD, OR REDISTRIBUTED TO THE PUBLIC, EXCEPT WITH EXPRESS WRITTEN PERMISSION FROM [*Company Name*].

TRANSFER RESTRICTIONS

- **POOR PROVISION:**

YOU MAY NOT TRANSFER, RENT, OR OTHERWISE DISPOSE OF THE SOFTWARE TO ANY OTHER PERSON.

ANALYSIS: The above provision is concise, but it fails to impress on the consumer the effect of a transfer or other transaction with respect to the Software. To fill in the gaps and ensure full understanding, the following paragraph expressly emphasizes that use of the license is personal to the consumer that purchased it.

- **BETTER PROVISION:**

THIS SOFTWARE IS LICENSED TO YOU ONLY. IF YOU CHANGE YOUR COMPUTERS, YOU MAY TRANSFER THE SOFTWARE FROM THE INITIAL SINGLE COMPUTER TO A NEW COMPUTER, PROVIDED THAT YOU CONTINUE TO USE THE SOFTWARE ON ONLY ONE (1) COMPUTER AT A TIME. YOU MAY NOT TRANSFER OR DISTRIBUTE COPIES OF THE SOFTWARE OR THE ACCOMPANYING MANUAL AND OTHER PRINTED MATERIALS TO OTHERS WITHOUT THE PRIOR WRITTEN CONSENT OF [*Company Name*]. ANY SUCH UNAUTHORIZED TRANSFER WILL TERMINATE THIS LICENSE AGREEMENT. EXCEPT AS PROVIDED IN THIS PARAGRAPH, YOU ARE PROHIBITED FROM TRANSFERRING, ASSIGNING, RENTING, LEASING, SELLING OR OTHERWISE DISPOSING OF THE SOFTWARE TEMPORARILY OR PERMANENTLY TO ANY OTHER INDIVIDUAL OR ENTITY.

TERMINATION OF LICENSE

- **POOR PROVISION:**

THIS LICENSE TERMINATES AUTOMATICALLY IF YOU DO NOT COMPLY WITH ITS TERMS OR IF YOU TRANSFER THE SOFTWARE.

ANALYSIS: A common practice in contracts is to provide for termination on written notice from one party to the other. Termination can occur automatically, but it is a good practice to indicate specifically that no notice is required for the termination to become effective.

- **BETTER PROVISION:**

THIS LICENSE TERMINATES AUTOMATICALLY WITHOUT NOTICE TO YOU IF YOU FAIL TO COMPLY WITH ANY PROVISIONS OF ITS. ON TERMINATION YOU ARE REQUIRED TO DESTROY THE WRITTEN MATERIALS AND ALL COPIES OF THE SOFTWARE, INCLUDING ANY MODIFIED COPIES.

CHAPTER 9

Parties to IP Rights, Part III: Finalizing Ownership and Use Rights

THE CREATION IS READY TO BE DISCLOSED PUBLICLY. You've covered all the salient points of market research, culture, manufacture, legal transport and customs regulations, and protection of your IP rights. You have sales outlets anxiously awaiting your products or representatives ready to learn your service methodology. Your IP rights are wrapped up securely in nondisclosure agreements, assignments, registrations, cautionary notices, shrink-wrap and other licenses, and you have a strategy of enforcement in place.

Now is the time to take one last look at your IP strategy. Have you protected your IP rights sufficiently so that you will not lose them at the time of public disclosure? Has your due diligence been adequate? What are the incentives for loyalty among your employees and representatives? Do your plans include education of the public and of your employees and representatives? You should consider whether you have accounted for the points listed here.

Creator

You are at the front of a chain: your creation will pass from you through various outlets to the ultimate consumer. To reap the value of the IP you have created, you must secure and actively assert your rights. It is wise to plan with the assistance of legal counsel. Keep in mind the following points as you formulate and implement your IP strategy:

EVALUATION OF IP NEEDS

- WHAT IP RIGHTS DO YOU HAVE AND DO YOU NEED TO PROTECT THEM?

  Identification of IP rights is an ongoing process, and reassessment of IP needs should be a significant part of the periodic planning and budgetary sessions that most successful businesses undertake at least annually. A company's IP policies should reflect the worth of the company's IP rights, and it is therefore important to track the value of those rights as the reputation and goodwill of the country spreads. If those rights are of high value, the company should protect them by preemptive not reactive means. You should review your IP strategy in terms of the following considerations:

- Is your idea or work actually unique or novel within your trade or industry?
- Is your trade or industry competitive, or is there little risk that your IP will be the subject of infringement?

- How much are you willing to spend on IP protection, and how much are you willing to risk to keep your IP budget minimal?
- Have you added the value of your IP assets into your company's balance sheet?

WISE IP SELECTION

■ HAVE YOU CHOSEN IP THAT WILL BE EASY TO REGISTER, PAINLESS TO DEFEND, AND FRUSTRATING TO INFRINGERS?

A proactive and strict IP strategy does not necessarily have to be expensive, provided you choose your IP wisely. Careful selection of your IP can deter infringement initially, and it can make proof of ownership less difficult when fighting infringement. As part of the selection process, a check on prior IP rights is also essential because you could lose substantial investment of time, effort, and money spent on product development, package design, and promotional materials if you are forced to withdraw your IP from the market in the face of a claim of infringement. Remember to consider factors such as the following:

- Have you made a preliminary survey of whether your IP will be attractive and acceptable cross-culturally?
- How did you derive your ideas and works of expression, and is that derivation sufficiently inventive, unusual, and creative?
- Are you confident that your IP rights do not infringe on the prior rights of another IP owner?
- Have you retained evidence of the creation and use of your IP?

PRESERVATION OF IP RIGHTS

■ HAVE YOUR IP RIGHTS BEEN PROTECTED AGAINST INFRINGEMENT BEFORE BEING RELEASED PUBLICLY?

A cost-benefit analysis of your IP rights should reveal that an ounce of prevention is worth a pound of enforcement. There are many ways of preserving your IP rights at reduced cost relative to fighting infringers through legal processes. Be certain to consider and quickly implement means of preserving your rights so as not to delay your marketing and production. You should consider whether costs can be reduced by any of the following means:

- Can your IP rights be registered by recognition or at central registries through bilateral, regional, or international treaties?
- Have you secured your IP rights through registration in your primary and secondary markets?
- What innovative means can be used with your IP that is released to the public to prevent easy duplication?
- Are your IP rights clearly identified by legal notices before being released to the public?
- Do you have a solid employee training program on the value and protection of your IP, and do you have a program of in-house security?

- What cost-effective method can you use to track your products from manufacture to the point of sale so that you can easily investigate unauthorized sales?

GRANT OF USE OR OWNERSHIP RIGHTS

■ WHAT PRECAUTIONS HAVE YOU TAKEN TO ENSURE THAT YOU WILL BE ABLE TO REALIZE A PROFIT FROM USE OR SALE OF YOUR IP RIGHTS?

Your IP rights will have no value unless they are used. Value tends to increase with use, which is why many companies have realized exponential growth through licensing, merchandising, and franchising their IP rights. Even an outright sale of ownership rights in IP can be profitable. The grant of use or ownership rights can also, however, become a nightmare of lost investment if the proper preventive steps are not taken. For this reason, it is essential to contact legal counsel for assistance in formulating these relationships, and you should additionally consider the following:

- Have you made a due diligence check of the other party to ensure that they have the appropriate authority, financial capacity, organizational capability, and clean history?
- Have you provided attractive incentives and educational programs, including training in IP rights, value, and dilution?
- Have you consider alternative, cost-effective remedies for termination, breach, and infringing activities?
- Do you have an independent monitoring and auditing system in place?

ENFORCEMENT OF IP RIGHTS

■ IS YOUR POLICY OF IP ENFORCEMENT PROACTIVE OR REACTIVE?

Strict and quick enforcement of IP rights is the best policy to ensure that your IP retains its value. Publicity and educational press releases about your strong enforcement policy can serve as a deterrent to infringement. You must be prepared to monitor use of your IP, investigate infringements immediately, and fight for your IP rights if necessary. Otherwise, your IP rights are liable to be diluted, infringers are likely to target you, and you are likely to lose your competitive advantage in terms of the value of your IP and the overly burdensome cost of protecting it. In any program of enforcement, you should take into account the following:

- Have you implemented a network of services and local representatives to locate infringement at a reduced cost?
- Where are infringements most likely to occur, and have you set up a system to monitor those markets periodically?
- Do you have an efficient quick-response team to investigate and squelch infringements?
- Have you developed attractive incentives for would-be infringers to seek licenses or other legitimate uses of your IP?
- Are you using innovative enforcement methods, including diplomatic trade channels, media releases, educational and cultural programs, and special promotions to increase consumer awareness and respect of your company?

Licensee or Franchisee or Assignee

As an important link in the chain between the creator and the consumer, you will benefit most by keeping both sides happy. While you must ensure that your own interests are protected, you also have a responsibility to protect the interests of the creator. If you fail to do so, you are likely to undermine your own business. In most arrangements with a creator, you will be signing a contract prepared by the other party's attorney. Be certain to obtain your own legal advice, and before signing carefully consider the following issues:

COMMITMENT TO RELATIONSHIP

■ IF THE CONTRACT CREATES AN ONGOING RELATIONSHIP, WHAT ARE THE INCENTIVES?

A license or franchise relationship is likely to continue for a lengthy period of time, but only if there is business growth plus an acknowledgement of trust and gratitude by both parties. A long-term contract should have built in incentives to reward the parties for their efforts and loyalty. You should consider whether your contract terms provide for the following:

- Does your contract allow sufficient time for you to establish and prove the quality and potential of the market?
- Is there any allowance for renegotiation of terms after a certain profit margin is attained, or are there automatic step-up incentives to account for growth?
- How reasonable and efficient are the means for renegotiating and amending the contract?
- Can the contract be amended through addendums, schedules, or other add-ons to avoid modification formalities and expenses?

AUTHORITY TO CONTRACT

■ HAVE YOU VERIFIED THE OWNERSHIP CLAIMS OF THE CREATOR?

A party who has no actual ownership rights cannot transfer rights of use or ownership to another. Any license or assignment that is not supported by actual ownership rights may be deemed invalid and attacked by third parties. Moreover, you will not be able to enforce such an agreement against a purported creator who in fact has no ownership interest. It is wise, therefore, to obtain written and verified evidence of ownership before committing to a contract. You should consider the following points:

- Is the creator an individual or business entity, and have you been given documentation showing that the business entity is in good standing and has authorized its representative to handle this transaction?
- Has the creator provided you with evidence of ownership, such as a certificate of registration in the name of the creator or an assignment of rights to the creator?
- Have you verified the creator's claim through an independent source, such as a search of the relevant IP registry or due diligence on the history of the company?

WARRANTIES OF VALUE

■ WHAT ASSURANCE DO YOU HAVE THAT THE IP RIGHTS AT ISSUE ARE IN FACT VALUABLE?

A license to use or contract to buy rights is a wasted investment if there is no market value in the rights, unless your intent is to purchase the rights to eliminate competition with your own business. Before committing to any agreement, you must decide on what you intend to do with the IP rights and you should determine whether those rights have value to your company. This determination should be made through an independent review of the situation. Do not rely on the information provided by the creator. You might review the following points:

- Can the IP rights be merged easily into, and will they enhance, your own business plan?
- If you gain use or ownership rights in the IP will you also gain a competitive edge, and is the cost of acquisition balanced by the anticipated gain?
- Will acquisition of the IP rights expand your markets, product lines, or services offered?
- Have you had favorable results in a preliminary survey of the potential markets for the IP rights?
- How strong is your competition and how easy will it be to gain a satisfactory and profitable market share?

LIABILITIES ON TERMINATION OR DEFAULT

■ WHAT ARE THE RISKS AND REMEDIES IF THE AGREEMENT ENDS IN A DISPUTE OR BY MUTUAL CONSENT?

The contract enforcement clauses are likely to be strict against your interest because the agreement has been drafted by the other party. Nevertheless, you can insist on certain procedures and remedies that will protect you from burdensome responsibilities in the event that you cannot perform to the standards required by the creator. You should review these extremely important clauses with your attorney to ensure that you understand your liabilities and have limited your risks as much as possible. Consider the following issues:

- Does the agreement encourage negotiation, mediation, or arbitration of disputes?
- Are there provisions that entitle you to remedies if the creator breaches the agreement, and are those remedies satisfactory?
- Does the agreement allow either party to cancel or terminate for justifiable reasons?
- Is there a grace period during which either party may try to comply or fix a breach before the agreement will be considered terminated?
- Does it provide for liquidated damages (contractual stipulated damages)?
- Is there a provision for an award of legal fees and costs to the prevailing party in any arbitration or litigation?
- If a forum is designated for dispute resolution, is it convenient to you?

Attorney for Creator

When finalizing your IP strategy, and particularly before signing any contracts for the use or sale of your IP rights, a visit to your attorney is essential. Your lawyer will point out the strengths and weaknesses of your strategy, suggest factors to be considered in your cost-benefit analysis, and review your proposed contracts. You should further seek advice on securing, monitoring, and enforcing your rights worldwide so that you will be prepared to act quickly and decisively to protect your IP rights from the very beginning which will make would-be infringers think twice about riding on your goodwill and cutting into your markets. Be certain to ask your attorney about the following issues:

EFFECTIVE IP STRATEGY

- From a legal standpoint, is your IP strategy sufficient to secure your rights and maintain the value of your IP? What additional factors should be included?
- What is the risk involved in adhering to an IP strategy that implements protection in stages, focusing first on primary markets and then expanding as the company's profits and sales grow?
- How much would it cost to secure and manage a worldwide IP portfolio and what would be the advantages and disadvantages?
- Is your company's in-house security sufficiently diligent for protection of your IP rights?

FORMATION OF USE OR SALE AGREEMENTS

- Is your agreement in compliance with requirements of the national laws in both your own country and the other party's country?
- What additional due diligence might be advisable before signing the contract and handing over knowledge of your IP rights to the other party?
- What evidence should be obtained to show that the other party has authority to make the contract?
- How can you monitor and independently audit the other party's production or rendering of services within the limits of the law?
- In practice, will you be able to effect the remedies within a quick time frame so that bad publicity and lengthy delays can be avoided or minimized?
- What will each remedy involve in terms of procedure, cost, and time?
- Are there any remedies available that would better protect your interests?

ENFORCEMENT OF IP RIGHTS

- What are the advantages and disadvantages of enforcement procedures available through civil, criminal, and administrative forums?
- What remedies are generally available against infringements, passing off, and unfair competition in various countries and how effective are these remedies?
- In general terms, what will each remedy involve in terms of procedure, cost, and time?

- Are there any international or regional forums where IP rights can be enforced, and how effective are those forums in terms of cost, time, and results?

Attorney for Licensee or Franchisee or Assignee

Before you sign any agreement to use or buy IP rights, be certain to have it reviewed by a lawyer who is familiar with the laws of your country and of the creator's country. The lawyer will be able to advise you on the strength or weakness of the contract, and may be able to help you negotiate terms that better protect your rights. Do not rely on the other party's counsel, because the other party's interests are in conflict with your own. To ensure that you know your legal rights and liabilities under the agreement, be certain to ask your attorney about the following issues:

VOID OR VOIDABLE PROVISIONS

- Do any country laws prohibit clauses for choice of forum or selection of the law to be applied when interpreting the agreement?
- Is arbitration a viable alternative that is recognized and upheld in the countries where the parties reside?
- Is a liquidated damages clause enforceable?
- On what grounds will a contract be deemed void or invalid?

FORMALITIES OF THE CONTRACT

- What evidence should be obtained to show that the other party has authority to make the contract?
- What evidence of IP ownership should be requested and how can it be verified?

WARRANTIES AND REMEDIES

- What warranties has the other party provided to you with regard to the value, ownership, and use of the IP rights?
- Can you rely on these warranties and what will be the legal effect of your reliance?
- In practice, will you be able to effect the remedies provided?
- What will each remedy involve in terms of procedure, cost, and time?
- Are there any remedies available that would better protect your interest?

CHAPTER 10

Key Issues Related to IP Rights Internationally

Societal Recognition of IP Rights

A prime reason that IP laws vary from country to country is that the concepts of property have developed differently among the societies of the world in two respects: recognition of intangible property rights and recognition of individual property rights.

Initially, recognition of intangible property rights occurred primarily in Europe, the Americas, and countries and territories under their influence. The laws of many countries have therefore failed until the modern era to protect property rights in intellectual works. Even today, some countries are more progressive than others in expanding their IP laws to cover new types of works.

In countries ruled under socialist or communist law, the political philosophy disfavors individual property rights in favor of communal rights. Although these countries have and are developing modern IP laws, enforcement of IP rights is often difficult because the populace has been educated to understand that property rights are common to all.

An international trader will therefore find more protection and ready enforcement of IP rights in some countries and regions of the world than in others. If a trader is operating in countries with minimal IP protection, the trader may need to take his or her own measures to protect IP from infringement as much as possible.

CULTURAL ISSUES RELATED TO DEVELOPMENT OF IP

Cultural differences will affect the value, meaning, and acceptance of your IP in foreign markets. The IP you choose to market or to use in connection with your products or services will be successful in capturing a significant market share only if you have taken into account cultural differences. You must be sufficiently flexible in developing and using your IP to ensure that the culture of your customers is respected. The success of your business depends on it.

In a commercial context, culture is a set of conventions that indicate the preferences of a society in relation to marketplace. These conventions suggest the etiquette, traditions, values, and living styles of a group of people. When trading internationally, you must be aware of and sensitive to other cultures, and you must adapt your IP to the preferences of the foreign market.

Culture applies to people, not to nations. Although it may be possible to identify an overall culture for a particular country, many subcultures are likely to exist. Once you have identified the foreign countries where you intend to market your IP and have learned the cultural rules that you think might apply, you should avoid clinging to the rules as preconceived notions. Flexibility and adaptation are extremely important, particularly in the fast pace of today's world where people are on the move, cultures are crossing country borders, and cultural rules are constantly evolving.

In researching and testing markets for your IP, you will need to follow some initial cultural guidelines to ensure successful acceptance of your IP. It will be important to determine whether a general protocol tends to be applied throughout the country or whether many subcultures are present. You will need to consider the size of your market in terms of these subcultures, and the means by which you can adjust your IP to appeal cross-culturally.

If you are meeting foreign traders interested in your IP, you will also need to be aware of the cultural protocol that is likely to arise at the first contact. Cultural issues include greetings, courtesies, business ethics, decision making, gender, meeting formalities, and business attire. Be certain that you approach these cultural issues with the proper attitude. Cultural missteps are inevitable and will be made on both sides. Humor will ease a tense situation, and respect and awareness are likely to bring acceptance.

Trends Toward Globalization and Uniformity

The treatment of IP rights has been long recognized as an indirect barrier to trade. Beginning in the 1800s, multilateral trade agreements related to IP rights have been adopted, two of the most famous being the Berne and Paris Conventions. Over the decades, these Conventions and many other agreements have come into effect and been strengthened by periodic amendments.

In the 1990s, giant steps were made toward globalization and uniformity in commercial practices worldwide, including the registration and protection of various types of IP rights. The Uruguay Round of the General Agreement on Tariffs and Trade (GATT), signed by 117 nations in 1993, took effect in 1995, resulting in creation of the World Trade Organization (WTO) and implementation of the Trade-Related Aspects of Intellectual Property Rights Agreement (TRIPS). Regional agreements encouraging trade and the protection of IP rights have included the North American Free Trade Agreement (NAFTA) of 1993 and the United States Andean Trade Preference Act (ATPA) of 1991.

Multilateral agreements specific to IP rights have also proliferated in recent years. The Trademark Law Treaty was adopted in 1994, and the Madrid Protocol was adopted in 1989 to amend and strengthen the Madrid Agreement, by which IP rights can be registered centrally for all member countries.

When you begin developing a global IP strategy, you will need to consider the expansion now underway in reducing trade barriers. Although some countries continue a self-imposed isolation, most have come to recognize that development and refinement of a global economic strategy is important to the growth and maintenance of a strong economy. Uniformity among countries facilitates the registration and protection of IP rights, and your global IP strategy should take advantage of the regional and international systems of protection being created.

At the same time, it is essential to take into account the limitations of the cross-border systems and the national differences that remain. Many of the international

Cultural Do's and Don'ts

WHEN YOU DEVELOP YOUR IP

DO consider whether it will be universally acceptable and desirable to consumers from different cultural backgrounds, including moral, religious, educational, historical, and geographical factors. Try to develop IP that can be easily modified to account for cultural differences. Be responsible for the creation of IP that has a positive influence on society.

DON'T try to please all people everywhere, because your R&D costs will be exorbitant. Avoid developing IP that has core features that are so rigid or restricted that they cannot be changed without great labor and expense. Do not cling to preconceived notions and generalities, but instead recognize subcultures within cultures.

WHEN YOU FIRST MEET A FOREIGN TRADER

DO use a title to show respect. Wait for the other party to initiate informality. Reply to inquiries immediately. Be friendly and enthusiastic but not overbearing. Allow the other trader equal speaking time. Confirm your understanding and the other trader's understanding, and be watchful of language barriers that affect mutual comprehension.

DON'T be in a hurry. Determine in advance whether it is common business practice in the other party's country to develop deals over time. If not, make your deal. If so, plan to establish a professional relationship before you sign any contracts. If you are seeking more than a one-time deal, you may need months or even a year to reach a long-term arrangement.

WHEN YOU SOCIALIZE TO ENCOURAGE BUSINESS

DO accept an invitation if your host graciously extends it. Go prepared with several conversational topics that might interest your host other than the business at hand. Research the cultural norms of gift exchanging, and consider a gift that represents your country.

DON'T offer to socialize if your host sticks to business or is constrained by time during meetings. Avoid criticism of your host's country and government, and do not raise sensitive topics such as politics, religion, or personal issues. Do not consume alcohol in excess.

and regional systems are new, and older ones are being amended periodically, so that the effect on IP rights is not always certain. In accepting and modifying national laws to comply with international agreements, each country is moving at its own pace, with its own preferences, and in accordance with its own priorities and agenda. Your IP strategy must be sufficiently flexible to allow for the varied and changing international IP scene.

Role of Politics

Political events have a major impact on the economy of a country, and therefore on the value of IP rights within that country. Government instability can devastate a country's markets, while a stable government can be a great asset. A strong and growing economy in turn tends to have a calming effect on political turmoil. Although some would argue that politicians should take less of a role in regulating the commercial affairs of private traders, the influence of politics will no doubt always be a major factor because these two forces are so entwined.

International trade plays such a significant role in a country's economy that governments throughout history have used direct and indirect trade barriers to force changes in the governments and policies of other countries. Trade barriers include boycotts, quotas, tariffs, import and export prohibitions, licenses, consumer and labeling requirements, and environmental regulations. A country's failure to adequately protect the IP rights of foreign traders is an indirect trade barrier. Foreign countries often use trade sanctions to influence another country's domestic and foreign policies and practices, and favorable trade preferences to reward countries that implement changes thought to be desirable in the international community.

As a global trader, you must stay in touch with political trends. Your IP strategy should reflect the political situation in various countries. You will need to decide whether you have a market for IP there, whether and how you can protect your IP there, and whether you might lose some value in your IP if you fail to protect it despite present difficulties.

TIP: Do not erase a country or region permanently from your list. Watch for laws and the political climate to change and look for new opportunities as trade barriers are relaxed. Before committing to do business in a particular market, you should consider whether the country's political past and current political climate are conducive to your trade. However, the past is not necessarily the deciding factor. Given international pressures toward peaceful encouragement of commercial exchange, your markets are more likely to expand than to be limited by historical disturbances.

Regulatory Laws

In any country where you use or exploit your IP rights, you are responsible for knowing the law. In many countries, IP law is bound tightly with unfair competition laws, and acts of unfair competition and infringement are often punished as crimes. Means of enforcing IP rights, including settlement negotiation, civil suits, and criminal prosecutions, are all subject to regulatory laws.

Regulatory laws relating to IP rights are in a state of flux throughout the world today. Many countries are conforming their laws and regulations to uniform international standards. New forms of intellectual property—particularly those related to computers and electronics—have given rise to new legal issues, requiring the development of new regulatory laws to set standards and provide protection.

It is essential that you know and understand the legal implications and boundaries of commerce in your own country and abroad. An attorney with international legal experience can advise you on the issues that you should know. You should select an attorney who will keep you advised of changes in domestic and foreign laws and practices that are likely to affect your IP rights.

Internet Issues

In the realm of IP rights, the Internet poses some thorny issues for global traders. Hundreds of thousands of business-related websites have been created, and thousands more are created every week. Top-level domain names (such as ".com",".org" and ".net") are also multiplying, including top-level domain names for national networks. Small and large business alike are creating websites and reserving primary and secondary domain names. They are, however, plagued by "cybersquatters" who register names likely to be used by both start-up companies and established brands.

The Internet's potential for reaching markets with relative ease and minimal expense is exciting, but the protection of IP rights on the Internet is particularly difficult. A person can digitize, compress, upload, download, copy and distribute IP to thousands and millions of users in different countries at a time. Protected materials—writings, sounds, graphics, photographs, and so forth—can be stored on a network and delivered quickly and cheaply through cyberspace. The opportunities are immense, but enforcement of IP rights, ensuring appropriate usage of IP, and collecting compensation for the creators are tremendous challenges. To add to the problem, international and national IP laws and practices have not kept up with technology.

The Internet is a public domain, and therefore individual rights in IP can be lost if the IP is not protected before being placed on the Internet. Most countries that recognize IP rights are applying their existing laws protecting trademarks and copyrights to IP on the Internet. However, the laws and regulations are far from settled, and they were developed while IP law was based on a territorial concept of marks that were primarily used locally or within a nation. Consumer confusion across borders was minimal and could be dealt with if and when it arose. On the World Wide Web, IP conflicts are no longer limited in geographical terms, and national laws do not necessary address the issues relevant to conflicts in cyberspace.

Global traders are well-advised to protect their IP by ensuring its registration prior to release on the Internet, registering their names and trademarks as domain names worldwide, and employing monitoring services for secure delivery and collection of compensation owed.

CHAPTER 11

IP Rights in Multi-National Forums

THE IMPORTANCE AND VALUE OF IP RIGHTS have been recognized in various international, regional, and bilateral treaties, agreements, and conventions. Recognition and protection have been primarily afforded to copyrights, patents, and trademarks (including service marks). Often, the protective provisions are fairly general and each member country is permitted to limit or somewhat modify the terms as specifically employed within its territory. For this reason, the international systems are not necessarily applied uniformly. However, at a minimum, global traders can rely on these systems for the recognition of IP rights in foreign jurisdictions. Of even greater benefit are the centralized registries by which IP owners can obtain relatively fast and cost-effective protection for their rights in multiple jurisdictions.

International Treaties Affecting IP Rights

In the context of IP rights, the multi-national and regional treaties, agreements, and conventions that affect IP rights may be grouped generally together in one of the following classifications. Please note that this list is not exclusive.

RECOGNITION OF IP RIGHTS AND FACILITATION OF HARMONIOUS NATIONAL IP SYSTEMS, INCLUDING:

- Association of South East Asian Nations (ASEAN)
- Berne Convention for the Protection of Literary and Artistic Works
- Brussels Convention Relating to the Distribution of Programme-Carrying Signals Transmitted by Satellite
- General Agreement on Tariffs and Trade (GATT)
- Geneva Convention for the Protection of Producers of Phonograms Against Unauthorized Duplication of Their Phonograms
- Madrid Agreement for the Repression of False or Deceptive Indications of Source of Goods
- Nairobi Treaty on the Protection of the Olympic Symbol
- North American Free Trade Agreement (NAFTA)
- Paris Convention for the Protection of Industrial Property
- Rome Convention for the Protection of Performers, Producers of Phonograms and Broadcasting Organizations
- Trade-Related Aspects of Intellectual Property Agreement (TRIPS), negotiated as part of the Uruguay Round of the General Agreement on Tariffs and Trade (GATT)
- Trademark Law Treaty (TLT)
- World Intellectual Property Organization Convention (WIPO)
- WIPO Copyright Treaty (Internet Treaty)
- WIPO Performances and Phonograms Treaty (Internet Treaty)

ESTABLISHMENT OF REGIONAL OR INTERNATIONAL IP DEPOSITORIES, INCLUDING:

- African Regional Intellectual Property Organization (ARIPO)
- Budapest Treaty on the International Recognition of the Deposit of Microorganisms for the Purposes of Patent Procedure
- Eurasian Patent Convention
- European Patent Convention
- Hague Agreement Concerning the International Deposit of Industrial Designs
- Lisbon Agreement for the Protection of Appellations of Origin and their International Registration
- Madrid Agreement and Protocol Concerning the International Registration of Marks
- Organization for African Property Intellectual (OAPI)
- Pan-American Treaty
- Patent Cooperation Treaty (PCT)

CREATION OF INTERNATIONAL CLASSIFICATION SYSTEMS TO FACILITATE INDEXING AND RETRIEVAL OF IP REGISTRATIONS, INCLUDING:

- Locarno Agreement Establishing an International Classification for Industrial Designs
- Nice Agreement Concerning the International Classification of Goods and Services for the Purposes of the Registration of Marks
- Strasbourg Agreement Concerning the International Patent Classification
- Vienna Agreement Establishing an International Classification of the Figurative Elements of Marks

Space limitations in this book prevent listing all of the bilateral treaties existing between various countries. Moreover, full coverage of all of these agreements is not feasible in this short volume. Therefore, the discussion is limited to a brief introduction of the agreements that have the broadest application, leaving each global trader to ask his or her own legal counsel about other treaties and agreements that might be relevant to a particular situation. A brief description of the selected agreements follows in alphabetic order.

Association of Southeast Asian Nations (ASEAN)

- IP RIGHTS: Recognition and harmonization for all IP rights
- EFFECTIVE DATES: ASEAN, 1967; Intellectual Property framework agreement, 1995
- MEMBER COUNTRIES: Brunei, Cambodia, Indonesia, Laos, Malaysia, Myanmar, Philippines, Singapore, Thailand, and Vietnam
- WEB CONTACT: www.us-asean.org

PURPOSE AND FUNCTION

The original members of the Association of Southeast Asian Nations (ASEAN) created this regional trading bloc in the 1960s to foster trade and social cooperation within their region. Since 1998, the countries of Cambodia, Laos, and Vietnam have been voted into the bloc. The primary function of ASEAN has been to promote political, economic, and social exchanges among its members and to afford them trade preferences, and therefore its focus has been on commercial and political stability and growth, not on the protection of IP rights.

BENEFITS TO THE IP OWNER

The ASEAN has no centralized system for registration or protection of IP rights, but by agreement in December 1995, the member states established a framework for such a system. The agreement sets a goal among the members to explore in general terms the establishment of a central office for registration and promotion of effective region-wide protection of IP rights. During the subsequent, periodic meetings of the ASEAN, no further progress has been made on a regional IP system.

On a more immediate level, the 1995 agreement requires member countries to undertake to standardize, automate, and strengthen their IP laws and enforcement systems. Member countries must implement national laws and practices consistent with the international TRIPS Agreement and must cooperate with each other in the protection and enforcement of IP rights. In addition, an arbitration or other alternative dispute resolution system is being created under the ASEAN agreement for use in settling disputes related to IP rights among nationals of the member states. As these measures are being carried out, international traders are the beneficiaries of more effective and efficient IP practices in each ASEAN country.

Berne Convention

- IP RIGHTS: Recognition and harmonization for copyrighted works
- EFFECTIVE DATES: 1886; amended and revised periodically, most recently 1979
- MEMBER COUNTRIES: Albania, Algeria, Antigua and Barbuda, Argentina, Armenia, Australia, Austria, Azerbaijan, Bahamas, Bahrain, Bangladesh, Barbados, Belarus, Belgium, Belize, Benin, Bolivia, Bosnia and Herzegovina, Botswana, Brazil, Bulgaria, Burkina Faso, Cameroon, Canada, Cape Verde, Central African Republic, Chad, Chile, China, Colombia, Congo, Congo D.R., Costa Rica, Côte d'Ivoire, Croatia, Cuba, Cyprus, Czech Republic, Denmark, Dominica, Dominican Republic, Ecuador, Egypt, El Salvador, Equatorial Guinea, Estonia, Fiji, Finland, France, Gabon, Gambia, Georgia, Germany, Ghana, Greece, Grenada, Guatemala, Guinea, Guinea-Bissau, Guyana, Haiti, Holy See, Honduras, Hungary, Iceland, India, Indonesia, Ireland, Israel, Italy, Jamaica, Japan, Jordan, Kazakhstan, Kenya, Korea [South], Kyrgyzstan, Latvia, Lebanon, Lesotho, Liberia, Libya, Liechtenstein, Lithuania, Luxembourg, Macedonia (former Yugoslav Republic), Madagascar, Malawi, Malaysia, Mali, Malta, Mauritania, Mauritius, Mexico, Moldova, Monaco, Mongolia, Morocco, Namibia, Netherlands, New Zealand, Nicaragua, Niger, Nigeria, Norway, Oman, Pakistan, Panama, Paraguay, Peru, Philippines, Poland, Portugal, Qatar, Romania, Russian Federation, Rwanda, Saint Kitts and Nevis, Saint Lucia, Saint Vincent and the Grenadines, Senegal, Sierra Leone, Singapore, Slovakia, Slovenia,

South Africa, Spain, Sri Lanka, Sudan, Suriname, Swaziland, Sweden, Switzerland, Syria, Tajikistan, Tanzania, Thailand, Togo, Trinidad and Tobago, Tunisia, Turkey, Ukraine, United Kingdom, United States, Uruguay, Venezuela, Yugoslavia, Zambia, Zimbabwe

- WEB CONTACT: www.cepic.org/berne1.htm, www.cepic.org/berne2.htm

PURPOSE AND FUNCTION

The Berne Convention for the Protection of Literary and Artistic Works confers rights on owners of literary and artistic works that are protected by copyright. It requires member countries to enact national legislation in compliance with the international standards set forth in the Convention. Adopted in 1886, the Convention has been periodically amended to extend copyright coverage as new technologies develop.

BENEFITS TO THE IP OWNER

In all Convention member states, a copyright arises in a work at the time it is fixed in a tangible medium, regardless of whether the owner seeks a copyright registration. The Berne Convention can be invoked in any member state to protect the copyright owner's economic rights (such as rights of reproduction, public performance, display, distribution, adaptation, and translation) and moral rights (such as rights to object to distortion, mutilation, or other modification of the work prejudicial to the owner's honor or reputation).

NOTE: Rights related to copyrights are protected internationally under other treaties. The owners of these related rights form intermediate links between the copyright owners and the performance, distribution, display, or other dissemination of the works to the public. Thus, the rights of performers, musicians, broadcasters, and producers are protected under the Rome Convention and the Geneva Convention. Information about these Conventions may be obtained from WIPO at www.WIPO.int.

Community Trademark and European Union

- IP RIGHTS: Regional registration of trademarks in Europe
- EFFECTIVE DATES: 1993; first filing available January 1, 1996
- MEMBER COUNTRIES: Austria, Belgium, Denmark, Finland, France, Germany, Greece, Ireland, Italy, Luxembourg, Netherlands, Portugal, Spain, Sweden, United Kingdom
- WEB CONTACT: www.germainmaureau.com/communo1.html

PURPOSE AND FUNCTION

A trader may file a single application for a Community Trademark, which when registered will be recognized and enforced in the member countries of the European Union. The European Union (EU), formerly known as the European Community (EC), is a regional organization created among the nations of Europe to bring about the elimination of trade barriers in its member states. Initially organized in 1958 at the Treaty of Rome, the EC consisted of three separate regional organizations (European Coal and Steel Community, European Atomic Energy Community, and

European Economic Community), which were separately administered until 1967 when their administrative functions were merged.

As part of the plan to reduce and eliminate trade barriers within the European region, the member countries of the EU perceived a need to harmonize their national trademark laws and eventually to create a central registry. The Community Trademark (CTM) came into being in 1993 as an alternative, although not a replacement, to national registrations. The first CTM filings were permitted in 1996.

BENEFITS TO THE IP OWNER

The CTM is a single trademark registration that covers all of the EU member states, and an IP owner need not then secure and maintain national registrations in these countries. The application is submitted to the Office for Harmonization in Alicante, Spain. "Priority filing" is available based on the Paris Convention, and the registration date of a national trademark will be recognized for purposes of establishing seniority as against a conflicting mark. The registration process is similar as for national trademarks, including a formal examination, substantive examination, and publication and opposition period. Once registered, a CTM mark is valid for ten years and is renewable for subsequent periods of the same duration, provided that the mark is in use.

A CTM filing has a few disadvantages. For example, the cost from filing a single CTM application to issuance of the certificate tends to be higher than for a single national registration, although it is less than for filing a national registration in every EU country. Another difficulty is that national registrations, particularly in the United Kingdom, Netherlands, and France, may have to be submitted to support applications in territorial possessions, a problem that will be solved as more and more territories gain independence and former territories enact their own laws. A third drawback to the CTM is that a registration can be rejected by any one of the member nations, and that rejection will affect the entire CTM application. The owner of a rejected application may request that the CTM application be converted into national registrations, in which event they may retain the priority date of the CTM application.

European Patent Convention

- IP RIGHTS: Regional registration of patents in Europe
- EFFECTIVE DATES: 1977; first filing in 1978
- MEMBER COUNTRIES: Austria, Belgium, Cyprus, Denmark, Finland, France, Germany, Greece, Ireland, Italy, Liechtenstein, Luxembourg, Monaco, Netherlands, Portugal, Spain, Sweden, Switzerland, United Kingdom, with extended protection to Albania, Latvia, Lithuania, Romania, and Slovenia
- WEB CONTACT: www.european-patent-office-office.org/index.htm

PURPOSE AND FUNCTION

A central registry was established for the filing of patents among European nations when the European Patent Convention (EPC) was signed in 1977. This Convention created the European Patent Office (EPO), which began accepting patents in 1978. The purpose of the central registry for patents is the same as the reason for the Community Trademark (CTM), that is, to harmonize the patent laws and reduce trade barriers related to IP rights among the member states. Unlike the CTM, the EPC is completely separate of the EU. Today, the EPO files approximately 100,000 patent applications every year.

BENEFITS TO THE IP OWNER

The filing of a single patent application has obvious time, labor, and cost savings, particularly if protection is sought in three or more countries. An EPC patent can be filed for any novel invention. The invention must not be barred by prior art, which includes everything made available to the public through written or oral description, by use, or in any other way that would allow the public to determine the nature of the invention.

A single application is submitted to the EPO in Munich, Germany or The Hague, Netherlands, and the patent undergoes only one examination—by the EPO, not by each member state. The procedures are similar to the usual international practices, requiring publication, the filing of a request to examine, and the payment of periodic annuities. However, extra expenses must be incurred to translate the patent into French and German, and once the patent is accepted, the official fees of each national office where protection is desired must also be paid.

Once granted, the EPC patent matures into individual national patents, one per member country, and the national patents are valid for 20 years from the date of the application.

General Agreement on Tariffs and Trade (GATT)

- IP RIGHTS: Recognition and harmonization for all IP rights
- EFFECTIVE DATES: 1948; amended periodically in Rounds
- MEMBER COUNTRIES: Albania, Algeria, Andorra, Angola, Antigua and Barbuda, Argentina, Armenia, Australia, Austria, Azerbaijan, Bahamas, Bahrain, Bangladesh, Barbados, Belarus, Belgium, Belize, Benin, Bhutan, Bolivia, Bosnia and Herzegovina, Botswana, Brazil, Brunei, Bulgaria, Burkina Faso, Burundi, Cambodia, Cameroon, Canada, Cape Verde, Central African Republic, Chad, Chile, China, Colombia, Congo, Costa Rica, Côte d'Ivoire, Croatia, Cuba, Cyprus, Czech Republic, D.P.R. [North] Korea, D.R. Congo, Denmark, Dominica, Dominican Republic, Ecuador, Egypt, El Salvador, Equatorial Guinea, Eritrea, Estonia, Ethiopia, Fiji, Finland, France, Gabon, Gambia, Georgia, Germany, Ghana, Greece, Grenada, Guatemala, Guinea, Guinea-Bissau, Guyana, Haiti, Holy See, Honduras, Hungary, Iceland, India, Indonesia, Iraq, Ireland, Israel, Italy, Jamaica, Japan, Jordan, Kazakhstan, Kenya, Korea [South] Republic, Kuwait, Kyrgyzstan, Laos, Latvia, Lebanon, Lesotho, Liberia, Libya, Liechtenstein, Lithuania, Luxembourg, Macedonia (former Yugoslav Republic), Madagascar, Malawi, Malaysia, Mali, Malta, Mauritania, Mauritius, Mexico, Moldova, Monaco, Mongolia, Morocco, Mozambique, Namibia, Nepal, Netherlands, New Zealand, Nicaragua, Niger, Nigeria, Norway, Oman, Pakistan, Panama, Papua New Guinea, Paraguay, Peru, Philippines, Poland, Portugal, Qatar, Romania, Russian Federation, Rwanda, Saint Kitts and Nevis,

Saint Lucia, Saint Vincent and the Grenadines, Samoa, San Marino, Sao Tome and Principe, Saudi Arabia, Senegal, Seychelles, Sierra Leone, Singapore, Slovakia, Slovenia, Somalia, South Africa, Spain, Sri Lanka, Sudan, Suriname, Swaziland, Sweden, Switzerland, Tajikistan, Tanzania, Thailand, Togo, Trinidad and Tobago, Tunisia, Turkey, Turkmenistan, Uganda, Ukraine, United Arab Emirates, United Kingdom, United States, Uruguay, Uzbekistan, Venezuela, Vietnam, Yemen, Yugoslavia, Zambia, Zimbabwe

- WEB CONTACT: www.fas.usda.gov/itp/Policy/Gatt/gatt.html

PURPOSE AND FUNCTION

The General Agreement on Tariffs and Trade (GATT) was initially considered an interim agreement when signed in 1948 by 23 nations in response to trade conflicts that contributed to the outbreak of World War II. Today, GATT is a key institution in world trade, with more than 170 member countries and a number of nonmember countries applying GATT principles. Its main purpose is to provide a forum for discussion of world trade issues with a goal of liberalizing and securing world trade, including the reduction of trade barriers and improvement of international trade relations. International negotiations are conducted at meetings known as "Rounds," and it was at the Uruguay Round that the member states created a new administrative framework for the GATT, namely the World Trade Organization (WTO).

BENEFITS FOR THE IP OWNER

In terms of IP rights, the primary benefits of GATT have been as follows:

- FORUM FOR IP AGREEMENTS. The GATT serves as a forum for the creation of multi-lateral agreements for the protection and enforcement of IP rights among member states.
- PROTECTION OF TRADE SECRETS. Member states have pledged to protect trade secrets owned by the residents and nationals of all member nations.
- COMPLIANCE WITH BERNE AND PARIS CONVENTIONS. All member states signing GATT must comply with the Berne and Paris Conventions.
- SPECIFIC AGREEMENT ON IP RIGHTS. Appended to GATT is the Agreement on Trade-Related Aspects of Intellectual Property (TRIPS), to which all of the member states are signatories and must be in compliance within a transitional period.

Nice Agreement

- IP RIGHTS: Creation of classification system for marks
- EFFECTIVE DATES: 1957; periodically revised, latest revision 1979
- MEMBER COUNTRIES: Algeria, Australia, Austria, Barbados, Belarus, Benelux [Belgium, Luxembourg, Netherlands (includes Aruba)], Benin, Bosnia and Herzegovina, China [includes Macau S.A.R.], Chile, Croatia, Cuba, Czech Republic, D.P.R. (North) Korea, Denmark [includes Faroe Islands], Dominica, Estonia, Finland, France, Germany, Greece, Guinea, Hungary, Iceland, Ireland,

Israel, Italy, Japan, Korea (South), Kyrgyzstan, Latvia, Lebanon, Liechtenstein, Lithuania, Macedonia (former Yugoslav Republic), Malawi, Moldova Republic, Monaco, Morocco, Norway, Poland, Portugal, Qatar, Romania, Russian Federation, Singapore, Slovakia, Slovenia, Spain, Suriname, Sweden, Switzerland, Tajikistan, Tanzania, Trinidad and Tobago, Tunisia, Turkey, Ukraine, United Kingdom, United States, Uruguay, Yugoslavia

- WEB CONTACT: www.uspto.gov/go/tac/doc/gsmanual/nice.htm www.wipo.org/eng/general/ipip/nice.htm

PURPOSE AND FUNCTION

The Nice Agreement is one of several multi-national treaties that establish an international classification system to make the identification and indexing of IP registrations feasible and more efficient among the member states. The concept of a classification system first developed on a national level, with each country creating its own classifications for purposes of identifying IP rights in connection with goods and services. World leaders soon recognized the national systems as indirect trade barriers, and therefore came together to create several international systems for IP registration. Specifically, the Nice Agreement provides for classifications of goods and services in connection with the registration of trademarks and service marks in the member nations. The Nice Classification has even been adopted or adapted by countries that have not yet become signatories.

BENEFITS FOR THE IP OWNER

In countries that adhere to the Nice Classification, the indexing of goods and services used in connection with trademarks and service marks is approximately the same. A trader may select from among 42 classes of goods and services, making applications in multiple jurisdictions more efficient. Moreover, the indices of trademarks and service marks are similar among the member states, making it easier to search for identical and similar marks for purposes of registration and enforcement of registered marks.

Some caution must be exercised when relying on the Nice Classification because member countries are allowed to make modifications and exceptions to the classification. Thus, some countries do not allow for registration of service marks at all, and some have refused to recognize retail services. An application for registration should always be submitted through local legal counsel who is familiar with the laws and rules of the particular country.

Madrid Union

- IP RIGHTS: Establishment of centralized registry for trademarks
- EFFECTIVE DATES: Madrid Agreement, 1891; Madrid Protocol, 1989; Common Regulations, 1996
- MEMBER COUNTRIES: Albania (A), Algeria (A), Antigua and Barbuda (P), Armenia (A&P), Austria (A&P), Azerbaijan (A), Belarus (A), Belgium/Benelux (A&P), Bhutan (A&P), Bosnia and Herzegovina (A), Bulgaria (A), China (A&P), Croatia (A), Cuba (A&P), Czech Republic (A&P), D.P.R. [North] Korea (A&P),

Denmark (P), Egypt (A), Estonia (P), Finland (P), France (A&P), Georgia (P), Germany (A&P), Greece (P), Hungary (A&P), Iceland (P), Italy (A&P), Japan (P), Kazakhstan (A), Kenya (A&P), Kyrgyzstan (A), Latvia (A&P), Lesotho (A&P), Liberia (A), Liechtenstein (A&P), Lithuania (P), Luxembourg/Benelux (A&P), Macedonia (Former Yugoslav Republic) (A), Moldova (A&P), Mongolia (A), Morocco (A&P), Mozambique (A&P), Netherlands/Benelux (A&P), Norway (P), Poland (A&P), Portugal (A&P), Romania (A&P), Russian Federation (A&P), San Marino (A), Sierra Leone (A&P), Singapore (P), Slovakia (A&P), Slovenia (A&P), Spain (A&P), Sudan (A), Swaziland (A&P), Sweden (P), Switzerland (A&P), Tajikistan (A), Turkey (P), Turkmenistan (P), Ukraine (A&P), United Kingdom (P), Uzbekistan (A), Vietnam (A), Yugoslavia (A&P)

(A) Signatory to Madrid Agreement

(P) Signatory to Madrid Protocol

- WEB CONTACT: www.wipo.org/eng/document/govbody/wo_gb_mm/index_32.htm

PURPOSE AND FUNCTION

The signatory countries to the Madrid Agreement Concerning the International Registration of Marks created a central bureau for the international registration of trademarks among the member countries. Initially signed in 1891, this Agreement has been amended periodically. In 1989, the Madrid Protocol Relating to the Madrid Agreement was signed to implement new features to address some of the problems with the Agreement that have kept some countries from joining. Known today as the Madrid Union, these Agreements are not limited to a particular region, but have member countries on nearly every continent with the exception of North and South America and Australia.

BENEFITS TO THE IP OWNER

The obvious advantage of applying for a Madrid Union trademark registration is that your trademark can gain recognition in all of the member states through a single application. However, life is never that easy, and neither is the registration or enforcement process under the Madrid Union. In fact, many countries have refused to join the Union because of perceived weaknesses in the system. The advantages of this registration must therefore be weighed against the disadvantages described in the subsequent paragraphs.

REGISTRATION OF IP RIGHTS

The International Registration Bureau of the Madrid Union is today operated by the World Intellectual Property Organization (WIPO). Registration of a trademark with the International Bureau is available to any subject or citizen of any country that is a member of the Madrid Union, provided that the applicant meets the following requirements:

1. The applicant must be domiciled in a member nation or must have a real and effective industrial or commercial establishment there;
2. The applicant must be the owner of the trademark; and
3. The applicant must have already registered or applied for registration of the trademark in his or her home country.

To register with the International Bureau, the owner of a pending or registered home country mark would next apply for Madrid Union registration through the authority appointed in his or her home country to handle such applications. Whether the registration process is efficient will therefore depend in part on the speed and agility of the appointed authority in the home country. Often, this authority is the same trademark office that receives domestic applications.

The appointed authority will then forward the application to the International Bureau, which will process it, register the mark, publish notice of the registration to all member countries, and notify each member country of the registration. At this stage, however, the mark is not yet protected in the member countries.

EFFECT OF MADRID REGISTRATION

Assuming that the international registration becomes effective, each country must treat the registration as if it were a national registration within that country. This treatment is one of the primary factors cited against the Union: the central registry is weakened by passing enforcement to the national level. In trying to appease all nations, the result is that uniformity in mark registration and enforcement is not achieved. Thus, protection ultimately depends on national acceptance, appeals depend on national procedures, and for the first five years of the registration, the continued existence of the international registration depends on the existence of the home country registration.

- National Acceptance or Rejection. Each member country has the right to accept or reject the registration, and they have an entire year within which to make that decision. Any of the member countries may reject the registration of a mark, provided the rejection is supported "by reasonable grounds." If the member country accepts the registration or fails to make a decision within the year, the mark registration will take effect as if it were a national registration in that country.

NOTE: For member countries that are signatories to the Madrid Protocol, the mark must be accepted within 18 months instead of 12 months (1 year). Thus, nearly 2 years could elapse before the mark is considered protected in the countries belonging to the Protocol.

An applicant may appeal a rejection only if the rejecting country has an appeal procedure. There is no appeal at the level of the International Bureau. An appeal in one country will not delay the effective date of registration in the other countries where the mark registration has been accepted.

- DURATION AND CANCELLATION. An international registration is valid for ten years and is renewable for additional ten-year periods.

NOTE: When seeking a Madrid Union registration, timing of the application is extremely important to ensure that you secure a priority date as early as possible. Your priority date determines whether you can claim a presumption of exclusive rights as against other registrants of the same or similar mark. If another party has an earlier priority date, your application may be rejected.

The International Registration will be deemed effective for ten years from the earliest of the following dates: (1) the official filing date of the home country registration, provided the international application is filed within six months of the home country filing date; (2) the date on which the international application is received by the home country appointed authority, provided within two months of that date the application is received in correct form by the International Bureau; or (3) the date the international application is received by the International Bureau.

The international registration will be canceled if, within the first five years of the international registration, the trademark owner's home country registration is refused or canceled. Protection can still be obtained by filing applications at each national registry that has declared acceptance of the mark, and if the national application is filed within three months of the cancellation or refusal, the national registry must give the owner's national registration the same priority date as that of the international registration.

- ENFORCEMENT AND TRANSFERS OF IP RIGHTS. For enforcement of exclusive rights, the owner of a Madrid Union registration must rely on the local procedures and remedies available within the particular member country where enforcement is sought. No central or cross-border enforcement mechanisms are available.

  If the owner of a Madrid Union registration decides to assign, license, or otherwise transfer rights in that registration to another party, that transfer will become effective in the designated countries provided it is recorded with the International Bureau. Ownership rights may be assigned or otherwise transferred to a party who is entitled by nationality or domicile to hold a Madrid Union registration only.

Paris Convention

- IP RIGHTS: Recognition and harmonization for all IP rights
- EFFECTIVE DATES: 1883; periodically amended every 10 to 15 years
- MEMBER COUNTRIES: Albania, Algeria, Antigua and Barbuda, Argentina, Armenia, Australia, Austria, Azerbaijan, Bahamas, Bahrain, Bangladesh, Barbados, Belarus, Belgium, Belize, Benin, Bhutan, Bolivia, Bosnia and Herzegovina, Botswana, Brazil, Bulgaria, Burkina Faso, Burundi, Cambodia, Cameroon, Canada, Central African Republic, Chad, Chile, China [includes Hong Kong S.A.R. and Macau S.A.R.], Colombia, Congo, Costa Rica, Côte d'Ivoire, Croatia, Cuba, Cyprus, Czech Republic, D.P.R. [North] Korea, D.R. Congo, Denmark [includes Faroe Islands], Dominica, Dominican Republic, Ecuador, Egypt, El Salvador, Equatorial Guinea, Estonia, Finland, France, Gabon, Gambia, Georgia, Germany, Ghana, Greece, Grenada, Guatemala, Guinea, Guinea-Bissau, Guyana, Haiti, Holy See, Honduras, Hungary, Iceland, India, Indonesia, Iran, Iraq, Ireland, Israel, Italy, Jamaica, Japan, Jordan, Kazakhstan, Kenya, Korea [South], Kyrgyzstan, Laos, Latvia, Lebanon, Lesotho, Liberia, Libya, Liechtenstein, Lithuania, Luxembourg, Macedonia (former Yugoslav Republic), Madagascar, Malawi, Malaysia, Mali, Malta, Mauritania, Mauritius, Mexico, Moldova, Monaco, Mongolia, Morocco, Mozambique, Netherlands [includes Netherland Antilles and Aruba], New Zealand [includes Cook Islands, Niue, and Tokelau], Nicaragua, Niger, Nigeria, Norway, Oman, Panama, Papua New Guinea, Paraguay, Peru, Philippines, Poland, Portugal, Qatar, Romania,

Russian Federation, Rwanda, Saint Kitts and Nevis, Saint Lucia, Saint Vincent and the Grenadines, San Marino, Sao Tome and Principe, Senegal, Sierra Leone, Singapore, Slovakia, Slovenia, South Africa, Spain, Sri Lanka, Sudan, Suriname, Swaziland, Sweden, Switzerland, Syria, Tajikistan, Tanzania, Togo, Trinidad and Tobago, Tunisia, Turkey, Turkmenistan, Uganda, Ukraine, United Arab Emirates, United Kingdom [includes Isle of Man], United States [includes Guam and Puerto Rico], Uruguay, Uzbekistan, Venezuela, Vietnam, Yugoslavia, Zambia, Zimbabwe

- WEB CONTACT: www.wipo.org/treaties/ip/paris

PURPOSE AND FUNCTION

The Paris Convention sets forth general standards and mandates that must be adopted and followed within the national laws of the member states to the Convention. This Convention, the full title of which is the *International Convention for the Protection of Industrial Property*, was the result of a final summit meeting of the world's leading statesman in March 1883. The stated objectives of the Convention were as follows: (1) to establish more unified rules for IP protection among the member states; (2) to strengthen protection and enforcement mechanisms; and (3) to encourage cross-border recognition of IP registrations, including priority filings and reciprocal protection. The intent of the member states was to facilitate international trade by eliminating conflicts among nations in the treatment of IP rights and unfair competition. These conflicts were, in effect, indirect barriers to trade.

The Convention is now administered by WIPO, and the TRIPS Agreement under GATT has extended the application of the Paris Convention to nations that are members of the World Trade Organization (WTO), regardless if they are direct signatories of the Convention itself. As a result, the Paris Convention is one of the most significant international agreements to global intellectual property protection today.

BENEFITS TO THE IP OWNER

Unlike the central IP registries created by regional pacts or the Madrid Union, the Paris Convention may seem to have merely a trickle-down effect on the average business owner. Its provisions are rather nebulous and are aimed at such a high political level—legislative and administrative rule-making bodies—that it is difficult to understand how these general terms could possibly apply in specific situations. But the application is very real, and the significance of the Convention provisions is extremely important to understand.

- WHO BENEFITS Individuals and business entities that are nationals or domiciliaries of a Paris Convention member country can claim application of the Convention provisions in transactions with citizens, nationals, or domiciliaries of any other Convention country. Nationals of nonmember nations are also protected by the Convention if they are domiciled or have a real and effective industrial or commercial establishment in a Convention country.

- PRIORITY DATE A very significant and immediate benefit to the owner of IP is the Convention provision on priority dates for IP registration. When an IP owner files for registration, a "priority date" is assigned to the application. That date raises a presumption of ownership in the applicant, and the applicant can oppose all later applications for registration of the same or similar IP by other parties.

The Paris Convention sets a six-month window of time for filing an application with a priority claim. During this time, an applicant for IP registration who is a national of one of the Convention countries is permitted to file for IP registration in other member countries using the priority date of the application first filed. In other words, a Paris Convention country will grant a priority date earlier than the actual filing date of the application, provided that the application is filed within six months of the date the application for registration of the same IP was filed in the first Convention country where the applicant sought IP registration. The earlier priority date assigned will be the same as the priority date for the application filed in the Convention country where registration was first sought.

EXAMPLE: If a Mexican national files an application for registration of a trademark in Mexico on April 3, 2010, that filing date commences a period of six months during which the same national may file for registration of the same mark in any one or more of the other Paris Convention countries and may claim the same priority filing date as was given in Mexico. If the Mexican national files applications to register the same mark in Argentina on May 23, 2010, in Sweden on July 18, 2010, and in Japan on September 15, 2010, each of those applications may claim a priority date of April 3, 2010.

- RECIPROCAL TREATMENT The requirement of reciprocity has served to break down indirect barriers against trade by eliminating preferential treatment of domestic IP rights, and made enforcement and protection of IP more available and effective for foreign companies. Each Convention member nation must treat IP registered by a foreign owner in the same manner as the IP registered by its own nationals. This means that the same standards of examination must be applied, the fees must be the same, and the terms of exclusivity must be the same. In addition, foreign and domestic IP owners must be afforded equal protection of their rights.
- UNIFORM TREATMENT The registration of IP in foreign countries has become easier to accomplish and maintain because of the provisions of the Paris Convention that require member states to conform their national IP systems to Convention standards.

  In the area of trademarks, business owners benefit from Convention provisions that require all member countries:

1. To recognize service marks and collective marks.
2. To register marks independently of registrations in other countries, meaning that the refusal or invalidation of a registration in one country will not automatically affect its validity in other Convention countries.
3. To allow reasonable time for an applicant to begin using a trademark, and justification of non-use if use is made mandatory.
4. To accept an application for registration of a mark that the same owner has registered in his or her home country, unless the mark cannot be registered under domestic law.

- WELL-KNOWN MARKS One of the most advantageous provisions of the Paris Convention is the one that protects well-known marks. The Convention states that the trademark authorities of a Convention country must refuse to register a mark if it constitutes a reproduction, imitation, or translation of, or is likely to cause confusion with, a mark that is considered in that country to be well-known as belonging to another party. Although this far-reaching prohibition is somewhat limited by the requirement that the well-known mark itself must be entitled to Convention protection and must be used for identical or similar goods or services, it can and often has been invoked to protect the famous marks of international traders. Moreover, the well-known mark provision in the Convention set the stage for the TRIPS Agreement, which expanded the protection accorded to well-known marks, as described subsequently in this chapter.

EXAMPLE: The ABC Company seeks to register its mark ABCCO in Cambodia in relation to cycle and car tires. This mark has become so popular worldwide that it is considered well-known. The Cambodian Trademark Registry refuses to register the trademark because a registration already exists for an identical mark for the same goods in the name of a Cambodian national. The ABC Company can file a petition to cancel the prior mark, and can invoke both Cambodian law and the Paris Convention provisions protecting well-known marks. If the ABC Company shows that its mark is known in Cambodia, even through "spill-over reputation" from media that has reached the population there, the Registry can approve the cancellation. Once the prior registration has been canceled, the ABC Company can then request the Registry to accept its application for registration.

Patent Cooperation Treaty

- IP RIGHTS: Establishment of centralized registry for patents
- EFFECTIVE DATES: 1970; amended in 1979 and 1984
- MEMBER COUNTRIES: Albania, Algeria, Antigua and Barbuda, Armenia, Australia, Austria, Azerbaijan, Barbados, Belarus, Belgium, Belize, Benin, Bosnia and Herzegovina, Brazil, Bulgaria, Burkina Faso, Cameroon, Canada, Central African Republic, Chad, China [includes Hong Kong S.A.R.], Congo, Costa Rica, Côte d'Ivoire, Croatia, Cuba, Cyprus, Czech Republic, D.P.R. [North] Korea, Denmark, Dominica, Estonia, Finland, France, Gabon, Gambia, Georgia, Germany, Ghana, Greece, Grenada, Guinea, Guinea-Bissau, Hungary, Iceland, India, Indonesia, Ireland, Israel, Italy, Japan, Kazakhstan, Kenya, Kyrgyzstan, Latvia, Lesotho, Liberia, Liechtenstein, Lithuania, Luxembourg, Macedonia (former Yugoslav Republic), Madagascar, Malawi, Mali, Mauritania, Mexico, Moldova Republic, Monaco, Mongolia, Morocco, Mozambique, Netherlands [includes Netherland Antilles and Aruba], New Zealand, Niger, Norway, Poland, Portugal, Romania, Russian Federation, Saint Lucia, Senegal, Sierra Leone, Singapore, Slovakia, Slovenia, South Africa, Spain, Sri Lanka, Sudan, Swaziland, Sweden, Switzerland, Tajikistan, Tanzania, Togo, Trinidad and Tobago, Turkey, Turkmenistan, Uganda, Ukraine, United Arab Emirates, United Kingdom [includes Isle of Man], United States [includes Guam and Puerto Rico], Uzbekistan, Vietnam, Yugoslavia, Zimbabwe
- WEB CONTACT: www.uspto.gov/web/offices/pac/dapps/pct/pct.htm

PURPOSE AND FUNCTION

The Patent Cooperation Treaty (PCT) established a central registry for inventors seeking patent protection in more than one country. The intent of the member states was to simplify and render more economical the process of obtaining such protection in several countries. It was believed that a more efficient and cost-effective system would also accelerate the public's access to technical information contained in the patent applications.

BENEFITS TO THE IP OWNER

If a patent owner is a resident or national of one of the PCT countries, the owner may file an international PCT application to protect the patent in one or more of the PCT member countries. A PCT filing is available for patents for inventions, utility models, and patents of addition, as well as for certificates of the same. The single PCT application will become valid in whichever of the member countries are designated by the applicant.

The documentation for a PCT filing is fairly similar to that which is filed at the national level. Claims, abstracts, descriptions, and drawings are all required. Some modification may be required to conform to the PCT regulations. The complexity of patent drafting is best left to an attorney.

TIP: If you are planning to file a PCT application, you should take steps to do so immediately after filing your national patent. Time limits are tight, and if the deadline is missed, there are no late filings.

Trademark Law Treaty (TLT)

- IP RIGHTS: Harmonization of national trademark laws
- EFFECTIVE DATES: October 27, 1994
- MEMBER COUNTRIES: Australia, *Burkina Faso, Cyprus, Czech Republic, Denmark, Egypt, *Guinea, Hungary, Indonesia, Ireland, Japan, Latvia, Liechtenstein, Lithuania, Moldova, Monaco, **Netherlands, Romania, Russian Federation, Slovakia, Spain, Sri Lanka, Switzerland, Trinidad and Tobago, Ukraine, United Kingdom, United States, Uzbekistan, Yugoslavia.

  **Not in force until three months after African Intellectual Property Organization (OAPI) deposits its instrument of accession.*

  ***Not in force until three months after Belgium and Luxembourg deposit instruments of ratification.*
- WEB CONTACT: www.uspto.gov/web/offices/com/sol/tmlwtrty

PURPOSE AND FUNCTION

The Trademark Law Treaty (TLT) is similar to the Paris Convention in that it does not establish a centralized registry or enforcement mechanism but merely requires the member countries to conform their national trademark systems to uniform guidelines. These guidelines include specific procedural requirements related to applications for registration and alterations and renewal of registrations. The TLT also offers a set of model forms for the use of its members.

Adopted in October 1994, the TLT now has more than 20 member states. Membership is open to nations that belong to WIPO, but fewer countries have acceded to the TLT because, prior to joining the TLT, a nation must already have implemented laws and procedures that conform to the uniform guidelines. Countries that have complied with the TRIPS Agreement can generally conform to the TLT guidelines with little effort, and therefore the TLT is becoming more generally accepted as countries modernize their trademark laws.

BENEFITS TO THE IP OWNER

The TLT provisions emphasize specific procedural requirements for registration and enforcement of trademarks, and therefore the effect of the TLT provisions on a global trader will be more obvious than the more general provisions of the Paris Convention or TRIPS. For example, traders in TLT countries will find that:

- Registration and renewal procedures will be similar among the different TLT countries because of uniform application guidelines.
- Documents filed with the trademark registrations will no longer need to be notarized or legalized by public and consulate officials.
- Local classifications of goods and services will no longer be a hindrance because TLT members must use the International Classification.
- Trademark registrations will be valid for 10 years with renewal periods of 10 years in TLT member countries.

Trade-Related Aspects of Intellectual Property Rights Agreement (TRIPS)

- IP RIGHTS: Recognition and harmonization for all IP rights
- EFFECTIVE DATES: January 1, 1995; agreement between WIPO and WTO, effective January 1, 1996.
- MEMBER COUNTRIES: Antigua and Barbuda, Angola, Argentina, Australia, Austria, Bahrain, Bangladesh, Barbados, Belgium, Belize, Benin, Bolivia, Botswana, Brazil, Brunei Darussalam, Burkina Faso, Burundi, Cameroon, Canada, Central African Republic, Chad, Chile, Colombia, Congo, Costa Rica, Côte d'Ivoire, Cuba, Cyprus, Czech Republic, D.R. Congo, Denmark, Djibouti, Dominica, Dominican Republic, Ecuador, Egypt, El Salvador, European Union, Fiji, Finland, France, Gabon, Gambia, Germany, Ghana, Greece, Grenada, Guatemala, Guinea, Guinea-Bissau, Guyana, Haiti, Honduras, Hong Kong S.A.R., Hungary, Iceland, India, Indonesia, Ireland, Israel, Italy, Jamaica, Japan, Kenya, Kuwait, Lesotho, Liechtenstein, Luxembourg, Macau S.A.R., Madagascar, Malawi, Malaysia, Maldives, Mali, Malta, Mauritania, Mauritius, Mexico, Mongolia, Morocco, Mozambique, Myanmar, Namibia, Netherlands, New Zealand, Nicaragua, Niger, Nigeria, Norway, Pakistan, Panama, Papua New Guinea, Paraguay, Peru, Philippines, Poland, Portugal, Qatar, Republic of Korea, Romania, Russian Federation, Rwanda, Saint Kitts and Nevis, Saint Lucia,

Saint Vincent and the Grenadines, Senegal, Sierra Leone, Singapore, Slovakia, Slovenia, Solomon Islands, South Africa, Spain, Sri Lanka, Suriname, Swaziland, Sweden, Switzerland, Tanzania, Thailand, Togo, Trinidad and Tobago, Tunisia, Turkey, Uganda, United Arab Emirates, United Kingdom, United States, Uruguay, Venezuela, Zambia, Zimbabwe

- WEB CONTACT: www.wto.org/english/tratop_e/trips_e/trips_e.htm

PURPOSE AND FUNCTION

One of the most important trade agreements to be concluded in the last decade was the Agreement Establishing the World Trade Organization (WTO), and annexed to it was a pact with an equally long title: the Trade-Related Aspects of Intellectual Property Agreement, known as TRIPS. These agreements took effect January 1, 1995. With the support of the substantial authority of the underlying WTO, TRIPS has effectively become the international standard for intellectual property protection.

The provisions of TRIPS closely relate to the treaties and conventions that have been administered by WIPO and its predecessor agencies for many years. For this reason, a cooperation agreement was signed between WIPO and the WTO, requiring these two agencies to work together to implement and administer TRIPS.

The purpose of TRIPS is to reduce trade barriers by promoting within the member nations the adoption of effective and adequate legal measures and procedures for the protection of all intellectual property rights. Rather than requiring specific, uniform procedures, TRIPS merely requires that the member countries meet certain minimum and fundamental standards of protection, leaving each nation free to determine its own method for implementing the TRIPS provisions.

BENEFITS TO THE IP OWNER

The TRIPS Agreement affects international traders in a fashion similar to the Paris and Berne Convention. In fact, TRIPS serves to strengthen the rights of those two conventions, both of which are incorporated by reference into TRIPS. Traders are indirectly and favorably affected as countries modernize their laws for the protection and enforcement of IP rights. These affects are being felt in all corners of the globe because TRIPS has been so widely accepted as part of the WTO Agreement.

WIPO Convention

- IP RIGHTS: Recognition and harmonization for all IP rights
- EFFECTIVE DATES: WIPO Convention, April 1970; mediation and arbitration rules, October 1, 1994; agreement between WIPO and WTO, January 1, 1996
- MEMBER COUNTRIES: Albania, Algeria, Andorra, Angola, Antigua and Barbuda, Argentina, Armenia, Australia, Austria, Azerbaijan, Bahamas, Bahrain, Bangladesh, Barbados, Belarus, Belgium, Belize, Benin, Bhutan, Bolivia, Bosnia and Herzegovina, Botswana, Brazil, Brunei, Bulgaria, Burkina Faso, Burundi, Cambodia, Cameroon, Canada, Cape Verde, Central African Republic, Chad,

Chile, China, Colombia, Congo, Costa Rica, Côte d'Ivoire, Croatia, Cuba, Cyprus, Czech Republic, D.P.R. [North] Korea, D.R. Congo, Denmark, Dominica, Dominican Republic, Ecuador, Egypt, El Salvador, Equatorial Guinea, Eritrea, Estonia, Ethiopia, Fiji, Finland, France, Gabon, Gambia, Georgia, Germany, Ghana, Greece, Grenada, Guatemala, Guinea, Guinea-Bissau, Guyana, Haiti, Holy See, Honduras, Hungary, Iceland, India, Indonesia, Iraq, Ireland, Israel, Italy, Jamaica, Japan, Jordan, Kazakhstan, Kenya, Kuwait, Kyrgyzstan, Laos, Latvia, Lebanon, Lesotho, Liberia, Libya, Liechtenstein, Lithuania, Luxembourg, Macedonia (former Yugoslav Republic), Madagascar, Malawi, Malaysia, Mali, Malta, Mauritania, Mauritius, Mexico, Moldova, Monaco, Mongolia, Morocco, Mozambique, Namibia, Nepal, Netherlands, New Zealand, Nicaragua, Niger, Nigeria, Norway, Oman, Pakistan, Panama, Papua New Guinea, Paraguay, Peru, Philippines, Poland, Portugal, Qatar, Republic of Korea, Romania, Russian Federation, Rwanda, Saint Kitts and Nevis, Saint Lucia, Saint Vincent and the Grenadines, Samoa, San Marino, Sao Tome and Principe, Saudi Arabia, Senegal, Seychelles, Sierra Leone, Singapore, Slovakia, Slovenia, Somalia, South Africa, Spain, Sri Lanka, Sudan, Suriname, Swaziland, Sweden, Switzerland, Tajikistan, Tanzania, Thailand, Togo, Trinidad and Tobago, Tunisia, Turkey, Turkmenistan, Uganda, Ukraine, United Arab Emirates, United Kingdom, United States, Uruguay, Uzbekistan, Venezuela, Vietnam, Yemen, Yugoslavia, Zambia, Zimbabwe

- WEB CONTACT: www.wipo.org/members/convention

PURPOSE AND FUNCTION

The World Intellectual Property Organization (WIPO) is an agency within the United Nations (UN) that works on an international level to promote protection of all types of intellectual property. The Convention came into force in 1970, and WIPO became a specialized agency of the UN in 1974. More than 90 percent of the world's countries are members of WIPO.

Since 1974, WIPO has been the agency that oversees administration of more than 20 multilateral treaties on intellectual property, including the Paris and Berne Conventions, the Madrid Union, and the TLT. In 1996, WIPO entered into a cooperation agreement with the World Trade Organization (WTO) to assist in administration of the TRIPS Agreement. In addition, it serves as a forum for the creation of new international treaties for the protection of IP rights, and provides technical assistance to countries that are developing and modernizing their IP laws and practices.

BENEFITS TO THE IP OWNER

Although WIPO operates on an international political level that is somewhat removed from the average trader, it has established lines of communication that are easily accessible worldwide. Its publications, news bulletins, and web sites are important resources for developments related to IP practices in countries throughout the world.

- MEDIATION AND ARBITRATION Traders in member countries can also take advantage of the mediation and arbitration programs that WIPO administers for resolution of disputes related to IP rights. A trader who wants to take advantage of WIPO mediation or arbitration may do so simply by including a provision in his or her written contract to submit disputes to the WIPO program or by agreeing after the dispute has arisen to submit to WIPO arbitration or mediation. Expedited arbitration may even be available, allowing a shortened time frame and reduced cost.

■ PROCEDURAL REQUIREMENTS Any party who is in a dispute with another party over intellectual property rights may request mediation, arbitration, or expedited arbitration of the dispute. To commence one of these procedures, the party must submit a form, called a Request for Mediation/Arbitration, to the WIPO Arbitration Center. The process is then determined by the rules provided by WIPO, copies of which are easily available from the central office for this organization.

Mediation and arbitration differ in their formalities and intent. Mediation tends to be less formal and allows for more participation by the parties in the process of settling their dispute. The intended result of mediation is for the parties to reach a settlement agreement. In arbitration, the parties submit claims and counterclaims in a process similar to a court trial. The papers and evidence are considered by the arbitrators, who then decide the claims.

CHAPTER 12

Fundamentals in Country Legal Systems: Generalities

BEFORE YOU CREATE OR ACQUIRE IP RIGHTS, you should become generally familiar with the legal systems and laws of other countries where you might desire protection for those rights. You should also have some awareness of the similarities and distinctions between the legal system of your own country and those of other countries.

It is not necessary for you to become an expert on these laws—you can leave that to your attorney. But you need some awareness to make certain that you are asking the right questions and gaining satisfactory protection. Fortunately, in the realm of IP, many of the distinctions tend to blend across country borders because most countries have recently developed or amended their IP laws and regulations to conform to international agreements, such as TRIPS.

Nevertheless, an understanding of country legal systems is important for two reasons. First, an awareness of legal systems will be useful in a general context when considering your business and marketing plans. If you know which countries have tended to follow common law versus socialist law, you can anticipate the treatment of your IP and the receptivity of the markets, and you can make advance modifications to secure your IP rights and to ensure popular acceptance. Second, if you are aware of how local laws have developed within the context of different legal systems, you will be better prepared when facing the specific requirements of a particular country. For example, if you understand the basic tenets of Germanic civil law and you are protecting your IP rights in Japan, you can make some assumptions as to what to expect because Japan's IP law was developed from Germanic civil law.

Legal Systems Worldwide

There are four major types of legal systems in the world: common law, civil law, Islamic (Shari'ah) law, and communist or socialist law. Many countries have adopted a combination of these legal systems, and in addition have retained some influences from various cultures that have crossed the borders in the past. For example, Japan looked to Germany when developing its modern laws, and therefore it follows the civil law system. The United States took much of its legal system from England, and therefore it follows common law. Malaysian law is a combination of common law, Islamic law, and Malay principles, and it is also influenced by Chinese and Muslim cultures. In Egypt, the civil law system combines French Civil Law with Islamic principles and some common law rules, reflecting lingering British and French influences. In Asia, Africa, and South America, and various island chains, many of the legal systems have been built on the foundations of former colonial masters—Brazil applies civil law reflecting its Portuguese history, while Singapore applies common law on account of its English heritage.

Common Law

Courts in England began creating and applying common law before statutes were adopted for that country. By the time statutes were drafted, the courts were well entrenched and a tremendous body of law, the common law, had already been established. The statutes served to confirm, codify (put into Code), limit, and supplement the common law of the courts. As a result, its distinguishing feature is its reliance on precedence established by judges in earlier cases. In other words, the courts in common law countries will apply and interpret statutes by following the principles developed in earlier judicial decisions. This does not mean that common law is static, that is, always the same from court decision to court decision. Quite the contrary, common law is ever expanding because the courts often extrapolate new principles from the old ones to apply in new factual situations, and sometimes they even reverse or limit their prior stance in the light of new circumstances. Also, court decisions must be made within the boundaries established by statutes, and therefore as legislative enactments change the statutes, court decisions will reflect the amendments made.

Countries that operate under a common law system are those that were at some time under the power of the British Commonwealth. These include England, the United States, Australia, Singapore, the Hong Kong S.A.R., and India. In these countries, IP rights can be established without registration of the IP, although the standards of proof tend to be more burdensome and the remedies less remunerative if the IP has not been registered pursuant to the statutes. Trials are typically before one judge. To insure a fair trial, complex rules and procedures have been developed, and an appeal process is available.

IP RIGHTS

The concept of IP rights was first developed in the common law system. Rights granted by statute and protected by court decisions vary from country to country, largely depending on the extent to which a country's laws are influenced by other systems of law and culture. The trend in adopting new IP laws is to be expansive rather than restrictive, with the result that more and more IP rights are being recognized and protected. The courts take an essential role in this progressive attitude by applying precedential case law and interpreting statutory law to cover IP rights that are on the fringes. Through the common law, protection for IP rights can sometimes be attained while the lawmakers are still making the laws.

Countries with common law systems usually offer satisfactory means of enforcing IP rights. Enforcement may be effected through court actions, although the bureaucracy in the courts can be a stumbling block in some places because of lengthy backlogs in setting trials. There are often alternative remedies available through custom agencies (national customs services) or through a registry of IP rights. Arbitration and mediation are commonly used, and even criminal proceedings can be brought to bear on an infringer.

Civil Law

Most countries that do not apply common law have civil law systems. Civil law is characterized by comprehensive and systematic compilations of statutes, known as Codes of Law, which govern most aspects of human endeavor. These countries have developed their Codes first and then their courts. Therefore judicial decisions are based on the legal principles set forth in the Codes.

Civil law systems use non-jury trials, except in criminal cases, and the courts are typically composed of a panel of judges. In comparison to common law systems, there are few well-defined rules of evidence, and minimal oral testimony or argument is permitted before the court. Most evidence and arguments are presented to the court in writing.

Legal decisions are generally based on one-time interpretations of the codified laws with minimal reference to preceding cases, although in some countries prior case decisions are recognized after the same decision has been made a certain number of times. As a result, the decision in any particular lawsuit is less predictable than it would be in a common law court, which will rely on precedential case law.

Examples of common law countries include Germany, France, and Japan.

IP RIGHTS

Most countries that have adopted civil law have selected to follow either the French or the Germanic systems. French civil law somewhat mirrors the common law philosophy that the recognition of IP rights forms a contract between the creator and society, that IP rights are a form of monopoly and should be limited, and that a person charged with infringement is a protector of society's right to free, uninhibited trade. In contrast, German civil law views IP rights as grants made by the state in its power as protector over its nationals. An infringer is considered to have taken away the right granted by the state, and the infringer has therefore acted against the state. For this reason, the fact that the grant might have been invalid is not in itself a defense to infringement.

In the context of IP rights, the primary difference between civil law jurisdictions and other legal systems is in matters of procedure. The judges in a civil law country typically are appointed shortly after graduating with a law degree, and they work their way up through the levels of the court system as they become more experienced. Heavy reliance is placed on the submission of written materials to the courts, there are minimal pre-trial procedures for the collection of evidence, and minimal evidentiary rules at trial. It is a frequent practice for the judge to take a role as a fact-finder, and even to question the parties and their attorneys. Issues that might be brought in a single action—such as the validity of an IP registration and the infringement of IP rights—often must be raised in separate actions and before different judges. Some countries have established specialist courts for hearing commercial and IP cases, and these courts have no jurisdiction to determine more general issues.

Islamic (Shari'ah) Law

In criminal, family, and personal injury matters, Moslem or Islamic countries apply the Law of Islam, originally derived from the Koran and the Sunna. The Koran is believed by its adherents to contain revelations of Allah to the Prophet Mohammed, and the Sunna is a recording of the Prophet's later teachings and actions. These sacred volumes do not contain detailed codes, but rather principles and precepts of the Muslim religion. Muslims do not modify these laws, because of their belief that after the Prophet's death the direct revelations of God ceased, and the words of God are immutable. With some exceptions, most Muslim countries no longer adhere to the strict traditional form of Shari'ah Law. Today, its application tends to be limited to family and estate succession law. Even these laws have been codified, so reference to the traditional texts is rarely made except when existing statutes and codes fail to cover a specific situation.

IP RIGHTS

Traditional Shari'ah law did not specifically deal with intangible property. For many years, IP rights were not recognized in these jurisdictions. To accommodate changes in modern societies and international business practices, most Muslim countries have adopted modified codes based on European legal models, particularly French or Napoleonic Code. A separate division of commercial courts or administrative tribunals usually handles matters involving IP rights in accordance with civil law concepts. Case decisions are based on the law; case precedents are not binding on later cases.

Communist and Socialist Law

A form of communism or socialism is used in the People's Republic of China, Cuba, the Democratic People's Republic of [North] Korea, Laos, and Vietnam. It originated from the Communist manifesto of Karl Marx and Friedrich Engels. The Manifesto is a philosophical mandate under which individual rights were subsumed for the good of all society on the assumption that the rights of each citizen inhere in the goals of the state. A code of laws was gradually developed from the Manifesto for the purpose of transforming society into a socialist and then a communist order, at which time the laws were supposed to cease because the new society would function smoothly without the need for rules and regulations. In fact, most countries operating under this type of government today are socialist, never having attained the ideal communist order.

Private individuals and entities rarely resort to the court system in a socialist state. The laws, rules, and practices tend to have strong ideological content that is unsuitable for interpreting commercial relationships. Court proceedings are open, direct, and heavily reliant on oral testimony and examination. Rules of evidence are minimal, and prior case decisions carry little weight. The court will consider all evidence presented, decide the relative value and importance of facts, and make a determination based on general legal principles and communist ideology.

Socialist nations are rapidly changing. Most are in the process of modernizing their economies and have found that they need to conform their commercial practices to the international business world. When doing business with traders of these nations, you must recognize that the unpredictable state of government bureaucracies makes business arrangements inherently unreliable. You will probably need to develop personal trust in your relationships and to educate your business partners with respect to the value of your IP rights. You should be certain that they understand the scope of their rights within your business relationship, and that they assist you in making and keeping your IP rights valuable within that country.

IP RIGHTS

In the socialist system, commercial and foreign trade is primarily operated by the state and individual property rights are given up to the community. Individual rights in IP have slowly developed in these countries, primarily because of pressure from traders who have begun operating internationally, and global companies that have demanded protection for their IP before doing business in a particular country.

Trademarks, patents, and copyrights can be registered under the local laws of all of the socialist nations. Most of these nations are members of at least one of the international treaties and conventions protecting IP rights, and therefore their local IP laws at least partially conform with international standards. These rights are being protected through adoption of laws and regulations based primarily on civil law models. However, their laws are conservative in recognizing IP rights and the process for amending them is cumbersome and lengthy. For this reason, registration may not be available for IP rights covering the newest types of technologies and creations, and no body of court law is available to encourage extension of the laws.

In practice, IP laws in socialist countries are applied through government policies that place the right of society as a whole above individual rights. As a result, the application and enforcement of laws related to individual IP rights is somewhat unpredictable and can depend on sudden shifts in state ideology.

The enforcement of IP rights in a communist nation is difficult at best. One must first collect sufficient evidence of the infringement, which is a cumbersome process made trickier by the inherent lack of recognition of individual property rights. Violations of trademarks are usually more easily detected than violations of patents or copyrights, and any investigation can be quite expensive.

Reliance on governmental authorities is usually not the most pragmatic means of enforcement. Administrative remedies are highly bureaucratic, subject to government policy shifts, and subject to substantial time delays. If criminal remedies are available, the penalties are often too harsh (even sometimes death for severe infringement) in comparison to the negative publicity that often flows from such actions (big, bad foreigner taking tiny local person to task).

The best means for enforcing IP rights tends to be through informal and creative ways, which means that as a trader in these countries, you take on some of the responsibility for increasing the level of IP recognition. This may take the form of using local representatives and publicity to educate the local populace about the significance of IP rights and the means for recognizing the real article. Local representatives can also be hired to approach and obtain informal cooperation of local government authorities to pressure infringers into changing their activities into legitimate operations. Diplomatic contacts can also be used to increase awareness and educate officials about the needs for respect and recognition of IP rights and for a means of immediate and satisfactory enforcement.

CHAPTER 13

Validity of IP Rights Locally: Specifics

ALL IP RIGHTS ARE NATIONAL IN ORIGIN. International treaties may offer recognition and protection of IP rights, but one of their foremost goals has been to require the harmonization of national laws and practices. While this goal has been somewhat successful, local variations are still very much in existence. When developing an international IP strategy, it is important to keep some of these variations in mind, particularly if failure to comply will mean loss of your IP rights.

A listing of all requirements for all IP rights for all countries will not fit in this chapter. The countries listed below are intended to provide a sampling of the issues and requirements of local laws that you might find relevant when deciding on your IP strategy. Keep in mind that this is a short list and other concerns may also be important to take into account before finalizing your strategy.

As you will see, there are trends in harmonization but also many differences in details. It should also be apparent that the protection of IP rights is not as easy as it may at first seem; merely filing an application for registration is not all there is to it! For advice on specific local legal requirements, always consult an attorney knowledgeable in the laws and practices of the particular country of interest.

Local Patent Laws

ARGENTINA

- PATENT REGISTRY: National Patent Registry, National Institute of Industrial Property (INPI), Ministry of Economic Affairs, Public Works and Public Services
- RIGHTS PROTECTED: Utility (industrially useful) inventions; pharmaceutical products
- NOVELTY REQUIREMENT: Invention is novel if it is not currently known in the industry
- SPECIAL DOCUMENTARY REQUIREMENTS: Power of attorney legalized by Argentine Consulate; Spanish translation of specification, claims, and abstract; if applicant is not the inventor, deed of assignment legalized by the Argentine Consulate; if priority is claimed, certified copy of the application or registration on which the priority claim is based
- DURATION: 20 years
- USE REQUIREMENTS: Annual annuities; if owner fails to work patent within three years of granting date or within four years of filing date
- RELATED RIGHTS: Utility models, with 10 year duration

AUSTRALIA

- PATENT REGISTRY: Patent Office, IP Australia, Department of Industry, Science, and Resources
- RIGHTS PROTECTED: Utility (one that is useful in industry) inventions of devices, substances, methods, processes, and improvements thereon; pharmaceutical, food product, plant variety, microorganism, and computer-related inventions; schemes and plans
- NOVELTY REQUIREMENT: Absolute novelty, meaning no description of an identical invention has been publicly disclosed by any means anywhere in the world, nor has the invention ever been demonstrated, sold, or discussed in public anywhere before the application filing date
- SPECIAL DOCUMENTARY REQUIREMENTS: Power of attorney simply signed; specification (consisting of description and claims) and drawings in English; if priority is claimed, copy of the application or registration on which the priority claim is based, with English translation
- DURATION: Patent for 20 years
- USE REQUIREMENTS: Annual annuities
- RELATED RIGHTS: Design and industrial models, with 1-year term and extension to a maximum of 16 years; integrated circuit layout rights, with 10-year term and extension to a maximum of 20 years

BRAZIL

- PATENT REGISTRY: National Industrial Property Institute (INPI), Ministry of Industry, Commerce, and Tourism
- RIGHTS PROTECTED: Utility (industrially useful) inventions of devices, substances, methods, processes, and improvements thereon; pharmaceutical, food product, plant variety, and microorganism inventions
- NOVELTY REQUIREMENT: Absolute novelty, meaning no description of an identical invention has been made available to the public by any communication means anywhere in the world, nor has the invention ever been demonstrated, sold, or discussed in public anywhere before the application filing date
- SPECIAL DOCUMENTARY REQUIREMENTS: Power of attorney simply signed; summary, specification (consisting of description and claims), abstract, and drawing with Portuguese translation; if applicant is not the inventor, deed of assignment notarized; if priority is claimed, certified copy of the application or registration on which the priority claim is based with sworn Portuguese translation
- DURATION: Patent for 20 years from filing date, but never less than 10 years from granting date; for vegetal species, for 15 to 18 years depending on type
- USE REQUIREMENTS: Annual annuities beginning in third year from filing date; if owner fails to work patent, it becomes subject to compulsory licensing

- RELATED RIGHTS: Utility models, with 15 year duration from filing date but never less than 7 years from granting date; industrial designs and models, with 10 years duration from filing date and three consecutive renewals of five years each

CANADA

- PATENT REGISTRY: Canadian Intellectual Property Office (CIPO), Department of Industry
- RIGHTS PROTECTED: Utility (industrially useful) inventions of machines, compositions of matter, manufactures, processes, and improvements thereon; pharmaceutical, food product, plant variety, and microorganism inventions
- NOVELTY REQUIREMENT: New invention, that is, identical invention has not been previously disclosed by or through the applicant so as to become available to the public more than one year before the filing date and not made previously available to the public or in a prior application by another person
- SPECIAL DOCUMENTARY REQUIREMENTS: Power of attorney simply signed; abstract, specification (consisting of description and claims), and drawings in English; if applicant is not the inventor, statement of assignment with English translation; if priority is claimed, copy of the application or registration on which the priority claim is based with English translation
- DURATION: Patent protection is for 20 years from filing date
- USE REQUIREMENTS: Annual annuities; if owner fails to work patent in compliance with Canadian law, patent becomes subject to compulsory licensing; no compulsory license is imposed for medical or pharmaceutical patents
- RELATED RIGHTS: Industrial designs, with 10-year term; integrated circuit topographies, with 10-year term from the application filing date or date of first commercial exploitation whichever is earlier.

CHINA

- PATENT REGISTRY: Patent Office, State Intellectual Property Office (SIPO), State Administration for Industry and Commerce (SAIC)
- RIGHTS PROTECTED: Utility (industrially useful) inventions of products, processes, and improvements thereon; pharmaceutical, agricultural, chemical, and microorganism inventions
- NOVELTY REQUIREMENT: New invention, that is, identical invention has not been publicly disclosed in publications anywhere in the world, publicly used or made known to the public by any means whatsoever, nor subject of any prior patent application filings, except applicant may still file within 6 months after disclosure of invention without applicant's consent or disclosure of it at an international exhibition sponsored or recognized by the Chinese government or at a prescribed academic or technological meeting
- SPECIAL DOCUMENTARY REQUIREMENTS: Power of attorney simply signed; specification (consisting of description and claims), and abstract, and drawing; report on prior art; if applicant is not the inventor, deed of assignment; if priority is claimed, copy of the application or registration on which the priority claim is based

- DURATION: Patent for 20 years
- USE REQUIREMENTS: Annual annuities beginning in year patent is granted; if owner fails to work patent within reasonable time (determined by SIPO), patent becomes subject to compulsory licensing
- RELATED RIGHTS: Design and utility models, with 10 year duration

EGYPT

- PATENT REGISTRY: Egyptian Patent and Trademark Office, Administration of Commercial Registration, Ministry of Supply and Internal Trade
- RIGHTS PROTECTED: Utility (industrially useful) inventions of products, processes, and improvements thereon; pharmaceutical, food processes, plant varieties
- NOVELTY REQUIREMENT: Absolute novelty, meaning the invention must not have become known through publication or use in Egypt or anywhere in the world prior to the filing date or priority date of the application
- SPECIAL DOCUMENTARY REQUIREMENTS: Power of attorney legalized by the Egyptian Consulate; two copies of specification (consisting of description and claims), drawing, and abstract with Arabic translation; if applicant is not the inventor, assignment deed legalized by the Egyptian Consulate; if applicant is company, certificate of existence legalized by the Egyptian Consulate; if priority is claimed, certified copy of priority documents with Arabic translation
- DURATION: 15 years initially and one five-year renewal with proof of justification for renewal; pharmaceutical patents for 10 years initially and one 10-year renewal
- USE REQUIREMENTS: Annual annuities; if owner fails to work patent within three years from grant date or ceases to work it for two consecutive years, patent is subject to compulsory licensing by third parties
- RELATED RIGHTS: Design and industrial models can be protected for five years initially with two five-year renewal periods

GERMANY

- PATENT REGISTRY: German Patent and Trademark Office
- RIGHTS PROTECTED: Utility (industrially useful) inventions of machines, compositions of matter, manufactures, processes, and improvements thereon; pharmaceutical, and food product inventions
- NOVELTY REQUIREMENT: New invention, that is, identical invention has not been previously disclosed in any prior art anywhere in the world; if inventor described or used the invention in public, patent must be filed within six months of such disclosure
- SPECIAL DOCUMENTARY REQUIREMENTS: Power of attorney simply signed; three copies of the specification (consisting of description and claims) drawing, and abstract with German translation; if applicant is not the inventor, deed of assignment; if priority is claimed, copy of the application or registration on which the priority claim is based

- DURATION: Patent for 20 years
- USE REQUIREMENTS: Annual annuities; if owner fails to work patent in compliance with German law, patent becomes subject to compulsory licensing
- RELATED RIGHTS: Designs, with 5-year initial term and three five-year renewals (maximum 20 years) and industrial models, with 3-year initial term and two-year renewals to a maximum of 10 years

HONG KONG S.A.R.

- PATENT REGISTRY: Hong Kong SAR Patent Registry, Intellectual Property Department, Ministry of Trade and Industry
- RIGHTS PROTECTED: Standard utility (industrially useful) inventions of products, processes, and improvements thereon and plant variety inventions; designated patents filed and granted in China, United Kingdom, or European Patent Organization; short-term utility inventions for products or processes having short commercial life
- NOVELTY REQUIREMENT: Absolute novelty, meaning invention has not been made available to public and is not in prior art available to the public anywhere in the world prior to the application filing date or priority date, except that inventor has 6-month period from first publication to file in China
- SPECIAL DOCUMENTARY REQUIREMENTS: Power of attorney simply signed; if a designated patent, copy of recording of patent from designated country and copy of published application; specification (consisting of description and claims), drawings, and abstract with English and Chinese translation; title with English and Chinese translation; if short-term patent, search report obtained from designated authority; if priority is claimed, copy of the application or registration on which the priority claim is based
- DURATION: Standard or designated patent for a maximum of 20 years and a short term patent for a maximum of eight years
- USE REQUIREMENTS: Annual annuities from end of third year after filing date; if owner fails to work patent, patent becomes subject to compulsory licensing
- RELATED RIGHTS: Design applied by industrial process and integrated circuit design, with 5-year initial term and 5-year renewals to maximum of 25 years.

JAPAN

- PATENT REGISTRY: Japanese Patent Office (JPO)
- RIGHTS PROTECTED: Utility (industrially useful) inventions of machines, compositions of matter, manufactures, processes, and improvements thereon; pharmaceuticals, food products; microorganisms, plant variety inventions
- NOVELTY REQUIREMENT: New invention, meaning invention has not been made public knowledge and has not been used publicly anywhere in the world through any means of communication, including electronic networks, except that inventor may file within 6 months of public disclosure
- SPECIAL DOCUMENTARY REQUIREMENTS: Power of attorney simply signed; specification (description and single claim) and drawing with Japanese

translation; if priority is claimed, certified copy of the application or registration on which the priority claim is based

- DURATION: Patent for 20 years
- USE REQUIREMENTS: Annual annuities; if owner fails to work patent in compliance with Japanese law, patent becomes subject to compulsory licensing
- RELATED RIGHTS: Utility models, with 6-year term; industrial designs with 15-year term

MEXICO

- PATENT REGISTRY: Mexican Institute of Industrial Property (IMPI)
- RIGHTS PROTECTED: Utility (industrially useful) inventions of machines, compositions of matter, manufactures, processes, and improvements thereon; processes for making food products or medical drugs or pharmaceuticals
- NOVELTY REQUIREMENT: Absolute novelty, meaning no disclosure of preceding material constituting industrial prior art to public anywhere at any time by any means through which the invention could be understood
- SPECIAL DOCUMENTARY REQUIREMENTS: Power of attorney signed and witnessed; specification (consisting of description and claims), drawing, and abstract with Spanish translation; if applicant is not the inventor, deed of assignment certified; if priority is claimed, certified copy of the application or registration on which the priority claim is based
- DURATION: Patent for 20 years
- USE REQUIREMENTS: Annual annuities
- RELATED RIGHTS: Design and industrial models, with 15 year duration

UNITED KINGDOM

- PATENT REGISTRY: The Patent Office, Ministry of Trade and Industry
- RIGHTS PROTECTED: Utility (industrially useful) inventions of products, processes, and improvements thereon; pharmaceutical and food product inventions
- NOVELTY REQUIREMENT: Absolute novelty, meaning no disclosure of identical invention anywhere in the world through any means before the application filing date
- SPECIAL DOCUMENTARY REQUIREMENTS: Two copies of specification (consisting of description and claims), abstract, and drawings in English; if applicant is not the inventor, statement of assignment in English; if priority is claimed, copy of the application or registration on which the priority claim is based in English
- DURATION: Patent for 20 years; medicinal patent may be renewed for one 5-year term
- USE REQUIREMENTS: Annual annuities; if owner fails to work patent in three consecutive years after grant, patent becomes subject to compulsory licensing

- RELATED RIGHTS: Design models, with 10-year term beginning on date of first marketing to maximum of 15 years from creation date; industrial models, with 5-year term and two 5-year renewals

UNITED STATES

- PATENT REGISTRY: United States Patent and Trademark Office (USPTO), US Department of Commerce
- RIGHTS PROTECTED: Utility (industrially useful) inventions of machines, compositions of matter, manufactures, processes, and improvements thereon; food products, pharmaceuticals, plant varieties, and business method inventions
- NOVELTY REQUIREMENT: New invention, meaning it must not be known or used by others in the US, it must not be patented or described in a printed publication anywhere in the world before being invented by applicant; and it must not be in public use or sale in the US more than one year before the application filing date
- SPECIAL DOCUMENTARY REQUIREMENTS: Declaration of ownership signed by applicant or person on applicant's behalf; specification (consisting of description and claims), abstract, and drawing in English; if applicant is not the inventor, deed of assignment; if priority is claimed, copy of the application or registration on which the priority claim is based
- DURATION: Patent for 20 years
- USE REQUIREMENTS: Maintenance fee levied three times periodically after grant of patent
- RELATED RIGHTS: Design patents, with 14-year term

Local Copyright Laws

ARGENTINA

- COPYRIGHT REGISTRY: National Copyright Registry, National Institute of Industrial Property (INPI), Ministry of Economic Affairs, Public Works and Public Services
- RIGHTS PROTECTED: Literary, artistic, dramatic, and musical works, including computer programs, performances, broadcasts, and sound recordings; works in public domain earn dues for benefit of government fund for art development
- SPECIAL DOCUMENTARY REQUIREMENTS: Power of attorney notarized; three copies of the work or, if visual art or film, description or sketch
- DURATION: For individual creator, lifetime plus 70 years; for cinematographic works, 50 years from first projection; for anonymous works of corporate bodies, 50 years from publication; for works first published after the author's death, 50 years from date of death; for photographic works, 20 years from publication date

AUSTRALIA

- COPYRIGHT REGISTRY: Copyright Office, Intellectual Property Branch, Attorney General's Department
- RIGHTS PROTECTED: Literary, artistic, dramatic, and musical works, including computer programs, performances, broadcasts, and sound recordings
- SPECIAL DOCUMENTARY REQUIREMENTS: None
- DURATION: For individual creator, lifetime plus 70 years from end of year of death; for works first published after the author's death, 70 years from end of year of first publication date for products published after 1955 (before 1955, 50 years); for films and sound recordings, 70 years from publication; for broadcasts, 50 years from year made

BRAZIL

- COPYRIGHT REGISTRY: National Industrial Property Institute (INPI), Ministry of Industry, Commerce, and Tourism
- RIGHTS PROTECTED: Literary, artistic, dramatic, and musical works, including performances, computer programs, broadcasts, and sound recordings
- SPECIAL DOCUMENTARY REQUIREMENTS: Declaratory document as to right of ownership, with Portuguese translation
- DURATION: For individual creator, lifetime plus 70 years from January 1 of year following author's death; for audiovisual works and photographs, 70 years from publication date; for computer programs, 50 years from January 1 of year following publication date

CANADA

- COPYRIGHT REGISTRY: Copyright Office, Canadian Intellectual Property Office (CIPO), Department of Industry
- RIGHTS PROTECTED: Literary, artistic, dramatic, and musical works, including computer programs, performances, sound recordings, and communication signals
- SPECIAL DOCUMENTARY REQUIREMENTS: None
- DURATION: For individual creator, lifetime plus 50 years from end of year of author's death

CHINA

- COPYRIGHT REGISTRY: Copyright Office, State Administration for Industry and Commerce (SAIC)
- RIGHTS PROTECTED: Literary, artistic, dramatic, and musical works, including computer programs
- SPECIAL DOCUMENTARY REQUIREMENTS: Power of attorney simply signed
- DURATION: For individual creator, lifetime plus 50 years; for computer programs, 25 years with one 25-year renewal

EGYPT

- COPYRIGHT REGISTRY: Administration of Commercial Registration, Ministry of Supply and Internal Trade
- RIGHTS PROTECTED: Literary, artistic, dramatic, and musical works, including computer programs
- SPECIAL DOCUMENTARY REQUIREMENTS: Power of attorney legalized by Egyptian Consulate; certificate of registration for the work in any other country; original and two copies of the work
- DURATION: Creator's lifetime plus 50 years

GERMANY

- COPYRIGHT REGISTRY: German Patent and Trademark Office
- RIGHTS PROTECTED: Literary, artistic, dramatic, and musical works, including computer programs
- SPECIAL DOCUMENTARY REQUIREMENTS: Power of attorney simply signed
- DURATION: For individual creator, lifetime plus 70 years; for cinematographic, photographs, performances, and broadcasts, 50 years after first published; for works first published more than 60 but less than 70 years after the author's death, 10 years from publication

HONG KONG S.A.R.

- COPYRIGHT REGISTRY: Trade Marks and Patent Office, Intellectual Property Department
- RIGHTS PROTECTED: Literary, artistic, musical, and dramatic works, including performances, films, broadcasts, and computer programs
- SPECIAL DOCUMENTARY REQUIREMENTS: No registration
- DURATION: For individual creator, lifetime plus 50 years; for performances, 50 years from end of year of performance

JAPAN

- COPYRIGHT REGISTRY: Japanese Patent Office (JPO)
- RIGHTS PROTECTED: Literary, artistic, dramatic, and musical works, including performances, broadcasts, films, and computer programs
- SPECIAL DOCUMENTARY REQUIREMENTS: None
- DURATION: For individual creator, lifetime plus 50 years

MEXICO

- COPYRIGHT REGISTRY: Mexican Institute of Industrial Property (IMPI)
- RIGHTS PROTECTED: Literary, artistic, dramatic, and musical works, including performances, broadcasts, films, and computer programs
- SPECIAL DOCUMENTARY REQUIREMENTS: Power of attorney notarized

- DURATION: For individual creator, lifetime plus 100 years for works after 2003

UNITED KINGDOM

- COPYRIGHT REGISTRY: None; rights are automatic
- RIGHTS PROTECTED: Literary, artistic, dramatic, and musical works, including performances, sound recordings, broadcasts, films, and computer programs
- SPECIAL DOCUMENTARY REQUIREMENTS: None
- DURATION: For individual creator, lifetime plus 70 years; for cinematographic works, 70 years after death of last surviving principal involved with the film; for sound recordings and broadcasts, 50 years

UNITED STATES

- COPYRIGHT REGISTRY: US Copyright Office, Library of Congress
- RIGHTS PROTECTED: Literary, artistic, dramatic, and musical works, including performances, sound recordings, computer programs, broadcasts, and films
- SPECIAL DOCUMENTARY REQUIREMENTS: For foreign work, one copy of work; for US work, two copies of work
- DURATION: For individual creator, lifetime plus 70 years; for works by company employees, anonymous works, and pseudonymous works, earlier of 95 years from publication or 120 years from creation

Local Trademark Laws

ARGENTINA

- TRADEMARK REGISTRY: National Trademark Registry, National Institute of Intellectual Property, Ministry of Economic Affairs, Public Works and Public Services
- RIGHTS PROTECTED: Trademarks for goods and services; registration of famous mark can be nullified if third party proves that registrant knew or should have known that it was owned by another person or that it was registered for purposes of selling it to another person
- CLASSIFICATION: International; single-class application
- SPECIAL DOCUMENTARY REQUIREMENTS: Power of attorney notarized; if priority is claimed, certified copy of the application or registration on which the priority claim is based
- DURATION: 10 years initially; 10-year unlimited renewals
- USE REQUIREMENTS: Interested third party may seek cancellation of a trademark based on the owner's nonuse during the five consecutive years prior to the date of filing for cancellation

AUSTRALIA

- TRADEMARK REGISTRY: Trademark Office, IP Australia, Department of Industry, Science, and Resources
- RIGHTS PROTECTED: Trademarks for goods and services; first to use can assert rights over first to register; overseas use will protect mark if it has created reputation in mark that extends to Australia
- CLASSIFICATION: International; multi-class application
- SPECIAL DOCUMENTARY REQUIREMENTS: Power of attorney simply signed
- DURATION: 10 years initially; 10-year unlimited renewals
- USE REQUIREMENTS: Interested third party may seek cancellation based on owner's nonuse for three consecutive years after registration and prior to the cancellation request

BRAZIL

- TRADEMARK REGISTRY: National Industrial Property Institute (INPI), Ministry of Industry, Commerce, and Tourism
- RIGHTS PROTECTED: Trademarks for goods and services; internationally well-known marks are protected without registration, and protection of well-known marks extends to all classes
- CLASSIFICATION: International; multi-class application
- SPECIAL DOCUMENTARY REQUIREMENTS: Power of attorney simply signed; affidavit of applicant's status and scope of business
- DURATION: 10 years initially; 10-year unlimited renewals
- USE REQUIREMENTS: Interested third party may seek cancellation based on owner's nonuse for five consecutive years after registration and prior to the cancellation action

CANADA

- TRADEMARK REGISTRY: Trade Marks Office, Canadian Intellectual Property Office (CIPO), Department of Industry
- RIGHTS PROTECTED: Trademarks for goods and services; well-known marks are protected if they have been "made known" in Canada
- CLASSIFICATION: No classifications in effect
- SPECIAL DOCUMENTARY REQUIREMENTS: Power of attorney simply signed; if priority is claimed, copy of application or registration on which the priority claim is based
- DURATION: 15 years initially; 15-year unlimited renewals
- USE REQUIREMENTS: Affidavit of use is required; marks not in use are expunged from the Register

CHINA

- TRADEMARK REGISTRY: Trademark Office, State Administration for Industry and Commerce (SAIC)
- RIGHTS PROTECTED: Trademarks for goods and services; famous mark designation may be granted by SAIC
- CLASSIFICATION: International; single-class application
- SPECIAL DOCUMENTARY REQUIREMENTS: Power of attorney simply signed; if priority is claimed, certified copy of the application or registration on which the priority claim is based
- DURATION: 10 years initially; 10-year unlimited renewals
- USE REQUIREMENTS: Registration may be cancelled for non-use

EGYPT

- TRADEMARK REGISTRY: Administration of Commercial Registration, Ministry of Supply and Internal Trade
- RIGHTS PROTECTED: Trademarks for goods and services
- CLASSIFICATION: International; single-class application
- SPECIAL DOCUMENTARY REQUIREMENTS: Power of attorney legalized by Egyptian Consulate; if applicant is a corporate entity, certified copy of Certificate of Incorporation or extract of entry in Commercial Register showing status, ownership, and business of entity; if priority is claimed, certified copy of the application or registration on which the priority claim is based
- DURATION: 10 years initially; 10-year unlimited renewals
- USE REQUIREMENTS: Interested third party may seek cancellation based on owner's nonuse for five consecutive years after registration and prior to the cancellation action

GERMANY

- TRADEMARK REGISTRY: German Patent and Trademark Office
- RIGHTS PROTECTED: Trademarks for goods and services
- CLASSIFICATION: International; multi-class application
- SPECIAL DOCUMENTARY REQUIREMENTS: Power of attorney simply signed; if priority is claimed, copy of the application or registration on which the priority claim is based
- DURATION: 10 years initially; 10-year unlimited renewals
- USE REQUIREMENTS: Interested third party may seek cancellation based on owner's nonuse for five consecutive years after registration and prior to the cancellation action

HONG KONG S.A.R.

- TRADEMARK REGISTRY: Trade Marks and Patent Office, Intellectual Property Department, Ministry of Industry and Trade

- RIGHTS PROTECTED: Trademarks for goods and services; famous marks are protected if known in Hong Kong
- CLASSIFICATION: International; single class application
- SPECIAL DOCUMENTARY REQUIREMENTS: If priority is claimed, certified copy of the application or registration on which the priority claim is based
- DURATION: Seven years initially; 14-year unlimited renewals
- USE REQUIREMENTS: Interested third party may seek cancellation based on owner's nonuse for five consecutive years after registration and prior to the cancellation action

JAPAN

- TRADEMARK REGISTRY: Japanese Patent Office (JPO)
- RIGHTS PROTECTED: Trademarks for goods and services; famous marks are protected if known in Japan
- CLASSIFICATION: International; single-class application
- SPECIAL DOCUMENTARY REQUIREMENTS: Power of attorney simply signed; if priority is claimed, certified copy of the application or registration on which the priority claim is based
- DURATION: 10 years initially; 10-year renewal periods
- USE REQUIREMENTS: Interested third party may seek cancellation based on owner's nonuse for three consecutive years after registration and prior to the cancellation action.

MEXICO

- TRADEMARK REGISTRY: Mexican Institute of Industrial Property (IMPI)
- RIGHTS PROTECTED: Trademarks for goods and services
- CLASSIFICATION: International; single-class application
- SPECIAL DOCUMENTARY REQUIREMENTS: Power of attorney signed and witnessed; if priority is claimed, copy of the application or registration on which the priority claim is based
- DURATION: 10 years initially; 10-year renewal periods
- USE REQUIREMENTS: Interested third party may seek cancellation based on owner's nonuse for five consecutive years after registration and prior to the cancellation action

UNITED KINGDOM

- TRADEMARK REGISTRY: The Patent Office, Ministry of Trade and Industry
- RIGHTS PROTECTED: Trademarks for goods and services
- CLASSIFICATION: International; multi-class application
- SPECIAL DOCUMENTARY REQUIREMENTS: If priority is claimed, copy of the application or registration on which the priority claim is based
- DURATION: 10 years initially; 10-year renewal periods

- USE REQUIREMENTS: Interested third party may seek cancellation based on owner's nonuse for 5 consecutive years after registration and prior to the cancellation action

UNITED STATES

- TRADEMARK REGISTRY: United States Patent and Trademark Office (USPTO), US Department of Commerce
- RIGHTS PROTECTED: Trademarks for goods and services
- CLASSIFICATION: International; multi-class application
- SPECIAL DOCUMENTARY REQUIREMENTS: If based on use, specimen showing mark as used in US federal commerce; if based on foreign registration, certified copy of the registration with English translation; if priority is claimed, copy of the application or registration on which the priority claim is based
- DURATION: 10 years initially; 10-year renewal periods
- USE REQUIREMENTS: Declaration of use prior to issuance of initial registration; declaration of use between fifth and sixth year of term; affidavit of use with renewal application

CHAPTER 14

Acquiring IP Rights: Letters of Instruction

IF YOU ARE NOT A NATIONAL OF THE SAME COUNTRY where you are seeking protection of IP rights, local laws usually require that you obtain assistance of local counsel to file and prosecute an application to register those rights. If you are seeking IP protection in your own home country, you may be able to file for registration directly without the assistance of an attorney or agent.

However, the terms you need to understand have rather technical meanings. For example, in United States trademark law the terms "use in commerce," "drawing," and "specimen" have particular meanings. In other countries, you may have to supply a "replica" but not a "specimen," and "use" is defined differently. If you are seeking copyright protection, you must usually supply the "best edition" or "best version." The requirements for patent registration are quite complex, and most countries require the filing to be made by a person qualified to practice in the patent field, regardless of whether you are a national of the country or a foreigner.

Accordingly, you may choose to instruct a legal professional, either an attorney or qualified agent, to file your application for registration. The following letter may be adapted to suit your needs, but it should serve as a basis for transmitting to your attorney or agent the information typically required in most countries for the registration of a trademark, copyright, or patent. You will need to select the attachment that is relevant to your type of filing, that is, copyright, patent or trademark.

Letter of Instruction

[your name and address]

[telephone, fax, and e-mail]

[date]

[name and address of legal counsel or agent]

DEAR [*Sir/Madam*]:

I AM ENCLOSING A DATA SHEET SETTING FORTH THE PARTICULARS OF MY [*work/invention/mark*] FOR WHICH I DESIRE TO OBTAIN FULL PROTECTION UNDER THE INTELLECTUAL PROPERTY LAWS OF [*country*]. ACCORDINGLY, PLEASE FILE AS SOON AS POSSIBLE APPLICATIONS FOR REGISTRATION WITH THE FACTS SHOWN IN THE DATA SHEETS.

IN THE ABSENCE OF CONTRARY INSTRUCTIONS, PLEASE APPLY FOR ALL NECESSARY EXTENSIONS OF TIME AND TAKE ALL STEPS REQUIRED TO PREVENT ABANDONMENT OR REJECTION OF THE APPLICATION FOR FAILURE TO PROSECUTE. IF ANY REGULAR FEES ARE DUE TO GOVERNMENT AGENCIES TO OBTAIN THE REGISTRATION, PLEASE PAY SUCH FEES WITHOUT MY SPECIFIC INSTRUCTION, AND DEBIT THE FEES TO ME IN YOUR INVOICE.

I REQUEST THAT YOU SEND ME INVOICES FOR WORK PERFORMED AS YOU ARE PERFORMING IT SO AS TO ALLOW ME TO KEEP MY CHARGES CURRENT. YOUR INVOICES SHOULD BE MARKED TO MY ATTENTION AT THE ADDRESS SHOWN ABOVE. YOUR ASSISTANCE IS VERY MUCH APPRECIATED.

IMMEDIATELY ON YOUR RECEIPT OF THIS LETTER, PLEASE ACKNOWLEDGE BY SENDING A FACSIMILE TO ME WITH ANY RELEVANT COMMENTS AND FORMS FOR FILING.

THANK YOU.

SINCERELY YOURS,

[*your name*]

[*If you seek copyright protection, on a separate page add a completed data sheet for each work*:]

TYPE OF WORK:

❑ Written work/no performance

❑ Entire magazine, newspaper, or other serial

❑ Work to be performed/multimedia work

❑ Collection of one author's contributions to periodicals

❑ Pictorial, graphic, or sculptural work

TITLE:

Current:

Previous/alternative:

❑ Published in a collection, periodical, or serial

TITLE OF COLLECTION/PERIODICAL/SERIAL:

PERIODICAL/SERIAL VOLUME:

NUMBER:

ISSUE DATE:

PAGES OF ARTICLE:

❑ Work consists of periodical or serial

VOLUME:

NUMBER:

DATE:

PUBLICATION FREQUENCY:

AUTHOR NAME:

BIRTH DATE:

DATE OF DEATH:

NATIONALITY:

STATE/COUNTRY OF RESIDENCE:

ANONYMOUS:

❑ Yes ❑ No

PSEUDONYMOUS:

❑ Yes ❑ No

WORK FOR HIRE

❑ Yes (author information is for the employer)❑ No

AUTHOR IS SAME AS PERSON CLAIMING COPYRIGHT

❑ Yes ❑ No

NATURE OF WORK

❑ Entire work

❑ Entire text and illustrations

❑ Coauthor of entire text

❑ Nondramatic literary work

❑ Magazine article

❑ Book

❑ Periodical/serial

❑ Novel

❑ Poetry

❑ Visual (describe)

❑ Compilation (describe added materials)

❑ Derivative (describe preexisting and added materials)

❑ Other ______________________________

YEAR WHEN WORK WAS COMPLETED:

Published: Country: ______________________________

Date (month/day/year): ______________________________

Previous registration: Reason for a new registration: ______________

Prior registration number and year: ____________

[*If you seek patent protection, add on a separate page:*]

EXACT INVENTION NAME (SUGGESTED FOR REGISTRATION): ______________

First conception of invention: Month and year: ______________

Available documentation: ______________

What gave you the idea? ______________

CONCISE, SINGLE SENTENCE DESCRIPTION OF THE INVENTION AND ITS PURPOSE (DO NOT RESTATE THE NAME): "THIS INVENTION RELATES TO

____

ATTACH ONE OR MORE OF THE FOLLOWING:

❑ Drawing (precise notations on size, parts, options, etc.)

❑ Prototype

❑ Photographs

❑ Video

ATTACH SHEETS SPECIFYING THE FOLLOWING:

a. Technical description of each part and its relation to the whole, including its materials, structure, optional features, size, shape, attachments, placement within the invention, and reference to drawing.

b. Description of the parts that can be upgraded, changed, enhanced, or modified for special purposes per consumer.

c. Description of advantages and benefits of the invention as a whole in comparison to other inventions.

d. Description of advantages and benefits of the parts in comparison to other inventions.

e. Description of operation and use of the invention, including potential use for environmental, health, recycling, or other public welfare concerns.

PRIOR RIGHTS:

TO YOUR KNOWLEDGE, HAS YOUR INVENTION EVER BEEN DESCRIBED IN ANY JOURNAL, PAPER, NEWSPAPER, PERIODICAL, BOOK, OTHER PATENT, OR ANY OTHER WRITTEN MATERIAL ANYWHERE IN THE WORLD? ❑ YES ❑ NO

TO YOUR KNOWLEDGE, IS THERE ANY INVENTION AVAILABLE THAT IS SIMILAR OR RELATED TO YOURS? ❑ YES ❑ NO

IF YES, DESCRIBE ON ATTACHED SHEET:

a. The available invention.

b. Use of the available invention.

c. Disadvantages and problems with the available invention.

d. Solutions developed by any other persons to resolve the problems.

e. Reasons why the solutions are not satisfactory.

DO YOU HAVE WRITTEN CONSENT TO USE THE PART OF YOUR INVENTION THAT HAS BEEN CREATED AND REGISTERED BY A THIRD PARTY?
❑ YES ❑ NO

TEXTS, PERIODICALS, AND OTHER REFERENCES RELEVANT TO THE INVENTION:

____

IDENTITY OF POSSIBLE COMPETITORS: ______________________

PUBLIC DISCLOSURES:

HAVE YOU HAD FAVORABLE COMMERCIAL INQUIRIES? ❑ YES ❑ NO

HAVE YOU SHOWN YOUR INVENTION TO ANY OTHER PARTY? ❑ YES ❑ NO

PERSONAL AND INDUSTRY INFORMATION:

INDUSTRY/TRADE RELEVANT TO INVENTION: ______________________________

HIGH-TECH INDUSTRY (FAST-PACED DEVELOPMENT OF TECHNOLOGY): ❑ YES ❑ NO

IS R&D USUALLY PUBLISHED WITHIN THE SCIENTIFIC/ENGINEERING COMMUNITY RELATED TO THIS INDUSTRY? ❑ YES ❑ NO

NUMBER OF YEARS YOU HAVE BEEN INVOLVED IN THIS INDUSTRY: __________

YOUR CURRENT TITLE: ______________________________

YOUR PRIMARY BUSINESS RESPONSIBILITY DURING THE PAST 5 YEARS:

____

YOUR FAMILIARITY WITH MARKETING IN THIS INDUSTRY/TRADE (1 TO 10 SCALE):

____

IDENTIFY INDUSTRY MEETINGS IN WHICH YOU PARTICIPATE:

____

IDENTIFY THE RESOURCES YOU USE TO KEEP UP WITH INDUSTRY/TRADE TRENDS: ______________________________

DESCRIPTION OF YOUR SPECIAL QUALIFICATIONS AS AN AUTHORITY ON CURRENT STATE OF THE ART IN YOUR INDUSTRY:

____

IS THIS INVENTION WITHIN THE SCOPE OF YOUR EMPLOYMENT OR COVERED BY AN ASSIGNMENT? IF YES, IDENTIFY THE EMPLOYER OR OTHER PARTY TO THE ASSIGNMENT. ❑ YES ❑ NO

[*If you seek trademark protection, add on a separate page:*]

APPLICANT NAME: ______________________________

ADDRESS: ______________________________

❑ INDIVIDUAL ❑ ENTITY TYPE: ______________________________

STATE/COUNTRY OF ORGANIZATION: ______________________________

TYPE OF BUSINESS (E.G., MERCHANT AND MANUFACTURER): ______________

MARK NAME: ______________________________

MARK DESCRIPTION: ______________________________

MARK DERIVATION: ______________________________

CLASS: ______________________________

SPECIFIC GOODS/SERVICES: ______________________________

COUNTRY OF REGISTRATION: ______________________________

COUNTRY AND DATE OF FIRST USE ANYWHERE: ______________________

DATE OF FIRST USE IN COUNTRY WHERE REGISTRATION IS SOUGHT: ________

METHOD OF COMMERCE USED IN COUNTRY WHERE REGISTRATION IS SOUGHT:

____

CLEAR REPRODUCTION OF MARK: ______________________________

CHAPTER 15

Acquiring IP Rights: Joint Collaboration Agreement

WHEN TWO OR MORE INDIVIDUALS WORK TOGETHER on an invention, a book or play, a musical score, or any other type of IP, they should first enter into a contract to cover their respective rights. A collaboration agreement will define their respective rights in the IP, not only among the creators themselves, but also in relation to third parties that seek to purchase or license the IP rights or infringe those rights. In the absence of an agreement, the rights of parties who have expended time and labor in a joint effort and who subsequently dispute those rights may be determined by statutory laws or court rulings that are not satisfactory to either party. Collaborating parties may modify the following form to reflect the particular arrangement and circumstances of their own situation. It may also be converted to letter format if the parties prefer a less formal contract.

Joint Collaboration Agreement

THIS COLLABORATION AGREEMENT IS MADE EFFECTIVE AS OF [*date*] BETWEEN [*name and address*] (FIRST COLLABORATOR) AND [*name and address*] (SECOND COLLABORATOR) (TOGETHER REFERRED TO AS THE COLLABORATORS). THE COLLABORATORS HAVE DECIDED TO [*describe collaboration,* E.G., RESEARCH AND DEVELOP AN INVENTION OR WRITE A BOOK/MUSICAL SCORE] JOINTLY, AND THEY NOW AGREE TO THE FOLLOWING TERMS AND CONDITIONS OF THEIR COLLABORATION:

1. AGREEMENT TO COLLABORATE THE COLLABORATORS AGREE TO COORDINATE AND COOPERATE IN JOINTLY CREATING THE INTELLECTUAL PROPERTY AS DEFINED IN THIS AGREEMENT. THIS AGREEMENT DOES NOT CREATE A PARTNERSHIP OR OTHER FORMAL ASSOCIATION AMONG THE COLLABORATORS, BUT MERELY FORMS A BASIS FOR COLLABORATION IN A JOINT EFFORT TO PRODUCE AND PUBLISH THE INTELLECTUAL PROPERTY.

2. INTELLECTUAL PROPERTY THE INTELLECTUAL PROPERTY THAT THE COLLABORATORS WILL JOINTLY CREATE CONSISTS OF A [*patent/book/musical score/other creation*] PROVISIONALLY ENTITLED [*title*] AND BRIEFLY DESCRIBED AS [*summary*]. THE COLLABORATORS HAVE TOGETHER DEVELOPED A WORKING [*plan/outline/specification/other*] OF THE INTELLECTUAL PROPERTY, WHICH IS ATTACHED TO THIS AGREEMENT AS EXHIBIT 1. ALL OF THESE CONCEPTIONS AND MATERIALS CONSTITUTE THE INTELLECTUAL PROPERTY REFERRED TO IN THIS AGREEMENT.

3. DIVISION OF LABOR IN CREATION THE COLLABORATORS SHALL HAVE THE FOLLOWING RESPONSIBILITIES IN JOINTLY CREATING THE INTELLECTUAL PROPERTY.

a. First Collaborator shall be responsible for [*describe or list,* e.g., researching and developing a prototype for the first phase of the Intellectual Property or writing the chapters of the Intellectual Property scheduled in this Agreement as first, fifth, and seventeenth through thirty-fifth, or writing and editing the entire Intellectual Property or writing the entire Intellectual Property.]

b. Second Collaborator shall be responsible for [*describe or list*, e.g., researching and developing a prototype for the second phase of the Intellectual Property or writing the remainder of the Intellectual Property or providing the research and story content for the Intellectual Property, editing the Intellectual Property, and supplying relevant photographs.]

4. OWNERSHIP OF INTELLECTUAL PROPERTY THE COLLABORATORS WILL OWN ALL RIGHTS IN THE INTELLECTUAL PROPERTY JOINTLY AND IN COMMON, AND THEIR RESPECTIVE RIGHTS SHALL PASS TO THEIR RESPECTIVE HEIRS, REPRESENTATIVES, AND ASSIGNS. MATERIALS AND INFORMATION COLLECTED BY EITHER COLLABORATOR FOR PURPOSES OF DEVELOPING, RESEARCHING, AND CREATING THE INTELLECTUAL PROPERTY SHALL BE OWNED BY BOTH COLLABORATORS AND MAY BE DISPOSED OF ONLY IF BOTH CONSENT IN WRITING. CONSENT SHALL NOT BE WITHHELD UNREASONABLY.

5. PUBLICATION OF INTELLECTUAL PROPERTY NEITHER COLLABORATOR HAS A RIGHT TO PUBLISH OR HAVE PUBLISHED THE INTELLECTUAL PROPERTY WITHOUT THE CONSENT OF THE OTHER, AND NEITHER COLLABORATOR MAY WITHHOLD SUCH CONSENT UNREASONABLY. ALL AGREEMENTS WITH COMPANIES FOR THE LICENSE, PUBLICATION, OR OTHER USE OF THE INTELLECTUAL PROPERTY SHALL BE WRITTEN AND MUST BE APPROVED AND SIGNED BY BOTH COLLABORATORS BEFORE TAKING EFFECT.

6. LICENSE, ASSIGNMENT, OR OTHER TRANSFER THE COLLABORATORS INTEND THAT THE INTELLECTUAL PROPERTY WILL BE OFFERED TO THIRD PARTIES FOR LICENSE, ASSIGNMENT, OR OTHER TRANSFER. THE TRANSACTION MUST BE MADE ON THE FOLLOWING TERMS, UNLESS THE COLLABORATORS AGREE IN WRITING OTHERWISE: [DESCRIBE].

7. DECISIONS AFFECTING INTELLECTUAL PROPERTY The Collaborators shall make all decisions, including business, editorial, and financial decisions, jointly. No changes to the Intellectual Property or agreement as to its use or disposition shall be valid without consent and signature of both Collaborators. Such consent and signature shall not be withheld unreasonably.

8. COST OF DEVELOPMENT, PRODUCTION, AND PUBLICATION ALL COSTS INCURRED JOINTLY OR BY EITHER COLLABORATOR IN THE RESEARCH, DEVELOPMENT, PRODUCTION, AND PUBLICATION OF THE INTELLECTUAL PROPERTY SHALL BE BORNE BY THE COLLABORATORS IN EQUAL SHARES, PROVIDED THAT SUCH COSTS ARE REASONABLE AND IF ANY ONE COST IS MORE THAN [*amount*], BOTH COLLABORATORS MUST APPROVE IT IN ADVANCE OF PAYMENT.

9. DIVISION OF PROFITS NET PROFITS FROM THE LICENSE, SALE, PUBLICATION, OR OTHER USE OF THE INTELLECTUAL PROPERTY SHALL BE DIVIDED BETWEEN THE COLLABORATORS IN EQUAL SHARES.

10. DERIVATIVE OR RELATED WORKS NEITHER COLLABORATOR WILL USE, INCORPORATE, OR OTHERWISE APPLY ANY INFORMATION OR MATERIAL THAT IS PART OF THE INTELLECTUAL PROPERTY IN ANY SUBSEQUENT WORK THAT MIGHT BE PROTECTED BY INTELLECTUAL PROPERTY RIGHTS, UNLESS THE OTHER COLLABORATOR AGREES IN WRITING. FOR [*time period*] AFTER COMPLETION OF THE INTELLECTUAL PROPERTY, NEITHER COLLABORATOR SHALL PREPARE OR OTHERWISE PARTICIPATE IN THE DEVELOPMENT AND PRODUCTION OF ANY WORK THAT IS RELATED OR IN DIRECT COMPETITION WITH THE INTELLECTUAL PROPERTY SUCH THAT PUBLICATION WOULD DIMINISH THE VALUE AND SALES OF THE INTELLECTUAL PROPERTY.

11. INFRINGEMENT OF RIGHTS If the rights of the Collaborators in the Intellectual Property are or may be infringed or otherwise invaded by a third party, the Collaborators may take, together or separately, any legal actions available to them to stop the infringement or invasion. If the

Collaborators take action together, they shall equally share all costs and damages resulting from such action. If only one Collaborator desires to takes action to stop an infringement or invasion, the consent of the other is not required. The single Collaborator acting alone may bring legal proceedings in the names of both Collaborators, but only at the cost and expense of the single Collaborator. The single Collaborator shall indemnify the other Collaborator against all losses in such a proceeding, but the single Collaborator shall also not be required to account to the other Collaborator for any amounts recovered in the proceeding, and such amounts shall belong to the single Collaborator who took the action.

12. ASSIGNMENTS EITHER COLLABORATOR MAY ASSIGN THE RIGHTS HELD IN THE INTELLECTUAL PROPERTY TO ANOTHER PARTY, BUT ONLY AFTER THE OTHER COLLABORATOR HAS CONSENTED IN WRITING. SUCH CONSENT SHALL NOT BE WITHHELD UNREASONABLY. THE DEVELOPMENT AND PRODUCTION OF THE INTELLECTUAL PROPERTY IS A PERSONAL WORK AND CANNOT BE ASSIGNED BY EITHER COLLABORATOR. IF IT IS ASSIGNED, THIS COLLABORATION AGREEMENT SHALL BE TERMINATED.

13. DEATH OR DISABILITY OF A COLLABORATOR IF ONE COLLABORATOR DIES OR BECOMES DISABLED WHILE THIS AGREEMENT IS IN EFFECT, THE OTHER COLLABORATOR HAS A RIGHT TO COMPLETE OR HIRE ANOTHER PERSON TO COMPLETE THE INTELLECTUAL PROPERTY, AND FURTHER HAS SOLE AUTHORITY TO PUBLISH, LICENSE, SELL, AND OTHERWISE TRANSFER THE INTELLECTUAL PROPERTY. THE DISABLED COLLABORATOR OR THE ESTATE OF A DECEASED COLLABORATOR SHALL BE ENTITLED TO A PROPORTIONATE SHARE OF THE INCOME RECEIVED FROM THE INTELLECTUAL PROPERTY, WHICH SHARE SHALL BE DETERMINED BY THE PORTION OF THE CONTRIBUTION MADE BY THAT COLLABORATOR AFTER DEDUCTION OF ALL EXPENSES AND COSTS FOR DEVELOPING, PRODUCING, AND PUBLISHING THE INTELLECTUAL PROPERTY.

14. TERMINATION OF AGREEMENT IF THIS AGREEMENT SHOULD TERMINATE FOR ANY REASON WHATSOEVER, THE COLLABORATORS UNDERTAKE TO PAY EQUALLY ALL COSTS INCURRED UP TO TERMINATION, TO SPLIT EQUALLY ALL NET PROFITS, AND TO ADHERE TO THE DUTIES IMPOSED BY PARAGRAPH 10. IF ANY DISPUTE ARISES BETWEEN THE COLLABORATORS THAT THEY CANNOT RESOLVE, THEY SHALL SEEK MEDIATION OR ARBITRATION THROUGH [*name an association*], AND THE DECISION IN THAT FORUM SHALL BE BINDING ON THEM. IN SUCH EVENT, EACH COLLABORATOR WILL BEAR THE RESPECTIVE ATTORNEY FEES, BUT THEY SHALL SHARE EQUALLY THE COSTS AND EXPENSES OF THE MEDIATION OR ARBITRATION.

15. ATTORNEY FEES THE PREVAILING PARTY IN ANY LEGAL ACTION REQUIRED FOR ENFORCEMENT OF THIS AGREEMENT SHALL BE ENTITLED TO AN AWARD OF REASONABLE ATTORNEY FEES AND THE COSTS OF THE ACTION.

16. ENTIRE AGREEMENT THIS AGREEMENT CONSTITUTES THE ENTIRE AGREEMENT BETWEEN THE COLLABORATORS. EACH COLLABORATOR ACKNOWLEDGES RECEIPT OF A COPY OF THIS AGREEMENT AND FURTHER ACKNOWLEDGES THAT NO PROVISIONS GOVERN THEIR RELATIONSHIP OTHER THAN THOSE WRITTEN IN THIS AGREEMENT.

17. GOVERNING LAW THIS AGREEMENT SHALL BE GOVERNED BY THE LAWS OF [*state/country*].

FIRST COLLABORATOR	**SECOND COLLABORATOR**
[*signature*]	[*signature*]
[T*yped name and title*]	[*typed name and title*]
[*date*]	[*date*]

CHAPTER 16

Acquiring IP Rights: Work Made for Hire Agreement

A WORK MADE FOR HIRE AGREEMENT alters the relationship of an employer and a freelance creator to allow the employer, not the creator, to acquire the IP rights in the creation. This agreement is required only if the creator is operating on a freelance basis for the employer. In such a case, the creator would be the owner of the IP rights under law, unless the parties agree otherwise in writing. If the creator is an employee, works created within the scope of the employment are presumed to be works made for hire without agreement between the parties, although the parties may change the ownership rights by express written agreement. For discussion of the technical term "work made for hire," see Chapter 1.

Work Made for Hire Agreement

USE OF FORM

The following form is placed in a letter format because this arrangement is often made informally through the mail without the parties ever meeting face to face. This type of contract is most commonly used for creations that are protected by copyright, and this form additionally focuses on creation of a manuscript for illustrative purposes. However, with slight modification it could instead apply to other types of works that can be protected by copyright, and even to other types of creations, including patents and marks.

WORK MADE FOR HIRE AGREEMENT

[*company name and address*]

[*telephone, fax, and e-mail*]

[*date*]

[*name and address of creator*]

DEAR [*Sir/Madam*]:

THANK YOU AGAIN FOR AGREEING TO PREPARE THE MANUSCRIPT, AS DEFINED IN THE FOLLOWING TERMS. WE CLARIFY AND EMPHASIZE AGAIN THAT YOU ARE PREPARING THE MANUSCRIPT AS AN INDEPENDENT CONTRACTOR AND THAT THE MANUSCRIPT IS ONE MADE FOR HIRE, WHICH MEANS YOU ARE RELINQUISHING ALL RIGHTS IN THE COPYRIGHT TO OUR COMPANY.

ACCORDINGLY, THIS LETTER CONSTITUTES THE ENTIRE AGREEMENT BETWEEN OUR COMPANY AND YOU FOR YOUR PREPARATION OF THE MANUSCRIPT ON THE FOLLOWING TERMS AND CONDITIONS:

1. TOPIC, FORM, AND SIZE YOU AGREE TO PREPARE [*title of manuscript*], CONSISTING OF APPROXIMATELY [*number*] WORDS, WHICH IS EXPECTED TO YIELD APPROXIMATELY [*number*] PUBLISHED PAGES ("THE MANUSCRIPT").

2. COMPENSATION FOR PERFORMANCE UNDER THIS AGREEMENT, OUR COMPANY AGREES TO PAY YOU [*amount*] WITHIN [*number*] [*days/weeks*] OF ACCEPTANCE OF THE MANUSCRIPT, AND IN ANY EVENT NO LATER THAN [*number*] [*days/weeks*] AFTER THE DATE WHEN THE MANUSCRIPT HAS BEEN SUBMITTED TO THE COMPANY.

3. WRITING SCHEDULE YOU AGREE TO SUBMIT THE FINAL MANUSCRIPT TO THE COMPANY ON OR BEFORE [*date*].

4. PRODUCTION OF MANUSCRIPT YOU WILL PREPARE AND PRESENT THE MANUSCRIPT IN AN ELECTRONIC FORM THAT IS COMPATIBLE WITH THE COMPANY'S SOFTWARE PROGRAMS, AS SPECIFIED IN WRITTEN INSTRUCTIONS PROVIDED TO YOU BY THE COMPANY. YOU NOW ACKNOWLEDGES RECEIPT OF THESE INSTRUCTIONS.

5. COMPANY'S ACTIONS REGARDING THE MANUSCRIPT THE COMPANY HAS THE RIGHT TO EDIT THE MANUSCRIPT IN ANY MANNER THAT THE COMPANY DEEMS FIT, INCLUDING WITHOUT LIMIT REWRITING, ADDING TO, DELETING FROM, CONDENSING, AND REORGANIZING. THE COMPANY HAS THE RIGHT TO REQUEST REASONABLE REVISIONS TO THE MANUSCRIPT TO CONFORM TO THE COMPANY'S SUBMISSION REQUIREMENTS PROVIDED TO YOU AT THE TIME OF CONTRACTING. YOU AGREE TO MAKE THE CHANGES, ADDITIONS, AND DELETIONS IN THE MANUSCRIPT THAT THE COMPANY MAY REQUEST FOR THIS REASON. YOU NOW ACKNOWLEDGE RECEIPT OF THE COMPANY'S SUBMISSION REQUIREMENTS.

6. TERMINATION OF AGREEMENT BY THE COMPANY IN ITS REASONABLE DISCRETION, THE COMPANY MAY REJECT ANY MANUSCRIPT THAT IT CONSIDERS IS OF DEFICIENT QUALITY OR FAILS TO MEET THE MANUSCRIPT SUBMISSION REQUIREMENTS PROVIDED TO YOU AT THE TIME OF CONTRACTING. ON REJECTING THE MANUSCRIPT, THE COMPANY MAY TERMINATE THIS AGREEMENT. IF THE MANUSCRIPT IS RETURNED FOR FURTHER WORK AND YOU FAIL TO REVISE IT SO THAT IT BECOMES ACCEPTABLE TO THE COMPANY, THE COMPANY MAY TERMINATE THIS AGREEMENT. IF THIS AGREEMENT IS TERMINATED, THE COMPANY SHALL RETURN YOUR UNPUBLISHED MATERIALS. IN SUCH EVENT, THE PARTIES SHALL BE RELEASED AND DISCHARGED FROM ANY CLAIMS GROWING OUT OF THIS AGREEMENT.

7. COPYRIGHT YOU UNDERSTAND AND AGREE THAT THIS MANUSCRIPT IS A "WORK MADE FOR HIRE" AND THAT THE COMPANY OWNS ALL RIGHT, TITLE, AND INTEREST IN THE MANUSCRIPT, INCLUDING THE COPYRIGHT. FURTHERMORE, IN THE EVENT THAT THIS MANUSCRIPT SHOULD BE FOUND BY A COURT OF LAW OR OTHERWISE NOT TO CONSTITUTE A WORK MADE FOR HIRE, YOU NOW ASSIGN AND TRANSFER TO THE COMPANY, ITS SUCCESSORS, AND ASSIGNS, ALL RIGHT, TITLE, AND INTEREST IN AND TO THE MANUSCRIPT AND ANY SUBSEQUENT UPKEEP, INCLUDING THE COPYRIGHT THEREIN AND ALL EXCLUSIVE COPYRIGHTS THROUGHOUT THE WORLD, FOR SUCH TERM AS IS NOW OR HEREAFTER AUTHORIZED BY LAW. THE COMPANY SHALL HAVE THE RIGHT, AS YOUR ASSIGNEE AND TRANSFEREE, TO SECURE COPYRIGHT REGISTRATION AND RENEWALS, IF ANY, IN ITS NAME. YOU MAY NOT REPRINT ANY MATERIAL FROM THE MANUSCRIPT, NOR GIVE PERMISSION TO ANYONE ELSE TO REPRINT THE MATERIAL, WITHOUT THE COMPANY'S PRIOR WRITTEN CONSENT. IF THIS AGREEMENT IS TERMINATED BEFORE THE DATE THE MANUSCRIPT IS PUBLISHED, THE COMPANY SHALL REASSIGN THE COPYRIGHT TO YOU.

8. AVOIDANCE OF INFRINGEMENT THE COMPANY'S POLICY IS THAT ALL MATERIALS THAT IT PUBLISHES MUST BE THE RESULT OF THE INDEPENDENT INTELLECTUAL EFFORTS OF THE AUTHORS. THE COPYING AND USE OF THE PUBLISHED MATERIALS OF OTHER AUTHORS, EVEN IF SUCH COPYING OR USE IS NOT LEGALLY ACTIONABLE, SHOULD BE DONE ONLY IN PURSUIT OF SUCH INDEPENDENT INTELLECTUAL EFFORT AND WITH PROPER ATTRIBUTION TO THE ORIGINAL SOURCES. EXCEPT FOR ORIGINAL MATERIAL CREATED BY YOU OR YOUR SUBCONTRACTING CONTRIBUTORS, THE MANUSCRIPT SHALL NOT CONTAIN ANY MATERIAL PROTECTED UNDER UNITED STATES COPYRIGHT LAW OR ANY OTHER LAW OF SIMILAR PURPOSE EXCEPT TO THE EXTENT OF "FAIR USE" AS THAT CONCEPT IS DEFINED IN SUCH LAWS, UNLESS YOU HAVE OBTAINED WRITTEN CONSENT TO REPRINT FROM THE PUBLISHER AND OWNER OF THE OTHERWISE PROTECTED MATERIAL AND SUPPLIED THAT CONSENT TO THE COMPANY WITH THE MANUSCRIPT. YOU MUST IDENTIFY ALL MATERIAL IN THE MANUSCRIPT FOR WHICH THE COPYRIGHT IS OWNED OR CLAIMED BY SUCH PUBLISHER AND OWNER. YOU SHALL BE SOLELY RESPONSIBLE FOR DETERMINING WHETHER THE MANUSCRIPT SATISFIES THE "FAIR USE" EXCEPTION. NOTWITHSTANDING THE FOREGOING, THE COMPANY MAY REFUSE TO PUBLISH ANY MATERIAL THAT IN ITS OWN JUDGMENT DOES NOT CONSTITUTE "FAIR USE."

9. CONFIDENTIALITY YOU AGREE THAT ANY INFORMATION PROVIDED BY THE COMPANY RELATING TO ITS PUBLICATION PLANS AND PROCESSES AND MARKETING PLANS AND PROJECTIONS FOR THE MANUSCRIPT IS PROVIDED IN CONFIDENCE, AND YOU AGREE NOT TO DISCLOSE SUCH INFORMATION WITHOUT THE COMPANY'S AUTHORIZATION, EXCEPT IN CONFIDENCE TO CO-CONTRIBUTORS AS NECESSARY IN THE PERFORMANCE OF YOUR OBLIGATIONS UNDER THIS AGREEMENT.

10. CONTRIBUTOR STATUS IN MAKING AND PERFORMING THIS AGREEMENT, THE PARTIES ACT AND SHALL ACT AT ALL TIMES AS INDEPENDENT CONTRACTORS, AND AT NO TIME SHALL EITHER PARTY MAKE ANY COMMITMENTS OR INCUR ANY CHARGES OR EXPENSES FOR OR IN THE NAME OF THE OTHER PARTY. YOU UNDERSTAND AND AGREE THAT YOU ARE NOT AN EMPLOYEE OF THE COMPANY AND ARE NOT ENTITLED TO PARTICIPATE IN ANY PENSION PLAN, UNEMPLOYMENT INSURANCE, BONUS, WORKER'S COMPENSATION INSURANCE, STOCK OR SIMILAR BENEFITS THAT THE COMPANY PROVIDES FOR ITS EMPLOYEES. YOU SHALL BE RESPONSIBLE FOR PERFORMING THE WORK UNDER THIS AGREEMENT IN A SKILLFUL MANNER AND SHALL BE LIABLE FOR THE CONSEQUENCES OF YOUR OWN ACTS AND/OR OMISSIONS, IF ANY. FURTHER, YOU SHALL BE RESPONSIBLE FOR ALL PAYMENTS OF INCOME TAXES, WITHHOLDING TAXES, AND OTHER TAXES, PENALTIES AND/OR OTHER SIMILAR CONTRIBUTIONS THAT HAVE ARISEN OR MAY ARISE OUT OF YOUR SERVICES UNDER THIS AGREEMENT.

11. CONFLICTING INTERESTS OF THE CONTRIBUTOR YOU WARRANT THAT YOU HAVE DISCLOSED TO THE COMPANY ANY SUBSTANTIALLY SIMILAR COMMERCIAL WRITING PROJECT PERFORMED OR AGREED TO BE PERFORMED BY YOU FOR ANOTHER PUBLISHER OR PERSON. YOU ARE NOT PRECLUDED FROM ENGAGING IN ANY SUCH WRITING PROJECT FOR ANOTHER PUBLISHER OR PERSON, AND YOU ARE FREE TO CONTRACT FOR SIMILAR SERVICES TO BE PERFORMED FOR OTHER PARTIES.

12. EDITORIAL ASSISTANTS AND CONTRIBUTORS AS AN INDEPENDENT CONTRACTOR, YOU MAY ENGAGE AT YOUR OWN EXPENSE ANY ASSISTANTS AND CONTRIBUTORS AS MAY BE DESIRED. IN NO EVENT WILL SUCH ASSISTANTS AND CONTRIBUTORS BE DEEMED TO HAVE BEEN EMPLOYED BY THE COMPANY, UNLESS OTHERWISE AGREED TO BY THE COMPANY IN WRITING.

13. MATERIALS, TOOLS, AND EQUIPMENT YOU SHALL FURNISH AT YOUR EXPENSE ALL MATERIALS, TOOLS, AND EQUIPMENT NEEDED BY YOU TO CARRY OUT THE WORK TO BE PERFORMED UNDER THIS AGREEMENT, EXCEPT AS OTHERWISE EXPRESSLY PROVIDED IN WRITING. THE ACCEPTANCE OR USE BY YOU OF ANY MATERIALS FURNISHED, LOANED, OR RENTED TO YOU BY THE COMPANY SHALL BE CONSTRUED TO MEAN THAT YOU ACCEPT FULL RESPONSIBILITY FOR THE LOSS OF OR DAMAGE TO SUCH MATERIALS AND FOR THE MAINTENANCE THEREOF.

14. ASSIGNMENT OF RIGHTS THE COMPANY MAY ASSIGN ANY OF ITS RIGHTS ARISING UNDER THIS AGREEMENT WITHOUT PRIOR NOTICE TO YOU AND WITHOUT YOUR CONSENT; HOWEVER, THE COMPANY SHALL NOT BE RELEASED FROM ANY OF ITS OBLIGATIONS UNDER THIS AGREEMENT WITHOUT YOUR SPECIFIC CONSENT. THIS AGREEMENT IS PERSONAL TO YOU, AND RIGHTS HEREUNDER GRANTED TO YOU ARE NOT ASSIGNABLE, NOR MAY THE OBLIGATIONS IMPOSED BE DELEGATED WITHOUT THE PRIOR WRITTEN CONSENT OF THE COMPANY. EXCEPT AS PROVIDED IN THE PRECEDING SENTENCE, THIS AGREEMENT SHALL INURE TO THE BENEFIT OF YOUR HEIRS, EXECUTORS, ADMINISTRATORS, AND ASSIGNS AND THE SUBSIDIARIES, SUCCESSORS, AND ASSIGNS OF THE COMPANY.

15. RETENTION OF MANUSCRIPT YOU MUST RETAIN AT LEAST ONE COPY OF THE MANUSCRIPT FINALLY SUBMITTED TO THE COMPANY FOR 60 DAYS AFTER DELIVERY OF THE MANUSCRIPT, OR UNTIL THE COMPANY AUTHORIZES DESTRUCTION, WHICHEVER OCCURS FIRST.

16. GOVERNING LAW THIS AGREEMENT SHALL BE CONSTRUED AS ENTERED INTO IN AND GOVERNED BY THE LAWS OF THE [*state/province, country*].

17. EFFECTIVE DATE THIS AGREEMENT IS MADE EFFECTIVE AS OF THE DATE FIRST WRITTEN ABOVE.

IF THIS AGREEMENT IS SATISFACTORY TO YOU, PLEASE SIGN WHERE INDICATED BELOW AND THE CONTRACT WILL THEN BE BINDING. PLEASE SIGN BOTH COPIES, RETAIN ONE FOR YOUR OWN RECORDS, AND RETURN THE OTHER TO US. WE LOOK FORWARD TO WORKING WITH YOU.

SINCERELY YOURS,

[*Company Name*]

[*signature*]

[*typed name*]

[*title*]

I UNDERSTAND AND AGREE TO THE TERMS OF THIS CONTRACT.

[*signature*]

[*typed name*]

CHAPTER 17

Protecting IP Rights: Nondisclosure Agreements

Protecting IP Rights: Nondisclosure Agreements

Prior to registration, IP rights in patents and marks consist of trade secrets. The disclosure of the IP could be deemed publication, and it could even place the IP into the public domain, in which event the IP rights could be lost. Although a copyright usually attaches when a creation is reduced to tangible form, a copyright can also be lost to the public domain if the owner publishes the work without identifying it as being subject to copyright. For these reasons, the owner of IP should take precautions to avoid losing the IP rights to the public at large. The following agreements cover disclosures made in three different situations: to a third party for acquiring capital or for licensing or selling the rights (Creator and Confidant Nondisclosure Agreement), to a publisher for purposes of protecting a copyright (Author and Publisher Nondisclosure Agreement), and to an employee who is leaving the employment of a company (Employer and Employee Nondisclosure Agreement).

Nondisclosure Agreement Between Creator and Confidant

USE OF FORM

This form is most useful when an individual IP owner is meeting private parties, venture capitalists, or similar persons. In an effort to make the agreement more acceptable to a company, it is written so as to impose mutual duties of confidentiality on both parties. However, many well-established companies may refuse to sign any nondisclosure agreement, because if the company is already developing the same or a similar creation you could later accuse it of stealing your own idea.

In fact, the company may require you to sign a waiver giving up your right to sue for infringement. Without the waiver, there will be no meeting.

To sell your creation, you may have to present a summarized version of your IP and trust the company to be honest. You could also try to waive your right to infringement claims in exchange for their acknowledgment that the specific presentation you are making is your own creation. In any event, you should always ensure that before disclosure you have also protected your IP rights, such as by means of an application for registration.

NONDISCLOSURE AGREEMENT

THIS AGREEMENT IS MADE AS OF [*date*] BY [*name and address of party*] (OWNER) AND [*name and address of party*] (CONFIDANT).

THE PARTIES STATE THAT THE PURPOSE OF THIS AGREEMENT IS AS FOLLOWS:

A. THE PARTIES ARE EXPLORING A BUSINESS OPPORTUNITY, AND ANY INFORMATION PROVIDED OR DISCUSSED BY EITHER PARTY IS INTENDED TO BE STRICTLY CONFIDENTIAL.

B. THE PARTIES EXPECT TO EXCHANGE CONFIDENTIAL INFORMATION, WHICH EACH MUST DIVULGE TO THE OTHER SO THAT THEY CAN EVALUATE WHETHER THE OWNER'S INTELLECTUAL PROPERTY AS DEFINED IN THIS AGREEMENT HAS ANY USE AND APPLICATION IN THE CONFIDANT'S BUSINESS.

C. THE PARTIES DESIRE TO PROTECT EACH OTHER'S RIGHTS IN ALL CONFIDENTIAL INFORMATION EXCHANGED AGAINST PUBLIC DISCLOSURE AND UNAUTHORIZED USE BY ANY PERSON, INCLUDING THE CONFIDANT AND THE OWNER.

ACCORDINGLY, IN CONSIDERATION OF THE MUTUAL PROMISES AND COVENANTS CONTAINED IN THIS AGREEMENT, THE PARTIES INTEND TO BE LEGALLY BOUND BY THE FOLLOWING TERMS AND CONDITIONS:

1. INTELLECTUAL PROPERTY RIGHTS THE PARTIES EACH HAVE SENSITIVE INFORMATION AND MATERIALS THAT ARE VALUABLE AND NOT GENERALLY KNOWN BY THE PUBLIC OR BY THEIR COMPETITORS. EACH PARTY ACKNOWLEDGES THAT THE OTHER'S RIGHTS IN THE INFORMATION AND MATERIALS CONSTITUTE VALUABLE AND PROPRIETARY INTELLECTUAL PROPERTY. THE INFORMATION AND MATERIALS CONSIST SPECIFICALLY OF THE FOLLOWING, WHICH SHALL BE REFERRED TO AS INTELLECTUAL PROPERTY:

a. Information and materials related to current and proposed products and services to be traded in commerce, including without limit drawings, descriptions and specifications, notes, memoranda, correspondence, graphs, technical know-how, designs, flow charts, plans and agreements for product development, and computer programs and electronic data.

b. Information and materials related to systems and plans for marketing, promoting, selling, licensing, and administering the current and proposed business, including marketing plans, accounting plans and computer programs, customer lists, industry data, sales data, and promotional materials not yet published.

c. Information and materials described in (a) and (b) that the Party has collected, compiled, organized, and treated as confidential, regardless of whether the Party created the materials or acquired them from other sources.

2. EXCEPTIONS THE DUTY OF CONFIDENTIALITY IMPOSED ON THE PARTIES SHALL NOT ARISE WITH REGARD TO ANY PORTION OF THEIR RESPECTIVE INTELLECTUAL PROPERTY THAT (A) WAS KNOWN BEFORE THE DISCLOSURE; (B) HAS BECOME PART OF THE PUBLIC DOMAIN THROUGH NO FAULT OR ACTION OF EITHER PARTY; OR (C) HAS BEEN RIGHTFULLY OBTAINED FROM A THIRD PARTY.

3. LIMITED PURPOSE OF DISCLOSURE THE PARTIES ARE DISCLOSING THEIR INTELLECTUAL PROPERTY SOLELY FOR THE CONFIDANT'S REVIEW AND EVALUATION OF WHETHER THE OWNER'S INTELLECTUAL PROPERTY IS OF INTEREST AND USE IN THE CONFIDANT'S BUSINESS. THE CONFIDANT MAY REVIEW AND TEST THE OWNER'S INTELLECTUAL PROPERTY FOR THE LIMITED TIME STATED IN PARAGRAPH 6. THE CONFIDANT HAS NO FURTHER RIGHTS TO CONTINUE REVIEWING OR USING THE OWNER'S INTELLECTUAL PROPERTY UNDER THIS AGREEMENT. THE OWNER'S CONSIDERATION OF ANY OF THE CONFIDANT'S INTELLECTUAL PROPERTY SHALL BE LIMITED TO THE SAME PURPOSE AND SAME PERIOD.

4. COVENANT OF CONFIDENTIALITY IN CONSIDERATION OF THEIR MUTUAL DISCLOSURES OF INTELLECTUAL PROPERTY, THE PARTIES SHALL TAKE ALL REASONABLE PRECAUTIONS TO AVOID DISCLOSURE OF THE INTELLECTUAL PROPERTY TO OTHER PERSONS OR TO THE PUBLIC AT LARGE. THE PARTIES SHALL KEEP THE INTELLECTUAL PROPERTY IN A SAFE PLACE THAT IS INACCESSIBLE TO OTHERS, SHALL NOT MAKE NOR PERMIT TO BE MADE ANY REPRODUCTIONS OF THE INTELLECTUAL PROPERTY, AND SHALL NOT MAKE ANY COMMERCIAL, PERSONAL, OR BUSINESS USE OF THE INTELLECTUAL PROPERTY WHATSOEVER. THE PARTIES MAY DISCLOSE THE INTELLECTUAL PROPERTY TO EMPLOYEES ONLY IF THEY NEED TO KNOW ABOUT IT FOR PURPOSES OF THEIR EMPLOYMENT AND THEY AGREE IN WRITING TO BE BOUND BY THE TERMS OF THIS AGREEMENT.

5. WARRANTY OF OWNERSHIP RIGHTS EACH PARTY WARRANTS THAT ALL RIGHTS IN ITS RESPECTIVE INTELLECTUAL PROPERTY ARE HELD BY THE RESPECTIVE PARTY, THAT EACH HAS THE RIGHT AND AUTHORITY TO DISCLOSE THIS INTELLECTUAL PROPERTY, AND THAT NO OTHER PERSONS KNOWN TO EITHER OF THEM HAVE CONFLICTING RIGHTS IN THIS INTELLECTUAL PROPERTY. THE PARTIES MAKE NO OTHER WARRANTIES.

6. RETURN OF THE INTELLECTUAL PROPERTY WITHIN THIRTY (30) DAYS, EACH PARTY SHALL RETURN ALL OF THE OTHER'S INTELLECTUAL PROPERTY BY PERSONAL DELIVERY, CERTIFIED OR REGISTERED MAIL, OR OTHER SAFE TRANSPORT AS REQUESTED BY THE RESPECTIVE PARTY. EACH PARTY AGREES AND UNDERTAKES TO DESTROY ALL NOTES, OTHER DOCUMENTS, AND COMPUTER DATA AND PROGRAMS MADE OR COPIED IN RELATION TO THE OTHER'S INTELLECTUAL PROPERTY. THIS AGREEMENT DOES NOT COVER INFORMATION OR MATERIALS THAT THE EITHER PARTY POSSESSED THROUGH INDEPENDENT ACQUISITION OR DEVELOPMENT PRIOR TO THE OTHER'S DISCLOSURE OF ITS RESPECTIVE INTELLECTUAL PROPERTY.

7. RETENTION OF ALL RIGHTS THE PARTIES HAVE NO INTENTION TO TRANSFER BETWEEN THEM ANY RIGHTS WHATSOEVER IN THEIR RESPECTIVE INTELLECTUAL PROPERTY. THE PARTIES UNDERSTAND AND AGREE THAT THEY RETAIN ALL RIGHTS OF OWNERSHIP IN THEIR RESPECTIVE INTELLECTUAL PROPERTY, AND NEITHER IS GRANTING NOR COMMITTING TO THE OTHER ANY RIGHTS WHATSOEVER IN THE INTELLECTUAL PROPERTY.

8. NO RELATIONSHIP THE PARTIES ACKNOWLEDGE THAT THEIR PLANS RELATING TO THE INTELLECTUAL PROPERTY ARE TENTATIVE AND THEIR DISCUSSIONS DO NOT REPRESENT ANY FINAL DECISIONS OR AGREEMENTS AS TO DEVELOPMENT OR USE OF THE INTELLECTUAL PROPERTY. THE PARTIES HAVE NO INTENTION TO ENTER INTO ANY AGENCY, PARTNERSHIP, VENTURE, OR OTHER SIMILAR ARRANGEMENT, AND THIS AGREEMENT SHALL NOT BE CONSTRUED AS CREATING SUCH AN ARRANGEMENT BETWEEN THEM.

9. PERIOD OF AGREEMENT THIS AGREEMENT SHALL BIND THE PARTIES UNTIL THEY HAVE ACQUIRED OTHER PROTECTION OF THEIR RESPECTIVE INTELLECTUAL PROPERTY, DISCLOSED PUBLICLY THEIR RESPECTIVE INTELLECTUAL PROPERTY, OR GIVEN EACH OTHER A WRITTEN RELEASE OF THE DUTIES UNDER THIS AGREEMENT.

10. REMEDIES AND ATTORNEY FEES THE PARTIES ACKNOWLEDGE AND UNDERSTAND THAT BREACH OF THIS AGREEMENT WILL CAUSE ONE OR BOTH OF THEM IRREPARABLE HARM AND THAT SUCH HARM CANNOT BE ADEQUATELY COMPENSATED BY MONEY DAMAGES. IN THE EVENT OF A BREACH OR THREATENED BREACH OF THIS AGREEMENT, THE PARTY WHO IS NOT IN BREACH SHALL THEREFORE BE ENTITLED TO SEEK THE FOLLOWING: (A) A RESTRAINING INJUNCTION TO PROHIBIT THE OTHER'S BREACH OR FURTHER BREACH; (B) ALL LEGAL REMEDIES AVAILABLE; AND (C) LIQUIDATED DAMAGES

IN THE AMOUNT OF [*dollar amount*]. THE PREVAILING PARTY IN A LEGAL ACTION RELATING TO THIS AGREEMENT SHALL BE ENTITLED TO RECOVER COSTS, EXPENSES, AND REASONABLE ATTORNEY FEES.

11. MODIFICATIONS OF AGREEMENT EVERY MODIFICATION, ADDITION, OR DELETION TO THIS AGREEMENT SHALL BE EFFECTIVE ONLY IF MADE IN WRITING AND SIGNED BY BOTH PARTIES.

12. LAW APPLICABLE TO AGREEMENT THE PARTIES MAKE THIS AGREEMENT PURSUANT TO THE LAWS OF [*state or country*], AND THEY INTEND THIS AGREEMENT TO BE CONSTRUED ACCORDING TO THOSE LAWS.

OWNER: [*business name*]

BY [*signature of authorized representative*]

[*typed name and title*]

[*date*]

CONFIDANT: [*business name*]

BY [*signature of authorized representative*]

[*typed name and title*]

[*date*]

Nondisclosure Agreement Between Author and Publisher

USE OF FORM

This second form is for use when an author approaches a publisher to seek a contract for publication of the author's work. This contract assumes that at least provisional protection has already attached to the work. Thus, the author should have already placed his or her work into a tangible medium for presentation to the publisher, which gives rise to copyright protection in most countries. This same contract may be used by an inventor who has a pending patent or an applicant for a pending trademark application.

An author, inventor, or trademark designer rarely has sufficient weight to negotiate a favorable contract, but this agreement serves to notify the publisher of the author's rights. Many publishers may refuse to sign this agreement, and may even refuse to review an author's work. Accordingly, most authors do not present the entire work to a prospective publisher until the publisher expresses interest in the work. If you also request a signature on this agreement, you will have put the publisher on notice that the work is confidential and subject to copyright. If the publisher later infringes the author's rights, the author will have some proof of the publisher's bad faith infringement.

To make this agreement less formal, it is placed in a letter format. It is also written with some humor because it must "catch the eye" of the publisher if your manuscript is going to be reviewed among the hundreds of unsolicited manuscripts that publishers receive. Accordingly, you can modify much of this letter to place it in your own style, while leaving the essential content on disclosure intact.

NONDISCLOSURE AGREEMENT

[*name and address of author*]

[*telephone, fax, and e-mail*]

[*date*]

[*name and address of publisher*]

DEAR SIR OR MADAM:

A CONFIDENTIAL MANUSCRIPT IS ENCLOSED. I HAVE TOILED AT GREAT LENGTH OVER THIS CREATION, AND I WOULD REQUEST YOUR HUMBLE REVIEW. PLEASE DO NOT BE TOO HARSH, AS I AM STILL RECOVERING FROM GIVING BIRTH TO IT. FOR YOUR FURTHER INFORMATION, I AM ALSO ENCLOSING A SHORT SUMMARY OF MY LIFE.

I WOULD DEEPLY APPRECIATE YOUR SIGNATURE AT THE BOTTOM OF THIS LETTER TO ACKNOWLEDGE THAT YOU HAVE RECEIVED MY UNBELIEVABLY SUPERB AND NOVEL WORK AND THAT YOU UNDERSTAND THAT I HAVE PROVIDED IT TO YOU FOR REVIEW ONLY. I REALIZE THAT THIS REQUEST IS A BIT COMMON AND PARANOID, AND IS RARELY ACCEDED TO BY PUBLISHERS OF YOUR LOFTY RANK, BUT HAVING YOUR FINE AUTOGRAPH IN MY GROWING COLLECTION WOULD MEAN SO MUCH TO ME.

AT THE MOMENT, I AM THE AUTHOR OF THIS SHINING WORK. JUST FOR YOU, I AM WILLING TO SWEAR ON A STAND AND WARRANT UNDER LAW THAT IT IS ALL MINE AND NOBODY ELSE'S. I AM, HOWEVER, ALSO WILLING TO SHARE, OR EVEN RELINQUISH MY RIGHTS TO, THE THRONE FOR AN AGREEABLE PRICE. OF COURSE, I DO HAVE CERTAIN MINIMAL DEMANDS. FOOD ON MY TABLE IS ALWAYS MY GOAL, ICING IS NICE. I AM AVAILABLE VIA VARIOUS ELECTRONIC MODES TO DISCUSS YOUR INTERESTS AND MY LIFESTYLE.

PLEASE BESTOW ON ME YOUR MOST FAVORABLE AND KINDEST RESPONSE.

IN HUMBLE GRATITUDE,

[*signature*]

[*typed name*]

DEAR [*author's name*]

I HAVE RECEIVED THE WORK TITLED "[*title of work*]" AND I UNDERSTAND THAT IT IS CONFIDENTIAL INFORMATION BELONGING TO YOU. I CAN ASSURE YOU THAT I WILL SAFEGUARD IT FROM PUBLIC DISCLOSURE AND UNAUTHORIZED USE. IF AFTER REVIEWING IT I REFUSE TO PUBLISH IT, I AGREE TO RETURN IT TO YOU.

[*signature*]

[*typed name*]

[*date*]

Nondisclosure Agreement Between Employer and Employee

When an employee is hired by your company, he or she should be required to sign an agreement that protects the trade secrets of your company. Often called a Confidentiality Agreement, this agreement is intended to emphasize the importance of nondisclosure of confidential information, and to memorialize the fact that the employee claims to have understood his or her duty to the employer. At the time an employee leaves your company, it is prudent to conduct an exit interview during which the employee is reminded of his or her duty to continue to keep the trade secrets confidential and to restore to your company all confidential materials he or she might posses. If trade secrets are disclosed by a former employee who is subject to a Confidentiality Agreement, the employer can prevent a third party from using the disclosed information in commerce.

CONFIDENTIALITY AGREEMENT

[*Employer's Letterhead*]

AGREEMENT OF CONFIDENTIALITY

1. DUTY TO COMPANY THE COMPANY HAS CLEARLY INFORMED ME THAT DURING MY EMPLOYMENT I WILL/WOULD BE GIVEN AND EXPOSED TO BUSINESS INFORMATION AND TRADE SECRETS THAT BELONG TO THE COMPANY. I UNDERSTAND AND AGREE THAT I SHALL KEEP THESE ITEMS COMPLETELY CONFIDENTIAL AND I SHALL NOT INTENTIONALLY DISCLOSE THEM TO ANY PARTY WHO IS NOT AUTHORIZED BY THE COMPANY. I FURTHER UNDERSTAND AND AGREE THAT I SHALL TAKE THE PRECAUTIONS DEEMED SUFFICIENT BY THE COMPANY AGAINST ACCIDENTAL DISCLOSURE TO ANY OTHER PARTY.

2. IDENTIFICATION OF PROPERTY I have reviewed the items listed on Exhibit A as being confidential business information and other intellectual property of the Company, and I confirm that I understand that these items have substantial value to the Company and that each of them must be treated with utmost confidentiality as stated in this Agreement. Further, I confirm my understanding that Exhibit A is not a complete list, and I therefore confirm that the Company can identify additional confidential business information and other intellectual property, and that such additional items shall be within the scope of this Agreement.

3. COMPLIANCE BY EMPLOYEE I CONFIRM THAT I HAVE READ, UNDERSTOOD, AND SIGNED AN EMPLOYMENT AGREEMENT WITH THE COMPANY, AND FURTHER THAT THE COMPANY HAS FURNISHED TO ME A COPY OF THE EXECUTED EMPLOYMENT AGREEMENT. BY SIGNING THIS ADDITIONAL CONFIDENTIALITY AGREEMENT, I CERTIFY THAT I HAVE COMPLIED AND WILL CONTINUE TO COMPLY WITH ALL OF MY OBLIGATIONS OF CONFIDENTIALITY AS PROVIDED IN THE EMPLOYMENT AGREEMENT. MY SIGNATURE ON THIS CONFIDENTIALITY AGREEMENT FURTHER CONFIRMS THAT I HAVE RECEIVED A COPY OF IT FROM THE COMPANY.

COMMENT: This confidentiality agreement assumes that the employer has wisely included confidentiality provisions in the employment contract effective during the employment. If not, this clause should be amended to avoid reference to the employment contract.

4. OWNER OF RIGHTS DURING MY EMPLOYMENT, I WILL BE CONTRIBUTING TO THE DEVELOPMENT OF THE COMPANY'S INTELLECTUAL PROPERTY. AS PROVIDED IN MY EMPLOYMENT AGREEMENT, I AGAIN ACKNOWLEDGE THAT ALL RIGHT, TITLE, AND INTEREST IN AND TO THIS INTELLECTUAL PROPERTY

BELONGS TO THE COMPANY, REGARDLESS OF WHETHER I CONCEIVE, DEVELOP, OR USE THE INTELLECTUAL PROPERTY.

COMMENT: If no provisions are made in the Employment Agreement, the reference to that Agreement should be deleted.

[IF THE EMPLOYEE IS LEAVING INCLUDE:]
5. WARRANTY BY EMPLOYEE I CERTIFY THAT I HAVE NO INTELLECTUAL PROPERTY BELONGING TO THE COMPANY IN MY POSSESSION, I HAVE NO COPIES OF ANY SUCH MATERIALS, AND I HAVE RETURNED ALL SUCH MATERIALS TO THE COMPANY INCLUDING, ALL, THOUGH NOT AN EXCLUSIVE LIST, THE FOLLOWING: OFFICE, COMPUTER, AND ELECTRONIC SYSTEM DOCUMENTATION; OFFICE, COMPUTER, PRODUCTION, SALES, AND OTHER MANUALS; OFFICE AND OTHER MEMORANDA RELATED TO OFFICE PROCEDURES, EMPLOYEES, AND OTHER CONFIDENTIAL MATTERS; TRAINING INSTRUCTIONS, MANUALS, AND PROGRAMS; COMPUTER SOFTWARE, COMPILERS, DATA STRUCTURES, ALGORITHMS, AND COMPUTER SOURCE CODE; COMPANY FORMULAS AND METHODOLOGIES; AND NOTEBOOKS, NOTES, JOURNALS, LOGS, DRAWINGS, PROPOSALS, OTHER DOCUMENTS OR MATERIALS, AND EXTRACTS OF SUCH MATERIALS.

I ACKNOWLEDGE THAT I HAVE READ AND UNDERSTOOD THE TERMS OF THIS AGREEMENT, AND ACCORDINGLY I SIGN BELOW ON [*date*].

[*signature*]

[*typed name of employee*]

CHAPTER 18

Protecting IP Rights: Cease and Desist Letter

AT THE FIRST SIGN OF AN INFRINGEMENT, you might choose to use a "cease and desist letter" to try to stop the suspected illegal activity. This procedure is a common and cost-effective method, and often produces results against individuals and smaller businesses, particularly if they have inadvertently "borrowed" your IP. It involves the sending of a letter such as the following directly to the infringer and demanding that the infringer stop all infringing activities and acknowledge your IP rights.

Although sending this letter is an inexpensive first step in fighting infringement, there are times when you may not want to use it. For example, you may have evidence that an infringer has substantial assets and production and holds a prior registration of your IP in another country. You may further discover that the infringer has gained exponential growth in market share, has hidden factories and untraceable suppliers, and has made blatant reference in advertising to your company or country as the source of goods. In such event, you can assume that the infringer knows of your IP rights and the value of your IP rights, and further that the infringer is trading on your reputation. You can further assume that a mere cease and desist letter is unlikely to have much effect against someone who is enjoying a substantial profit, but it is likely to tip off the infringer about your intentions, making it easier to hide the evidence that you will need to fight a successful court case. The strategies involved should be discussed with your legal counsel.

Cease and Desist Letter

USE OF FORM

The following letter is written in reference to your company. However, you would be wise to consult legal counsel prior to sending a cease and desist letter. A cease and desist letter that is sent without proper basis could lead to a suit against you for baseless threats made and damage to reputation. Furthermore, a cease and desist letter that comes from your legal counsel is likely to carry the extra weight of "the law" behind it.

CEASE AND DESIST LETTER

[*your company name and address*]

[*telephone, fax, and e-mail*]

[*date*]

[*name and address of infringer*]

DEAR SIR OR MADAM:

WE HAVE RECENTLY DISCOVERED THAT, WITHOUT ANY CONSENT FROM OUR COMPANY, [*your company's name*], YOU ARE [*describe infringing activity*, SUCH AS PRODUCING, SELLING, BUYING FOR SALE, AND/OR OTHERWISE PROMOTING, TRANSFERRING, AND/OR MAKING PRODUCTS], INCLUDING [*describe specific product or service*], THAT [*describe IP being infringed*, SUCH AS BEAR OUR COMPANY'S TRADEMARKS OR THAT ARE COPIES OF OUR COMPANY'S DESIGNS OR THAT ARE MADE BY MEANS OF OUR COMPANY'S PATENTED PROCESS].

OUR COMPANY, [*your company's name*], LOCATED AT [*address*] IS THE OWNER OF THE [*describe IP owned*], WHICH IS/ARE PROTECTED IN [*home country*] AND IN MORE THAN [*number*] COUNTRIES WORLDWIDE. OUR COMPANY PROTECTS, USES, AND PROMOTES ITS RIGHTS IN THIS INTELLECTUAL PROPERTY THROUGHOUT THE WORLD. WE HAVE HIGHLY VISIBLE ADVERTISING AND PROMOTIONAL CAMPAIGNS WITHIN THE [*industry/public at large*]. AS A RESULT, OUR NAME AND REPUTATION ARE WELL-KNOWN AND OUR PRODUCTS AND SERVICES ARE UNIQUELY ASSOCIATED IN THE MINDS OF THE TRADE AND PURCHASING PUBLIC WITH OUR COMPANY AND NO OTHER PERSON OR COMPANY.

YOUR USE OF OUR INTELLECTUAL PROPERTY IS A VIOLATION OF OUR EXCLUSIVE RIGHTS GRANTED IN OUR REGISTRATION, AND FURTHER IT IS LIKELY TO CONFUSE THE PUBLIC AND MAY AMOUNT TO UNFAIR COMPETITION. WE ARE CERTAIN THAT YOU DO NOT WANT TO FOSTER SUCH CONFUSION, TO CONVEY A FALSE AND MISLEADING IMPRESSION AS TO THE SOURCE OF PRODUCTS AND SERVICES, OR TO TRADE ON OUR REPUTATION.

THEREFORE, WE DEMAND THAT YOU:

1. CEASE AND DESIST ALL USE OF OUR COMPANY'S INTELLECTUAL PROPERTY IMMEDIATELY.

2. DESTROY OR ORDER THE DESTRUCTION OF ALL SAID INFRINGING MATERIALS, INFORMATION, PRODUCTS, AND OTHER ITEMS NOW IN YOUR POSSESSION OR THAT COME INTO YOUR POSSESSION IN THE FUTURE.

3. CEASE AND DESIST FROM USING ANY INTELLECTUAL PROPERTY CONFUSINGLY SIMILAR TO OUR COMPANY'S INTELLECTUAL PROPERTY.

4. TAKE ALL NECESSARY STEPS TO TRANSFER IMMEDIATELY TO OUR COMPANY ANY AND ALL REGISTRATIONS OF INTELLECTUAL PROPERTY THAT ARE IDENTICAL OR SIMILAR TO OUR COMPANY'S INTELLECTUAL PROPERTY.

5. TAKE ALL NECESSARY STEPS TO AVOID ANY FURTHER INFRINGING ACTIONS IN RELATION TO OUR COMPANY'S INTELLECTUAL PROPERTY.

6. PERMIT REPRESENTATIVES OF [*your company's name*] TO INSPECT YOUR PREMISES DURING REASONABLE BUSINESS HOURS AND WITHOUT ADVANCE NOTICE TO ENSURE THAT INFRINGING PRODUCTS ARE NOT PRESENT.

7. EXECUTE THIS LETTER BELOW AND RETURN IT TO US BY [*date*] AS YOUR WRITTEN ASSURANCE THAT YOU WILL SUBSCRIBE TO THE FOREGOING.

PLEASE NOTE THAT AN INFRINGER MAY FACE SUBSTANTIAL CIVIL LIABILITY, INCLUDING AN AWARD OF DAMAGES AND ATTORNEY FEES FOR WILLFUL VIOLATION AND WILLFUL INFRINGEMENT OF OUR COMPANY'S INTELLECTUAL PROPERTY. IF YOU HAVE QUESTIONS CONCERNING YOUR RESPONSIBILITIES AS STATED HERE, YOU ARE ADVISED TO CONSULT LEGAL COUNSEL. NOTHING IN THIS LETTER SHOULD BE CONSTRUED AS A WAIVER OF ANY OF OUR COMPANY'S RIGHTS, ALL OF WHICH ARE EXPRESSLY RESERVED.

IF WE DO NOT HEAR FROM YOU ON OR BEFORE [*date*], WE SHALL TAKE ALL NECESSARY LEGAL STEPS TO STOP THE INFRINGEMENT OF OUR INTELLECTUAL PROPERTY.

SINCERELY,

[*your company's name*]

[*signature*]

[*typed name and title*]

ENCLOSED: REGISTRATION

I, ______________________ (NAME), AS THE ______________________ (TITLE) OF ______________________ (NAME OF COMPANY OR STORE) LOCATED AT ____ (ADDRESS, CITY, STATE, COUNTRY) HEREBY AGREE AND UNDERTAKE TO CEASE AND DESIST ALL ACTIVITIES AS STATED IN THE ABOVE LETTER WITH REGARD TO ALL AND ANY OF THE INTELLECTUAL PROPERTY OWNED BY [*your company's name*]. FURTHER, I AGREE AND UNDERTAKE TO DESTROY OR ORDER THE DESTRUCTION OF ALL SAID INFRINGING MATERIALS, INFORMATION, PRODUCTS, AND OTHER ITEMS NOW IN MY POSSESSION OR THAT COME INTO MY POSSESSION IN THE FUTURE. I ALSO AGREE AND CONFIRM THAT REPRESENTATIVES OF [*your company's name*] MAY INSPECT MY PREMISES DURING REASONABLE BUSINESS HOURS AND WITHOUT ADVANCE NOTICE TO ENSURE THAT INFRINGING PRODUCTS ARE NOT PRESENT. I UNDERSTAND THAT INFRINGEMENT OF INTELLECTUAL PROPERTY IS A SERIOUS OFFENSE AND THAT I MAY BE LIABLE FOR DAMAGES TO [*your company's name*], AND FURTHER THAT [*your company's name*] HAS WAIVED NO RIGHTS WHATSOEVER IN THIS REGARD BY THIS CEASE AND DESIST LETTER.

EXECUTED ON ______________________ (*date*).

BY: ______________________ (*company name*)

______________________ (*signature*)

______________________ (*printed name*)

______________________ (*printed title*)

CHAPTER 19

Protecting IP Rights: Settlement Memorandum

WHETHER LEGAL PROCEEDINGS AGAINST A SUSPECTED INFRINGEMENT have commenced or are merely threatened, the parties involved would be wise to try to settle the dispute amicably. If legal proceedings are brought, the parties will incur substantial expenses for attorney fees, court costs, investigative and discovery costs, and other litigation related expenses. They are also likely to suffer harm to their reputation among consumers and industry traders, loss of sales, loss of production, and potentially loss of the business. Settlement negotiations can take time, but they are usually accomplished in private without harmful publicity.

The following Memorandum is not a full-fledged Settlement Agreement. It is merely the first agreement put into writing by two parties who have negotiated the basic terms of a settlement. By preparing a Memorandum, the parties can concentrate on the most significant, core provisions of the settlement. Once the basic settlement is agreed, the relationship of the parties will be determined and they can proceed with conducting their business while they wait for the attorneys to prepare and finalize a complete Settlement Agreement with all the nuances and subtleties of a detailed contract.

Settlement Memorandum

THIS SETTLEMENT MEMORANDUM SHALL TAKE EFFECT AS OF [*date*] BETWEEN [*name and address*] (FIRST PARTY) AND [*name and address*] (SECOND PARTY).

THE PARTIES ACKNOWLEDGE THE FOLLOWING:

a. The First Party has rights to Intellectual Property as stated in this Memorandum and is seeking to protect those rights.

b. The Second Party has used and/or registered intellectual property similar to the Intellectual Property claimed by the First Party, but the Second Party is not admitting to any illegal or infringing use of said Property by signing this Memorandum or otherwise by entering into settlement with the First Party.

ACCORDINGLY, THE PARTIES AGREE TO THE FOLLOWING TERMS AND CONDITIONS:

1. INTELLECTUAL PROPERTY THE FIRST PARTY OWNS ALL RIGHTS IN THE FOLLOWING INTELLECTUAL PROPERTY: [*list particulars*, INCLUDING NAME OR TITLE, REGISTRATION NUMBERS, AND OTHER IDENTIFYING INFORMATION].

2. NO RIGHTS THE SECOND PARTY CLAIMS NO RIGHTS WHATSOEVER IN ANY OF THE INTELLECTUAL PROPERTY OWNED BY THE FIRST PARTY, NOR IN ANY IDENTICAL OR SIMILAR INTELLECTUAL PROPERTY.

3. DISCLOSURE AND TRANSFER OF IP REGISTRATIONS THE SECOND PARTY HAS DISCLOSED TO THE FIRST PARTY ALL OF THE SECOND PARTY'S PENDING APPLICATIONS AND ISSUED REGISTRATIONS OF INTELLECTUAL PROPERTY THAT IS SIMILAR OR IDENTICAL TO THE INTELLECTUAL PROPERTY OF THE FIRST PARTY. THESE APPLICATIONS AND REGISTRATIONS ARE LISTED IN SCHEDULE A ATTACHED TO THIS MEMORANDUM. WITHIN FOURTEEN (14) DAYS OF THE EFFECTIVE DATE OF THIS MEMORANDUM, THE SECOND PARTY SHALL APPLY TO ALL REGISTRIES TO ABANDON OR CANCEL SUCH APPLICATIONS OR REGISTRATIONS, OR ON WRITTEN REQUEST OF THE FIRST PARTY, TO TRANSFER THEM TO THE FIRST PARTY. THE SECOND PARTY SHALL PROVIDE THE FIRST PARTY WITH CERTIFIED RECEIPTS SHOWING THAT THE APPLICATIONS AND REGISTRATIONS HAVE BEEN ABANDONED, CANCELLED, OR TRANSFERRED.

4. DISCLOSURE AND TRANSFER OF COMPANY AND TRADE REGISTRATIONS AND NAMES THE SECOND PARTY HAS DISCLOSED TO THE FIRST PARTY ALL REGISTERED AND UNREGISTERED COMPANY AND TRADE NAMES THAT THE SECOND PARTY HAS USED AND THAT ARE SIMILAR OR IDENTICAL TO THE INTELLECTUAL PROPERTY OF THE FIRST PARTY. THESE NAMES AND REGISTRATIONS ARE LISTED IN SCHEDULE B ATTACHED TO THIS MEMORANDUM. WITHIN FOURTEEN (14) DAYS OF THE EFFECTIVE DATE OF THIS MEMORANDUM, THE SECOND PARTY SHALL SELECT A NEW COMPANY AND TRADE NAME THAT HAS NO RELATION OR LIKENESS TO THE INTELLECTUAL PROPERTY OF THE FIRST PARTY WHATSOEVER. WITHIN THIS SAME TIME, THE SECOND PARTY SHALL APPLY TO ALL REGISTRIES TO ABANDON OR CANCEL ITS REGISTRATIONS OF SUCH NAMES, AND FURTHER SHALL BEGIN TO ELIMINATE THEIR USE AND APPLICATION OF SUCH NAMES AS REQUIRED WITHIN THIS MEMORANDUM. CERTIFIED RECEIPTS SHOWING CANCELLATION OR ABANDONMENT SHALL BE PROVIDED TO THE FIRST PARTY.

5. NO USE OF SIMILAR OR IDENTICAL PROPERTY AS OF FORTY-FIVE (45) DAYS FROM THE EFFECTIVE DATE OF THIS MEMORANDUM, THE SECOND PARTY SHALL HAVE CEASED MANUFACTURING, PRODUCING, APPLYING, FORMULATING, REPRESENTING, SELLING, PROMOTING, ADVERTISING, OR OTHERWISE USING IN ALL RESPECTS ALL INTELLECTUAL PROPERTY THAT IS SIMILAR OR IDENTICAL TO THE INTELLECTUAL PROPERTY OF THE FIRST PARTY.

6. DESTRUCTION OF SIMILAR OR IDENTICAL PROPERTY AS OF FORTY-FIVE (45) DAYS FROM THE EFFECTIVE DATE OF THIS MEMORANDUM, THE SECOND PARTY SHALL OBLITERATE ALL INTELLECTUAL PROPERTY THAT IS SIMILAR OR IDENTICAL TO THE INTELLECTUAL PROPERTY OF THE FIRST PARTY. THIS ACTION MUST BE TAKEN, WITHOUT LIMIT, IN RESPECT OF [*describe depending on type of intellectual property*, E.G., ALL PROCEDURES AND METHODS USED BY THE SECOND PARTY OR ALL LITERARY WORKS PRODUCED, SOLD, OR OTHERWISE USED BY THE SECOND PARTY OR ALL NAMES AND SIGNS THAT APPEAR ON ALL REAL ESTATE, INCLUDING WITHOUT LIMIT BUILDING FIXTURES, AND ON ALL ARTICLES IN THE SECOND PARTY'S POSSESSION OR OTHERWISE AVAILABLE FOR THE SECOND PARTY'S USE, INCLUDING WITHOUT LIMIT ALL OF THE SECOND PARTY'S TRADE LISTINGS, ADVERTISING, PROMOTIONAL MATERIALS, SIGNS, PANELS AND BILLBOARDS, STATIONERY, BUSINESS CARDS, LABELS, INVOICES, RECEIPTS, PACKAGING, BAGS, CONTAINERS, DESK AND COUNTER PENCIL CANS, NOTEPADS, CALENDARS, AND OTHER ACCESSORIES, PRINTING PLATES, STAMPS, AND SIMILAR EQUIPMENT].

7. NO REPRESENTATION AND NO INTERFERENCE FROM THE EFFECTIVE DATE OF THIS MEMORANDUM, THE SECOND PARTY SHALL NEVER REPRESENT NOR IN ANY WAY HOLD OUT TO ANY PERSON WHATSOEVER THAT THE FIRST PARTY OWNS OR IN ANY WAY IS CONNECTED OR ASSOCIATED WITH THE

SECOND PARTY. FURTHERMORE, THE SECOND PARTY SHALL NEVER OPPOSE OR INTERFERE WITH ANY OF THE FIRST PARTY'S PENDING APPLICATIONS FOR THE REGISTRATION OF ITS INTELLECTUAL PROPERTY, NOR SHALL IT EVER SEEK CANCELLATION OF SUCH REGISTRATIONS.

8. FORMAL AGREEMENT THE PARTIES INTEND THAT THIS MEMORANDUM WILL BECOME THE BASIS OF A FORMAL AGREEMENT OF SETTLEMENT BETWEEN THEM. THIS MEMORANDUM CONTAINS THE MOST SIGNIFICANT PROVISIONS OF THEIR AGREEMENT. ANY ADDITIONAL PROVISIONS THAT MAY BE ADDED TO THE FORMAL AGREEMENT OF SETTLEMENT BETWEEN THE PARTIES SHALL NOT IN ANY WAY WHATSOEVER MODIFY THE PROVISIONS OF THE MEMORANDUM WITHOUT THE EXPLICIT CONSENT OF BOTH PARTIES IN WRITING.

9. CONFIDENTIALITY THE PARTIES AGREE AND UNDERTAKE NOT TO DISCLOSE ANY TERMS AND CONDITIONS OF THEIR MEMORANDUM AND OF THEIR FORMAL AGREEMENT OF SETTLEMENT, AND THEY SHALL KEEP THE TERMS CONFIDENTIAL.

10. COSTS EACH PARTY SHALL BEAR ITS OWN COSTS, CHARGES, AND EXPENSES RELATING TO THIS SETTLEMENT.

11. CONSIDERATION IN CONSIDERATION OF THE UNDERTAKINGS BY THE SECOND PARTY IN THIS MEMORANDUM, THE FIRST PARTY AGREES TO DISMISS ANY LEGAL PROCEEDINGS THAT MAY HAVE BEEN COMMENCED AND FURTHER AGREES TO WAIVE ALL CLAIMS THAT THE FIRST PARTY MAY HAVE HAD AGAINST THE SECOND PARTY. HOWEVER, THIS AGREEMENT AND WAIVER SHALL NOT AFFECT ANY FUTURE CLAIMS THAT THE FIRST PARTY MAY HAVE, NOR SHALL IT AFFECT THE FIRST PARTY'S RIGHTS IN THE EVENT THAT THE SECOND PARTY BREACHES THIS MEMORANDUM OR THE FORMAL AGREEMENT OF SETTLEMENT.

12. COOPERATION THE PARTIES AGREE TO DO ALL THINGS AND EXECUTE ALL DEEDS, INSTRUMENTS, TRANSFERS, OR OTHER DOCUMENTS AS MAY BE NECESSARY OR DESIRABLE TO GIVE FULL EFFECT TO THE PROVISIONS OF THIS AGREEMENT AND THE TRANSACTIONS CONTEMPLATED.

IN AGREEMENT AND UNDERSTANDING, THE PARTIES NOW SIGN AND DATE THIS MEMORANDUM BELOW.

FIRST PARTY: [*Company Name*]

BY [*signature of authorized representative*]

[*typed name and title*]

[*date*]

SECOND PARTY: [*Company Name*]

BY [*signature of authorized representative*]

[*typed name and title*]

[*date*]

CHAPTER 20

Transferring IP Rights: Assignment Contract

A PARTY WHO TRANSFERS ALL RIGHTS IN IP makes an assignment. This type of transfer is sometimes referred to as an "all rights transfer." Once the assignment becomes effective, the party no longer owns any rights whatsoever in the IP. This form is a short form for the assignment of IP rights only. If an assignment of IP rights is being made as part of the sale of a business, the parties will usually make a single, long, and complex agreement that incorporates the IP assignment within it. In any event, the assignment of IP rights must usually be made in writing to be recognized and enforceable under the laws of most countries. In addition, most countries require that the assignment be recorded against the registration of the IP rights. For a form that may be used in recording IP rights, see Chapter 22.

Assignment Contract

THIS ASSIGNMENT IS MADE ON [*date*] BETWEEN [*name and address*] ("THE ASSIGNOR") AND [*name and address*] ("THE ASSIGNEE").

THE PARTIES ACKNOWLEDGE THE FOLLOWING:

A. THE ASSIGNOR HOLDS ALL RIGHTS, TITLE, AND INTEREST IN THE FOLLOWING, WHICH SHALL BE REFERRED TO AS "THE INTELLECTUAL PROPERTY": [*list identifying information*, SUCH AS THE NAME OR TITLE AND REGISTRATION NUMBERS OF THE IP].

B. THE ASSIGNOR HAS AGREED TO SELL TO THE ASSIGNEE FOR GOOD AND VALUABLE CONSIDERATION THE INTELLECTUAL PROPERTY ON THE TERMS AND CONDITIONS STATED IN THIS ASSIGNMENT.

NOW THIS ASSIGNMENT SHALL BE AS FOLLOWS:

1. TRANSFER IN CONSIDERATION OF THE SUM OF $[*amount*], NOW PAID BY THE ASSIGNEE TO THE ASSIGNOR (THE RECEIPT OF WHICH THE ASSIGNOR ACKNOWLEDGES), THE ASSIGNOR ASSIGNS TO THE ASSIGNEE ALL RIGHTS, TITLE, AND INTEREST IN THE INTELLECTUAL PROPERTY THROUGHOUT THE WORLD TO HOLD THE SAME UNTO THE ASSIGNEE ABSOLUTELY FOR THE FULL PERIOD OF PROTECTION FOR THE INTELLECTUAL RIGHTS AS GRANTED BY LAW AND FOR ALL RELEVANT RENEWALS AND EXTENSIONS. THE RIGHTS, TITLE, AND INTEREST TRANSFERRED SHALL INCLUDE WITHOUT LIMIT ALL OF THE FOLLOWING:

a. All benefits, privileges, and advantages of or arising out of or to be derived from the Intellectual Property.

b. All property, rights, title, interests, claims, and demands of the Assignor in and to the Intellectual Property.

c. All rights to sue third parties for infringement of the Intellectual Property and for all common law remedies with respect to the Intellectual Property.

d. All rights to recover damages in respect of all acts of infringement, passing off, unfair competition, and other similar acts that have occurred at any time after or prior to the date of this Assignment.

2. WARRANTY THE ASSIGNOR WARRANTS THE FOLLOWING:

a. The Assignor is the owner of the Intellectual Property and of all rights in such Property, and the Assignor has good right to assign the Intellectual Property unto the Assignee.

b. The Intellectual Property is an original creation and does not infringe in any way whatsoever on the rights of any third party.

c. The Assignor is entitled to enter into this Assignment and to transfer the Intellectual Property to the Assignee free of any encumbrances.

d. All Intellectual Property rights transferred are good, valid, and existing.

e. The Intellectual Property rights, title, and interest can be exercised, held, and enjoyed by the Assignee without any interruption or claim from the Assignor or any person or persons lawfully or equitably claiming under or in trust for the Assignor.

3. FURTHER ACTIONS BY ASSIGNOR AT THE REQUEST AND EXPENSE OF THE ASSIGNEE, THE ASSIGNOR WILL EXECUTE, PERFECT OR OTHERWISE ACT TO ENSURE THAT ALL RIGHTS, TITLE, AND INTEREST ARE ASSIGNED TO THE ASSIGNEE, THAT ALL ADDITIONAL DOCUMENTS AND INSTRUMENTS ARE EXECUTED TO CARRY OUT THIS ASSIGNMENT, AND IN THE EVENT OF INFRINGEMENT OR PASSING OFF, THAT ALL REQUIREMENTS ARE SATISFIED TO ENABLE THE ASSIGNEE TO COMMENCE, CARRY ON, AND PROSECUTE NECESSARY AND PROPER ACTIONS AND PROCEEDINGS AS SHALL OR MAY BE REASONABLY REQUIRED.

4. INDEMNIFICATION THE ASSIGNOR COVENANTS WITH THE ASSIGNEE THAT THE ASSIGNOR WILL KEEP THE ASSIGNEE INDEMNIFIED FROM AND AGAINST ALL ACTIONS, CLAIMS, PROCEEDINGS, COSTS, AND DAMAGES INCURRED OR AWARDED AND PAID ON ACCOUNT OF ANY BREACH OR NONPERFORMANCE OF THE ASSIGNOR WITH REGARD TO THE WARRANTIES MADE BY THE ASSIGNOR IN THIS ASSIGNMENT, OR WITH REGARD TO ANY CLAIM BY A THIRD PARTY THAT WOULD CONSTITUTE SUCH A BREACH IF PROVEN.

5. **ASSIGNMENT** THE ASSIGNEE SHALL HAVE THE RIGHT TO ASSIGN THE BENEFIT OF THIS ASSIGNMENT TO ANY THIRD PARTY.

6. ENTIRE TRANSACTION THE PARTIES CERTIFY THAT THIS TRANSACTION IS NOT PART OF A LARGER TRANSACTION OR A SERIES OF TRANSACTIONS FOR WHICH THE AMOUNT OR VALUE, OR THE AGGREGATE AMOUNT OR VALUE, OF THE CONSIDERATION EXCEEDS $[*amount*].

ACCORDINGLY, THE PARTIES HAVE EXECUTED THIS AGREEMENT BELOW.

ASSIGNOR: [*Company Name*]
BY [*signature*]
[*typed name*]
[*title*]

ASSIGNEE: [*Company Name*]
BY [*signature*]
[*typed name*]
[*title*]

CHAPTER 21

Transferring IP Rights # 1

LICENSE AGREEMENT

BY MEANS OF A LICENSE AGREEMENT, the owner of IP rights may transfer some but not all of the rights in the IP to another party. For example, the owner can retain ownership of the IP while allowing others to use the IP for a fee paid to the owner. A license may cover one or more of the IP owner's rights. For example, a license may be limited to use of the IP as a consumer, to translations of the IP, or to use of the IP in relation to a specific product or service only. A license is always either exclusive or nonexclusive. If it is exclusive, the license grants the IP rights to a single person within a certain scope of operation, such a particular industry, region, country, or city. If the license is nonexclusive, the owner of the IP rights is free to grant the same rights to other persons at the same time.

License Agreement

THIS AGREEMENT IS MADE ON [*date*] BETWEEN [*name and address*] ("THE OWNER") AND [*name and address*] ("THE USER").

THE PARTIES ACKNOWLEDGE THE FOLLOWING:

A. THE OWNER IS THE PROPRIETOR OF THE INTELLECTUAL PROPERTY, WHICH CONSISTS OF THE FOLLOWING: [*list identifying information,* SUCH AS THE NAME OR TITLE AND REGISTRATION NUMBERS OF ALL IP BEING LICENSED].

B. THE USER DESIRES TO USE THE INTELLECTUAL PROPERTY IN RELATION TO [*describe briefly and generally intended use*].

THE PARTIES NOW AGREE AS FOLLOWS:

1. THE OWNER PERMITS AND THE USER AGREES AND UNDERTAKES TO USE THE INTELLECTUAL PROPERTY IN ACCORDANCE WITH THE INSTRUCTIONS AND DIRECTIONS OF THE OWNER AND IN CONFORMITY WITH THE REQUIREMENTS PROVIDED BY THE OWNER TO THE USER, SO THAT SUCH USE SHALL BE IN COMPLIANCE WITH THE STANDARDS ESTABLISHED BY THE OWNER.

2. THIS AGREEMENT SHALL APPLY TO THE FOLLOWING USES OF THE INTELLECTUAL PROPERTY: [*describe each specific use*].

3. THIS AGREEMENT SHALL APPLY [*worldwide, or specify a geographical area*].

4. THE PARTIES [*do/do not*] INTEND THAT THE USER SHALL ENJOY THE EXCLUSIVE RIGHT OF PERMITTED USE OF THE INTELLECTUAL PROPERTY. THE OWNER [*expressly reserves the/shall have no*] RIGHT TO ESTABLISH OR MAINTAIN EXISTING ARRANGEMENTS FOR THE PERMITTED USE OF THE INTELLECTUAL PROPERTY BY OTHER PARTIES.

5. THE OWNER SHALL BE ENTITLED TO ALL OF THE FOLLOWING RIGHTS:

a. To inspect at any time during business hours the User's premises or other location where use of this Intellectual Property by the User or its authorized representatives is occurring.

b. To reject any use of the Intellectual Property that the Owner believes is not equal to the quality and standards established by the Owner.

c. To demand from time to time for purposes of inspection and analysis to be supplied with materials, information, samples, test results, and other similar items used or produced by the User in connection with the Intellectual Property.

6. THE USER RECOGNIZES AND ADMITS THAT THE OWNER HOLDS RIGHTS OF OWNERSHIP AND TITLE TO THE INTELLECTUAL PROPERTY, AND THE USER FURTHER UNDERTAKES AS FOLLOWS:

a. Never to do or cause to be done any act, deed, or thing that will in any way impair or put in issue the validity of the Intellectual Property or that will otherwise set up any adverse claim against the Owner's rights in the Intellectual Property.

b. At all times use the Intellectual Property in accordance with the laws that govern such use.

c. Never to take any steps or institute any action whatsoever to suppress any infringement of the Intellectual Property or to apply to cancel any conflicting or infringing registrations of other intellectual property, without the prior consent of the Owner.

7. THIS AGREEMENT SHALL CONTINUE IN FORCE UNTIL TERMINATED ON OCCURRENCE OF ANY OF THE FOLLOWING EVENTS:

a. By either Party giving advance written notice to the other Party, which notice must be received at least [*number*] months prior to the stated termination date.

b. By the Owner giving advance written notice of breach of this Agreement by the User, provided such notice is received by the User at least [*number*] months prior to the stated termination date and provided that, within [*number*] months of the notice of breach, the User fails to remedy or take steps approved by the Owner to remedy the breach.

c. If either Party makes any composition with its creditors, a receiver is appointed for the whole or any part of its assets, an order is made or resolution passed for winding up or otherwise liquidating its business, or a substantial part of its assets becomes subject to seizure.

8. ON TERMINATION OF THIS AGREEMENT, THE RIGHTS OF THE PARTIES SHALL BE AS FOLLOWS:

a. The User shall immediately discontinue all use of the Intellectual Property.

b. Except with the Owner's written approval, the User shall remove all representations of the Intellectual Property from all materials, inventory, advertising and directory listings, computers, manuals, and any other items that are in the User's possession.

c. The Owner may apply to cancel the entry of the User as a Registered User against the registration of the Intellectual Property, and the User agrees to execute all necessary documents to effect such cancellation.

d. After termination of this Agreement, the User shall continue to be bound the duties required in Clause 5 of this Agreement.

ACCORDINGLY, THE PARTIES HAVE EXECUTED THIS AGREEMENT BELOW.

ASSIGNOR: [*Company Name*]

BY [*signature*]

[*typed name*]

[*title*]

ASSIGNEE: [*Company Name*]

BY [*signature*]

[*typed name*]

[*title*]

CHAPTER 22

Transferring IP Rights # 2

DEED OF ASSIGNMENT OR LICENSE

WHEN TRANSFERRING ALL IP RIGHTS (assigning) or rights to use (licensing), the IP owner must fix the transfer in a written agreement. The laws of most countries require a written contract to achieve the transfer. In the absence of a written contract, the assignment or license may be considered invalid and therefore may be unenforceable in a particular country.

After the parties sign the assignment or license agreement, the party who acquires new rights in the IP should seek to protect those rights in all countries covered by the agreement. In many countries, the entire agreement, or a short form called a deed that references the agreement, must be recorded in the relevant IP registry to be recognized by the courts and to be effective notice to third parties. The party acquiring the IP rights should review the local law or contact local counsel to determine the requirements.

If recordal of a Deed is possible, most parties prefer to use it. The reason is simple: a recordal places a document on public record. The purpose of the recordal is merely to notify the Registry and third parties of the rights transferred and the new party who is authorized to own or use the IP. Therefore, the entire agreement need not be disclosed to accomplish this purpose. A short Deed will suffice.

In fact, the acquiring party is well advised to obtain the requirements and necessary forms before executing the agreement itself for two reasons. First, both parties to the assignment or license often need to sign the documents for recording. This can easily be accomplished at the same time that the agreement is signed, but thereafter the party transferring the rights, particularly for an assignment, is often more difficult to locate to obtain a signature. Second, many countries have enacted a time limit for recording a transfer, after which penalties for late recording will have to be paid. This period can be rather short, even 30 days from the date of the agreement.

Deed of Assignment or License

USE OF FORM

This form is provided only for purposes of illustration. It has been left largely in legalese because it is a deed, which is a statutory form that has not changed much from medieval times. The essential elements of the Deed do not vary much from country to country, but many countries prefer that you use a form that is preprinted and often in dual language—English and the official language of the country. Such forms are best obtained from local counsel. If you use the following form, be certain to choose throughout the terminology that refers to an assignment or a license, as appropriate to your situation.

DEED OF [ASSIGNMENT/LICENSE]

THIS [*ASSIGNMENT/LICENSE*] IS MADE ON [*date*]

BETWEEN:

[*Name of first party*], [*an individual/a company organized and existing under the laws of (state/country)*] WITH [*domicile/registered office*] AT [*full street address*]

("ASSIGNOR"/"LICENSOR");

AND

[*Name of second party*], [*an individual/a company organized and existing under the laws of (state/country)*] WITH [*domicile/registered office*] AT [*full street address*]

("ASSIGNEE"/"LICENSEE")

WHEREAS:

PURSUANT TO AN AGREEMENT [*of even date with this Deed/dated (date)*] BETWEEN THE [*Assignor/Licensor*] AND THE [*Assignee/Licensee*] (THE "PRINCIPAL AGREEMENT") THE [*Assignor/Licensor*] AGREED TO [*sell/transfer*] AND THE [*Assignee/Licensee*] AGREED TO PURCHASE INTER ALIA [*all rights in/rights to license and use*] THE INTELLECTUAL PROPERTY, DETAILS OF WHICH ARE SET OUT IN THE SCHEDULE TO THIS DEED, [*if all rights are being assigned, add:* TOGETHER WITH THE GOODWILL ASSOCIATED WITH THOSE RIGHTS AND ALL UNREGISTERED INTELLECTUAL PROPERTY AS DEFINED WITHIN THE PRINCIPAL AGREEMENT] (TOGETHER REFERRED TO AS "INTELLECTUAL PROPERTY").

THE [*Assignor/Licensor*] HAS AGREED TO ENTER INTO THIS [*Assignment/License*] TO ASSIGN TO THE [*Assignee/License*] [*all its rights, title and interest/specific rights of use*] IN AND TO THE INTELLECTUAL PROPERTY.

NOW IT IS AGREED AS FOLLOWS:

PURSUANT TO AND IN CONSIDERATION OF THE PAYMENT REMITTED BY THE [*Assignee/Licensee*] TO [*the Assignor/the Licensor/or name of payee for and on behalf of the Assignor/Licensor*] OF THE SUM PAYABLE IN RESPECT OF THE INTELLECTUAL PROPERTY AND IN ACCORDANCE WITH THE PRINCIPAL AGREEMENT (RECEIPT OF WHICH SUM THE [*Assignor/Licensor*] HEREBY ACKNOWLEDGES), THE [*Assignor/Licensor*] NOW [*assigns/transfers*] TO THE [*Assignee/Licensee*] [*all of its rights, title, and interest/a right of license and use*] IN AND TO THE INTELLECTUAL PROPERTY, [*if all rights are being assigned add:* INCLUDING, WITHOUT LIMITATION, ALL RIGHTS, PRIVILEGES, AND ADVANTAGES ATTACHING THERETO TO HOLD UNTO THE ASSIGNEE ABSOLUTELY AND (EXCEPT AS DISCLOSED IN THE PRINCIPAL AGREEMENT) FREE FROM ALL LIENS (AS DEFINED IN THE PRINCIPAL AGREEMENT) AND WITH THE INTENT THAT THE ASSIGNEE SHALL BE ABSOLUTELY ENTITLED TO ANY REGISTRATIONS GRANTED ON ANY PENDING APPLICATIONS OF THE INTELLECTUAL PROPERTY, TOGETHER WITH THE RIGHT TO SUE FOR AND RETAIN FULL AND EFFECTIVE RELIEF IN RESPECT OF EVERY ACT OF INFRINGEMENT OF THE INTELLECTUAL PROPERTY OCCURRING PRIOR IN TIME TO OR AFTER THE DATE OF THIS ASSIGNMENT],

[*If all rights are being assigned, include:* THE ASSIGNOR HEREBY RELINQUISHES IN FAVOR OF THE ASSIGNEE ANY AND ALL RIGHTS IT MAY HAVE TO THE INTELLECTUAL PROPERTY AND ALL RELATED MATERIALS OR IMAGES

THEREOF, AND THE ASSIGNOR EXPRESSLY ACKNOWLEDGES THE ASSIGNEE'S RIGHTS THERETO.]

AT THE REQUEST OF THE [*Assignee/Licensee*], THE [*Assignor/Licensor*] SHALL EXECUTE ALL SUCH FURTHER DOCUMENTS, FORMS, AND AUTHORIZATIONS AND SHALL DEPOSE OR SWEAR ANY DECLARATION OR OATH TO TAKE ANY OTHER ACTION, INCLUDING WITHOUT LIMITATION COMPLETING ANY INTRA-GROUP [*assignment/license*] AND NAME AND ADDRESS CHANGES PENDING AT THE DATE OF THIS [*Assignment/License*], AS MAY BE REQUIRED BY OR WHICH MAY, IN THE REASONABLE OPINION OF THE [*Assignee/Licensee*], OTHERWISE BE NECESSARY FOR [*if all rights are being assigned,* VESTING ANY RIGHT, TITLE, AND INTEREST IN AND TO THE INTELLECTUAL PROPERTY IN THE ASSIGNEE *or if rights of use are being licensed* TRANSFERRING THE SPECIFIC LICENSE AND USE RIGHTS IN THE INTELLECTUAL PROPERTY TO THE LICENSEE]. THE COST OF SUCH ACTIONS SHALL BE ALLOCATED AS IS SET OUT IN THE PRINCIPAL AGREEMENT.

THIS DEED OF [*Assignment/License*] MAY BE EXECUTED IN ONE OR MORE COUNTERPARTS, EACH OF WHICH SHALL BE DEEMED AN ORIGINAL, AND WHICH TOGETHER SHALL CONSTITUTE THE SAME AGREEMENT.

THIS DEED OF [*Assignment/License*] AND ITS TERMS SHALL BE GOVERNED BY AND CONSTRUED IN ACCORDANCE WITH [*state/country*] LAW AND THE PARTIES SUBMIT TO THE NON-EXCLUSIVE JURISDICTION OF THE [*state/country*] COURTS IN RELATION TO ALL MATTERS ARISING OUT OF THIS ASSIGNMENT.

IN WITNESS WHEREOF THIS [*Assignment/License*] HAS BEEN EXECUTED BELOW BY OR ON BEHALF OF THE PARTIES.

THE SCHEDULE

[*list identifying information of the IP, such as title or name and application or registration number*]

ASSIGNOR/LICENSOR: [*Company Name*]

BY: [*signature*]

[*typed name*]

[*title*]

ASSIGNEE/LICENSEE: [*Company Name*]

BY: [*signature*]

[*typed name*]

[*title*]

CHAPTER 23

Transferring IP Rights # 3

Addendum to Unrecorded Assignment or License

THE LAWS OF MANY COUNTRIES require the recording of agreements to assign, license or otherwise transfer some or all rights in IP to another entity or individual. Failure to record can mean that the agreement will be deemed void by the legal forums in the particular country, and therefore unenforceable between the parties to the agreement. In addition, or sometimes alternatively, the agreement can be considered invalid as against third parties (someone who is not a party to the agreement). In either event, if commercial transactions have continued in relation to the IP rights transferred, the IP owner can end up losing the IP rights, or at least be unable to enforce exclusivity in them, because the IP owner will be deemed to have acquiesced in the unauthorized (i.e., infringing) use of the IP.

If business operations have continued AND you have an agreement that has not been recorded against your IP registrations, you need to determine whether you can immediately record it. You may be able to record the agreement with payment of a penalty fee, or you may have to execute a new agreement (assuming the other party will consent) and have it recorded. If you can still record the agreement, you may want to execute the Addendum to IP Transfer Agreement shown here in order to "close the gap" between the effective date of the transfer and the recordal date. This Addendum makes no modification of the initial IP Transfer Agreement, but simply requires full disclosure and transfer of IP rights that may be implied by law in the absence of recordal of the IP Transfer Agreement.

If the IP Transfer Agreement is an assignment, in which all property rights are transferred without reservation, the disclosures and transfers in this Addendum will be made FROM the former IP owner (assignor) TO the new IP owner (assignee). If the IP Transfer Agreement is a license or other agreement merely giving some property rights (e.g., the right to use the IP) but reserving ownership rights, the disclosures and transfers are made FROM the party who is licensed (authorized user) TO the IP owner (licensor). This form may be adapted for the particular situation of the two parties.

You should also consider an immediate survey of the markets to determine whether any third-party infringement is occurring and whether you need to take action. *The following form will not resolve a problem with a third-party infringer.* It is unlikely that a third-party infringer will quickly bow to your claimed IP rights if you have failed to record the agreement as required by law. You may need to consider other means of enforcement.

Addendum to IP Transfer Agreement

THIS ADDENDUM TO THE [*name of IP Transfer Agreement*], WHICH IS DATED [*date*] (HEREINAFTER "THE PRINCIPLE AGREEMENT"), SHALL TAKE EFFECT AS OF [*date*], BETWEEN [*name and address of assignor/licensor*], WHICH IS [*a/an*] [*description and nationality*] (HEREINAFTER THE ["*Assignor*"/ "*Licensor*"]), AND [*name and address of assignee/licensee*], WHICH IS [*a/an*] [*description and nationality*] (HEREINAFTER THE "ASSIGNEE"/ "LICENSEE"). THIS ADDENDUM IS MADE PURSUANT TO PARAGRAPH [*number*] OF THE PRINCIPLE AGREEMENT, AND IT IS INTENDED TO CLARIFY THE TERMS OF THE PRINCIPLE AGREEMENT WITH RESPECT TO [*country*].

COMMENT: The parties identified in the clause should be the same as the parties in the Principle Agreement, and they should also execute the Addendum. The words used to identify each party (e.g., assignor/assignee) should also be the same as the words used to refer to each one in the Principle Agreement. In the last sentence of the above clause, reference should be made to a relevant paragraph in the Principle Agreement that allows amendment or correction of the Agreement by the parties.

THE PARTIES ACKNOWLEDGE THAT THE [*Assignee/Licensee*] HAS BEEN OPERATING A BUSINESS IN [*country*] PURSUANT TO THE PRINCIPLE AGREEMENT EXECUTED WITH THE [*Assignor/Licensor*];

ACCORDINGLY, THE PARTIES AGREE TO BE BOUND BY THE FOLLOWING PROVISIONS:

1. THE PARTIES AGREE THAT THE [*Assignee's/Licensee's*] OPERATIONS IN [*country*] WILL CONTINUE IN ACCORDANCE WITH THE PRINCIPLE AGREEMENT, BY WHICH THE [*if assignment*, ASSIGNOR HAS TRANSFERRED TO THE ASSIGNEE ALL RIGHTS, TITLE AND INTEREST IN *or if license*, LICENSOR HAS TRANSFERRED THE RIGHT TO USE WITHIN *(country)*] ANY OR ALL OF THE INTELLECTUAL PROPERTY SET FORTH IN EXHIBIT A TO THIS ADDENDUM (HEREINAFTER REFERRED TO AS THE INTELLECTUAL PROPERTY). THE PARTIES FURTHER ACKNOWLEDGE THAT THEY ARE BOUND BY THE TERMS AND CONDITIONS OF THE PRINCIPLE AGREEMENT.

2. [*If assignment*, THE ASSIGNOR ACKNOWLEDGES AND AGREES THAT IT HAS ASSIGNED TO THE ASSIGNEE ALL RIGHTS AND INTEREST, INCLUDING GOOD WILL, IN THE INTELLECTUAL PROPERTY PURSUANT TO THE PRINCIPLE AGREEMENT. ALL USES OF THE INTELLECTUAL PROPERTY IN (*country*) SHALL INURE TO THE BENEFIT OF ASSIGNEE *or if license*, THE LICENSEE ACKNOWLEDGES AND AGREES THAT IT HAS ACQUIRED NO RIGHTS WHATSOEVER, WHETHER BY USAGE OR OTHERWISE, OVER THE LICENSOR'S INTELLECTUAL PROPERTY OTHER THAN THE LICENSING RIGHTS GRANTED PURSUANT TO THE PRINCIPLE AGREEMENT. ALL USES OF THE LICENSOR'S INTELLECTUAL PROPERTY BY THE LICENSEE SHALL INURE TO THE BENEFIT OF LICENSOR.]

3. [*If assignment*, THE ASSIGNOR ACKNOWLEDGES THAT THE ASSIGNEE HOLDS EXCLUSIVE RIGHT, TITLE, AND INTEREST IN AND TO THE INTELLECTUAL PROPERTY, AND THE ASSIGNOR AGREES THAT IT SHALL NOT AT ANY TIME ACT OR CAUSE ANY ACTION CONTESTING, IMPAIRING, OR TENDING TO IMPAIR ANY PART OF THE ASSIGNEE'S RIGHT, TITLE AND INTEREST, *or if license*, THE LICENSEE ACKNOWLEDGES THAT THE LICENSOR HOLDS EXCLUSIVE RIGHT, TITLE, AND INTEREST IN AND TO THE LICENSOR'S INTELLECTUAL PROPERTY, AND THE LICENSEE AGREES THAT IT SHALL NOT AT ANY TIME ACT OR CAUSE

ANY ACTION CONTESTING, IMPAIRING, OR TENDING TO IMPAIR ANY PART OF THE LICENSOR'S RIGHT, TITLE AND INTEREST.]

4. [*If assignment*, THE ASSIGNOR SHALL NOT IN ANY MANNER REPRESENT THAT IT HAS ANY OWNERSHIP IN THE INTELLECTUAL PROPERTY, *or if license* THE LICENSEE SHALL NOT IN ANY MANNER REPRESENT THAT IT HAS ANY OWNERSHIP IN THE LICENSOR'S INTELLECTUAL PROPERTY OR REGISTRATION THEREOF.]

5. IN THE EVENT THAT THE PRINCIPLE AGREEMENT IS SET ASIDE OR OTHERWISE INVALIDATED FOR ANY REASON WHATSOEVER, THIS ADDENDUM SHALL TERMINATE AT THE SAME TIME, AND THE PARTIES SHALL COMPLY FULLY WITH THE TERMINATION PROVISIONS OF THE PRINCIPLE AGREEMENT.

6. THE [*Assignor/Licensee*] AGREES TO COMPLETE, SIGN, AND FILE ALL DOCUMENTS AND AGREEMENTS NECESSARY TO COMPLETE THE REGISTRATION OF THE PRINCIPLE AGREEMENT IN [*country*].

7. [*If license, include* THE LICENSEE WARRANTS THAT IT HAS USED THE INTELLECTUAL PROPERTY ONLY WITHIN THE PROVISIONS OF THE PRINCIPLE AGREEMENT AND THAT IT HAS NOT APPLIED, REGISTERED, OR USED ANY INTELLECTUAL PROPERTY IDENTICAL OR SIMILAR TO THE INTELLECTUAL PROPERTY EXCEPT WITHIN THE PROVISIONS OF THE PRINCIPLE AGREEMENT. MOREOVER, THE LICENSEE WARRANTS THAT IT HAS NOT TAKEN ANY ACTION THAT WOULD OR MIGHT INVALIDATE OR DILUTE THE INTELLECTUAL PROPERTY REGISTRATIONS OR TITLE TO THE LICENSOR'S INTELLECTUAL PROPERTY.]

8. [*If license, include* THE LICENSEE DECLARES THAT ANY REGISTRATION OR USAGE OF THE INTELLECTUAL PROPERTY HAS NOT AND WILL NOT CREATE JOINT RIGHTS OF OWNERSHIP BETWEEN THE PARTIES IN THE INTELLECTUAL PROPERTY. THE LICENSEE HEREBY WAIVES ANY AND ALL CLAIMS THAT IT COULD ASSERT IN THE INTELLECTUAL PROPERTY OTHER THAN BASED ON ITS LICENSING RIGHTS GRANTED BY, AND EXERCISED IN COMPLIANCE WITH, THE PRINCIPLE AGREEMENT. THE LICENSEE WILL NOT ATTEMPT TO VARY OR CANCEL ANY REGISTRATIONS OF THE INTELLECTUAL PROPERTY IN (*country*) OR ANY OTHER COUNTRY, NOR ASSIST ANY OTHER PERSON OR ENTITY TO DO SO.]

9. [*If assignment, include* THE ASSIGNOR SHALL NOT ATTEMPT TO CAUSE THE PRINCIPAL AGREEMENT TO BE SET ASIDE OR OTHERWISE INVALIDATED MERELY ON THE GROUND THAT THE PRINCIPLE AGREEMENT HAS NOT BEEN RECORDED AGAINST THE INTELLECTUAL PROPERTY.]

10. ANY BREACH OR OTHER VIOLATION OF THIS ADDENDUM WILL RESULT IN IMMEDIATE TERMINATION OF THE ADDENDUM AND THE PRINCIPLE AGREEMENT, UNLESS THE BREACH OR VIOLATION IS WAIVED BY THE OTHER PARTY IN WRITING. THE PARTIES ACKNOWLEDGE THAT ANY BREACH OR OTHER VIOLATION OF THIS ADDENDUM WILL RESULT IN THE DILUTION OR DESTRUCTION OF VALUABLE RIGHTS IN THE INTELLECTUAL PROPERTY, REPUTATION, AND GOODWILL AND WILL CAUSE GREAT AND IRREPARABLE HARM TO THE OTHER PARTY. THESE DAMAGES WILL BE IMPRACTICAL OR IMPOSSIBLE TO MEASURE, AND THEREFORE MONETARY DAMAGES WILL NOT BE ADEQUATE COMPENSATION FOR THE HARM. THEREFORE, REGARDLESS OF WHETHER THE BREACH OR OTHER VIOLATION OCCURS BEFORE OR AFTER TERMINATION OF THIS ADDENDUM, THE [*Assignor/Licensee*] ACKNOWLEDGES THAT THE OTHER PARTY SHALL BE ENTITLED TO APPLY FOR AND RECEIVE FROM ANY COURT OF COMPETENT JURISDICTION A TEMPORARY RESTRAINING ORDER, PRELIMINARY INJUNCTION, AND/OR PERMANENT INJUNCTION WITHOUT HAVING TO PROVE DAMAGES OR POST ANY BOND OR OTHER SECURITY, AND THE [*Assignor/Licensee*] SHALL STIPULATE TO BEING

ENJOINED FROM FURTHER BREACH OR OTHER VIOLATION OF THIS ADDENDUM AND/OR FURTHER INFRINGEMENT OR IMPAIRMENT OF SUCH RIGHTS. THIS RELIEF SHALL BE IN ADDITION TO AND NOT IN SUBSTITUTION OF ANY OTHER REMEDIES AVAILABLE.

11. [*If license, include* THE LICENSEE WARRANTS THAT IT IS IN FULL COMPLIANCE WITH ALL LAWS GOVERNING TAXATION, LICENSING, IMMIGRATION, LABOR, AND BUSINESS OPERATIONS.]

12. TO THE EXTENT THAT PROVISIONS IN THE PRINCIPLE AGREEMENT CONFLICT WITH PROVISIONS IN THIS ADDENDUM, THE PROVISIONS IN THIS ADDENDUM ARE DEEMED TO BE CONTROLLING.

13. IF ANY MATERIAL PROVISION OF THIS ADDENDUM SHOULD BE HELD INVALID, VOID, OR OTHERWISE UNENFORCEABLE BY A COURT OF COMPETENT JURISDICTION, EITHER PARTY SHALL HAVE THE RIGHT TO TERMINATE THIS ADDENDUM IMMEDIATELY.

IN WITNESS WHEREOF, THE PARTIES HAVE CAUSED THIS ADDENDUM TO BE EXECUTED AS OF THE DAY AND YEAR FIRST WRITTEN AT THE BEGINNING OF THIS ADDENDUM.

ASSIGNOR/LICENSOR: [*Company Name*]

BY: [*signature*]

[*typed name*]

[*title*]

ASSIGNEE/LICENSEE: [*Company Name*]

BY: [*signature*]

[*typed name*]

[*title*]

CHAPTER 24

Glossary

FOR A COMPREHENSIVE LISTING of international trade, economic, banking, legal and shipping terms, we recommend the *Dictionary of International Trade, 8th Edition,* also by World Trade Press.

For definitions of various intellectual properties, refer to Chapter 1, Intellectual Property (IP) Basics. For details about international treaties and unions, refer to Chapter 11, IP Rights in Multinational Forums.

ABRIDGEMENT (copyright) See DERIVATIVE WORK.

ABSTRACT (PATENT) A summary included with a patent application and generally placed at the front of a registered patent to describe briefly the nature, structure, and purpose of the invention.

AFRICAN REGIONAL INTELLECTUAL PROPERTY ORGANIZATION (ARIPO) An agreement between the African states of Kenya, Malawi, and Sudan to cooperate and coordinate in the registration of IP rights.

AGENCY A relationship between two parties, the first of whom (the agent) represents, acts for, and binds the other (the principal) in accordance with the oral or written instruction of the principal. In some countries, an agency can be created only by a written agreement or power of attorney entered into by a principal and agent. See AGENT; PRINCIPAL; POWER OF ATTORNEY.

AGENT An individual or legal entity authorized to act on behalf of another individual or legal entity (the principal). An agent's authorized actions will bind the principal, such as when the owner of a book protected by copyright authorizes another person to sell the rights to publish the book to a third party. Within the intellectual property laws of many countries, "agent" is given a special meaning as a person or company that has qualified under the law to file for the protection of intellectual property rights. These "agents" need not be qualified as lawyers, but they must usually have technical, scientific, or legal training. See AGENT; PRINCIPAL; POWER OF ATTORNEY.

ALL RIGHTS RESERVED (COPYRIGHT) A term that appears in many copyright notices for purposes of securing protection under the Buenos Aires Convention, by which the United States and Latin American countries agreed to reciprocal protection rights in copyrighted works. This term is of little significance today because other international treaties have superceded the Buenos Aires Convention, and these other treaties do not require use of this term.

AMENDMENT An addition, deletion, or other change in a legal document or legislation.

ANDEAN GROUP An alliance of Latin American countries, also known as the Andean Pact. The Group was formed in 1969 to promote regional economic integration, including integration of intellectual property rights, among medium-sized countries within the Andean region. Members include Bolivia, Colombia, Ecuador, Peru, and Venezuela. Address: Andean Group: Avenida Paseo de la Republica 3895; Casilla Postal 18-1177; Lima 18, Peru; tel: + (14) 41-4212; telex: 20104 PE; fax + (14) 42-0911.

ANNUITY (patent)) A fee imposed by law to maintain the validity of a patent registration. If an annuity payment is not made timely, the patent may lapse.

ANTHOLOGY (copyright) See COMPILATION WORKS.

ANTICIPATED (patent) An invention that is so similar to an earlier patent that it is not considered to be novel, and therefore cannot be registered as a patent. An invention may be anticipated by the existence of prior art or public use or display that precedes in time the filing of the patent. See PRIOR ART, and PUBLICATION.

ANTICIPATION (patent) SEE PRIOR ART.

ANTI-COMPETITION AGREEMENT See COVENANT NOT TO COMPETE.

ANTI-SHELVING CLAUSE A clause in a license agreement by which the licensee agrees to use commercially the intellectual property rights licensed within a stated period of time and not to merely "put the licensed rights on a shelf." This clause places an affirmative duty on the licensee to use or lose the rights to the license.

ANTI-TRUST LAW A statute that prohibits business operations intentionally aimed at unfairly dominating a market such that in practice a monopoly results, and further prohibiting business arrangements between companies by which they cooperatively engage in practices that result in the restriction or restraint of free trade, such as price fixing or bid rigging. Example: A company that shares its trade secret with only one of its competitors pursuant to an agreement by which the two companies plan to cooperate and corner the market is likely to be in violation of antitrust laws.

APEC See ASIA PACIFIC ECONOMIC COOPERATION.

APPELLATIONS OF ORIGIN Name of geographical place used in connection with products or services sold in commerce and originating from that location. Appellations are not considered trademarks because they are used to indicate a place of origin, not to distinctly identify a trader's goods or services.

ARCHIVAL COPY (copyright) An authorized copy of software made by the party who uses the software. Parties who "buy" software are actually purchasing a restricted license to use it, and they are not permitted to copy it, with one exception: a single copy may be made and kept in a secure place for purposes of having a copy to ensure against damage or loss of the original. This right is protected by law in some countries (for example, the US Computer Software Protection Act) and is also granted by most software program license agreements. If the software is transferred or destroyed, the archival copy must also be transferred or destroyed.

ARIPO See AFRICAN REGIONAL INTELLECTUAL PROPERTY ORGANIZATION.

ARM'S LENGTH TRANSACTION A transaction in which both parties have similar bargaining power during the negotiation and finalization of the arrangement and in which the parties exchange consideration of equivalent or nearly equivalent value. For example: an assignment of IP rights between unrelated parties is an arm's length transaction if the assignor receives valuable consideration based on the assessed value of the IP rights and the assignee gains IP rights that are in fact worth the consideration paid.

ART see Prior Art

ASEAN See ASSOCIATION OF SOUTHEAST ASIAN NATIONS.

ASIA PACIFIC ECONOMIC COOPERATION (APEC) An informal forum in which ministerial leaders of Asia Pacific countries gather for discussion of economic issues that affect their region and their specific countries. Members include Australia, Brunei, Canada, China, Hong Kong S.A.R., Indonesia, Japan, Korea (South), Malaysia, Philippines, Singapore, Thailand, Taiwan, and the United States. Address of the Secretariat: 438 Alexander Road 19-01; Singapore 0315; tel: + 276 1880; fax: + 276 3602.

ASSIGNEE A person or legal entity who is granted a property ownership right previously held by another party (the assignor). See ASSIGNOR; ASSIGNMENT.

ASSIGNMENT A transfer of property ownership rights, including title, interest, and benefits in the property, from the owner (the assignor) to another individual or legal entity (the assignee), who then becomes the owner of the property rights. See ASSIGNEE; ASSIGNOR. See also LICENSE.

ASSIGNOR The owner of a property right who transfers that ownership right to another party (the assignee). See ASSIGNEE; ASSIGNMENT.

ASSOCIATION OF SOUTHEAST ASIAN NATIONS (ASEAN) A trade and economic pact formed in 1967 to promote political, economic, and social cooperation among its members. Members: Brunei, Cambodia, Indonesia, Malaysia, Philippines, Singapore, and Thailand. Address: ASEAN, Jalan Sisingamangaraja; PO Box 2072; Jakarta, Indonesia; tel: + (21) 712 272.

BELGIUM, NETHERLANDS, LUXEMBOURG ECONOMIC UNION (BENELUX) An economic and political cooperation pact created to encourage economic activity among the three member nations, including a central Registry for trade marks, service marks, copyrights, and patents. Address: BENELUX, 39 rue de la Regence; 1000 Brussels, Belgium; tel: + (02) 519-38-11; fax + (02) 513-42-06.

BENELUX See BELGIUM, NETHERLANDS, LUXEMBOURG ECONOMIC UNION.

BERNE CONVENTION See INTERNATIONAL UNION FOR THE PROTECTION OF LITERARY AND ARTISTIC WORKS.

BEST EDITION (copyright) The highest quality version of a work protected by copyright. Most copyright registration laws require the party seeking copyright to deposit with the registry the best edition at the time the application for registration or deposit is made.

BEST MODE (patent) A disclosure of an invention that is sufficient in detail to allow a person of ordinary skill in the same technology to build or develop it. When filing a patent, the inventor must disclose the best mode because the inventor is granted a monopoly over the invention, but only in exchange for improving public knowledge of the technology.

BONA FIDE In or with good faith, honesty, and sincerity. A bona fide trade mark application, for example, is one that has been made by a trade mark owner who has actual and sincere intent and belief that he or she will use the mark in connection with the commercial sale of goods and that the mark is not an infringement on the rights of any other IP owner.

BUENOS AIRES CONVENTION See ALL RIGHTS RESERVED.

CAUTIONARY NOTICE A notice published in a public or legal newspaper or other periodical commonly circulated for purposes of informing the public at large about protected rights in a trademark or service mark. A cautionary notice is most commonly used when a country has no laws protecting trademarks or service marks. It may also be published to alert the public to infringement activities and to identify distinctive features of the IP belonging to the rightful owner.

CEASE AND DESIST A letter sent (usually by legal counsel) to notify a person or company that they are quite possibly infringing on the IP rights of the sender or sender's client.

CLAIM (patent) A statement in a patent application that describes the invention in the precise and formal language required by the patent registry. The claims contained in a patent will determine the scope of the patent and the breadth of protection given, but if claims are too broad there is a likelihood that the invention may have common characteristics with prior art and therefore cannot be patented. A patent application will usually contain a number of claims that define different aspects of the invention. An INDEPENDENT CLAIM is one that describes the invention without reference to any other claims. A DEPENDENT CLAIM is one that refers to other claims.

CLASSIFICATION (mark) Numbered categories of goods and services based on their type and used for limiting the scope of trademark or service mark protection to a particular specification of goods or services.

CLASSIFICATION (patent) Numbered categories of patents based on the type of invention and used for indexing and finding registered and pending patents. In general, a classification is assigned by a Registry because of the complexity and importance of classifications. For example, in the US, an invention may be classified within one or more of 66,000 classes.

COMBINATION IN RESTRAINT OF TRADE See RESTRAINT OF TRADE.

COMMUNITY TRADEMARK A trademark or service mark filed and registered in a single Registry established pursuant to the European Union (formerly the European Community) and protected in all of the European Union member nations. The Registry is called the Office of Harmonization of the Internal Market and is located in Alicante, Spain.

COMPILATION WORKS A work consisting of pre-existing works and materials that are chosen, collected, and presented in a novel fashion.

COMPULSORY LICENSE See LICENSE.

CONFIDENTIALITY AGREEMENT An employment agreement in which the employee agrees to hold in confidence all trade secrets learned during the employment. It is preferable to have a written confidentiality agreement because proof can be more easily established in court in the event that the employee breaches the agreement. Such an agreement can be implied by a court if there is proof that a duty of trust or confidentiality existed during the employment. See related definition at NONDISCLOSURE AGREEMENT.

CONSIDERATION An item of value passed from one contracting party to the other as an inducement to make the contract, and without which the contract is not binding. For example, the owner of an IP right may transfer that right to another person, and that transfer will be considered valid provided valuable consideration has been received in return.

CONVENTION FOR THE PROTECTION OF INDUSTRIAL PROPERTY See PARIS CONVENTION.

CONVENTION FOR THE PROTECTION OF PRODUCERS OF PHONOGRAMS AGAINST UNAUTHORIZED DUPLICATION OF THEIR PHONOGRAMS A multinational agreement created in 1971 by member nations to harmonize protection of audio reproductions, including any material in which sound can be fixed, reproduced, and communicated.

CONVENTION ON THE MEANS OF PROHIBITING AND PREVENTING THE ILLICIT IMPORT, EXPORT, AND TRANSFER OF OWNERSHIP OF CULTURAL PROPERTY A multinational agreement signed in 1970 by member nations to recognize the rights of countries to their cultural property and to harmonize the treatment of illegal activities related to removing cultural property from its homeland.

COPY (copyright) A copy refers to a tangible form of an expression that is retained for any period of time, regardless of how brief. Examples include photocopies, audio and visual tape recordings, programs and documents on computers and diskettes, and programs held in computer memory. The right to make a copy is exclusive to the owner of the copyright.

COPYRIGHT Exclusive rights in a work of authorship that is original, conceived with creativity, and fixed in a tangible medium.

COPYRIGHT NOTICE See NOTICE OF IP RIGHTS.

COVENANT NOT TO COMPETE A contractual provision by which one party promises not to compete against the other for a specific time or within a specific region. For example, a covenant may be included within a contract for employment to prevent an employee from taking a job with a competing company or within a contract for the sale of a business to prevent the seller from competing with the purchaser of the business. The covenant must be restricted, such as by time or geographical location, to be enforceable, and usually the purpose of the covenant is to protect the trade secrets of the company. In some places, covenants not to compete in employment contracts are prohibited by law and cannot be enforced, but such covenants in contracts for the sale of a business are usually enforced.

CREDIT LINE A spoken or written statement of acknowledgment used in connection with an IP work to identify the author or creator of that work. If the work is created by one author or creator, the credit line will simply identify the same. If the work of other authors is also incorporated, several credit lines are usually included to indicate use by permission, and the permission to use is commonly conditioned on the inclusion of a credit line to show ownership and source of the work.

CROSS-LICENSING A license arrangement by which patent owners agree to cooperate in the use of each other's inventions for producing goods that use several different inventions without having to pay royalties to each other.

CYBER-SQUATTING The bad faith registration of an Internet domain name that is similar or identical to the trademark of a well-known company. Such a registration is usually made for purposes of selling that name back to the company. Most Internet service providers now have procedures for cancellation of these names, and a growing number of countries are enacting laws by which companies can seek injunctions and damages against cyber-squatters.

CTM See COMMUNITY TRADEMARK

DERIVATIVE WORK A new work that is based on a prior work already protected by copyright.

DESIGN PATENT A patent for a design that is a nonfunctional part of a functional manufactured article.

DILUTION (MARK) A decrease in the value, reputation, and distinctiveness of a mark because a competitor's use of a same or similar mark tends to taint indirectly the mark's reputation or reduce its distinctiveness. For example, the use of the trademark IBM on a pornography magazine is a dilution of the mark. Dilution is not a direct infringement, and therefore many countries have enacted anti-dilution laws to provide remedies to companies that are faced with this situation.

DOCTRINE OF EQUIVALENTS (patent) A test developed and used by courts to decide whether a patent is being infringed based on whether another invention alleged to be infringing does the same work in substantially the same way to achieve the same result as the prior patented invention. See READ ON DOCTRINE.

DUE DILIGENCE (INVESTIGATION) The attention and care given to discover and evaluate facts in support of a statement.

EUROPEAN PATENT CONVENTION (EPC) An agreement between European nations to centralize and standardize patent law and procedure by establishing a central office (European Patent Office) for patent filings among the member nations. Once granted, the patent matures into individual patents—one in each country. Address: European Patent Office; Erhardtstrasse 27; 8000 Munich 2; Germany; tel: (89) 2399-0; Fax (89) 2399-4465.

EUROPEAN PATENT OFFICE See EUROPEAN PATENT CONVENTION.

FAIR USE (copyright) An exception to the exclusive rights accorded to an owner of a copyright by which a third party can use the copyrighted work without the owner's permission and without threat of liability for infringement. A third party may copy, restate, or otherwise use work (within limits) that is subject to copyright in connection with one of the following: scholarly or research activity, critique or commentary on the work (including parodies), news reporting, or teaching.

FIRST SALE DOCTRINE (copyright) With a few exceptions, a copyright owner's rights over a legal copy of a work end when the work is first sold. The purchaser is free to destroy, sell, lend, or otherwise dispose of the work in any manner whatsoever. However, the purchaser cannot make additional copies of the work, because that is an infringement of the copyright. Exceptions to this rule are made by law, and therefore they vary from country to country. For example, countries that have enacted computer software protection statutes typically prohibit the purchaser of a computer program from later renting or otherwise lending a copy to the public for any commercial benefit.

FIRST TO FILE LAW A law that gives IP rights to the party who first files an application to register the rights, regardless of whether the party was first to use the IP. Sometimes referred to as "race statutes," these laws award a party who is first in line at the registry without accounting for the rights of a party who has already used the IP, whether that use has occurred within or outside of the country.

FIRST TO INVENT LAW (patent) A law that awards IP rights in a patentable invention to the party who can prove that he or she was first to conceive the invention. If another party applies to register the patent first, the party who claims to have conceived the invention first may file an interference or opposition against the application to reclaim the IP rights.

FIRST TO USE LAW (marks) A law that awards IP rights in a trademark or service mark to the party who can prove that he or she used the mark first. In some countries, first use is recognized only if the use was made within the country. The laws of other countries acknowledge IP rights in a mark first used outside the country, particularly if the mark has become well-known in other jurisdictions.

FREELANCE Persons or companies that create works that are commissioned by or sold to publishers of such works.

GATT See GENERAL AGREEMENT ON TARIFFS AND TRADE.

GENERAL AGREEMENT ON TARIFFS AND TRADE (GATT) A multilateral trade treaty that has been negotiated by member countries in progressive meetings beginning in 1987 and continuing every few years. The major goal of GATT is to harmonize trade requirements and reduce trade friction and barriers among the member nations. Included within GATT are provisions related to the recognition and treatment of IP rights among the member nations. The GATT treaty has established the World Trade Organization (WTO) as the regulatory body for enforcing compliance. The GATT provisions for protection of intellectual property are contained within the Trade Related Aspects of Intellectual Property Rights (TRIPS) agreement.

GRANT OF RIGHTS (copyright) The assignment of all copyright rights from the author to a publisher in advance of publication and in exchange for payment or future royalties.

IDENTIFYING MATERIAL (copyright) A deposit of part of a work or a representation of the entire work with the Copyright Office, which is permitted in lieu of depositing the entire work whenever the work is difficult to deposit as a whole.

INDUSTRIAL DRAWINGS Schematic, process, and other drawings that portray an industrial process or manufacturing machinery.

INDUSTRIAL PROPERTY A form of intellectual property rights, commonly referring to IP rights in property developed and used specifically for commercial application, such as patents, trademarks, trade secrets, and appellations of origin.

INDUSTRIAL SECRET A trade secret that is mechanical, technological, scientific, or technical in nature, such as a secret process, machine, formula, manufacturing method, or unregistered industrial design. Some countries, such as the US, treat industrial secrets the same as trade secrets, affording them protection only if they have not been publicly disclosed. Other countries, such as France, Germany, and Japan, make a distinction for industrial secrets, affording them protection even if the general process or method related to the industrial secret is patented or otherwise publicly known. For example, the process of making ceramics is widely known in Japan, but factors that make ceramics a commercial success (product mixture, glaze mixture, firing temperature and time, and so forth) may be protected as industrial secrets.

INTANGIBLE PROPERTY A type of property that can be owned and transferred, but that is not tangible because one cannot observe it with any of one's senses. A book can be seen, held, and read, but the exclusive ownership right to the intellectual creation from which the presentation of the material was derived cannot be seen, held, or read. The ownership right may be represented by a registration notice, but the copyright itself is intangible.

INTELLECTUAL PROPERTY (IP) Intangible property rights in works created by a person's intellect. These rights can be protected if the works are novel, unique, or otherwise original, and they include copyrights, trademarks, service marks, patents, designs, trade secrets, traditional indigenous knowledge, and appellations of origin.

INTER ALIA Among other things.

INTERFERENCE An administrative procedure for determining patent rights when two patents or pending patents claim the same invention.

INTERNATIONAL CONVENTION FOR THE PROTECTION OF PERFORMERS, PRODUCERS OF PHONOGRAMS, AND BROADCASTING ORGANIZATIONS A 1961 multinational agreement intended to identify and harmonize among the member states the laws and legal treatment related to the IP rights of performers, phonogram producers, and broadcasters in live, taped, and recorded performances.

INTERNATIONAL UNION FOR THE PROTECTION OF INDUSTRIAL PROPERTY (PARIS CONVENTION) Founded in 1883, amended periodically, and today administered by the WIPO, this international agreement was intended to harmonize national patent and trademark treatment and to prevent discrimination against cross-border registrants and users of industrial property.

INTERNATIONAL UNION FOR THE PROTECTION OF LITERARY AND ARTISTIC WORKS (BERNE CONVENTION) An international agreement that was originally concluded at Berne, Switzerland, in 1886 by representatives of participating countries to provide for the recognition and treatment of rights in intellectual property among the signatories. The member countries agreed to protect copyrighted works by foreign authors in the same fashion as works by national authors and to extend copyright protection in a work for at least the life of the author plus 50 years. All countries that are signatory to GATT must also adhere to the Berne Convention. Also known as the Berne Convention or Berne Union, it has been revised periodically (Stockholm 1967 and Paris 1971) and it is now administered by the World Intellectual Property Organization (WIPO). See WORLD INTELLECTUAL PROPERTY ORGANIZATION.

LICENSE An agreement by which the owner of intellectual property rights (the licensor) authorizes another party (the licensee) to use the intellectual property in exchange for royalties or other compensation and with the restriction that the owner retains full ownership rights in the intellectual property. A license may grant exclusive use for a particular time, territory, or trade, or it may be nonexclusive.

A SHRINK-WRAP LICENSE is an agreement by which software publishers limit use of the software by the consumer. The license agreement is usually enclosed within the packaging so it cannot be read until after the software is purchased, but it must allow for a refund if the consumer refuses to accept the terms of the license.

A SITE LICENSE is granted by software publishers to a company that installs a number of copies of the software on several individual computers. The site license generally provides for a reduced rate for each copy of the software needed. In some countries, the law or the courts may impose against the owner of IP a COMPULSORY LICENSE, under which the owner must allow use of the IP by certain licensees and under certain conditions in exchange for compensation to the owner. For example, a compulsory license will arise by US law if, after a nondramatic musical composition is recorded and distributed to the public, the copyright owner refuses to permit any other company to record the music for distribution to the general public for private use. In such event, the law compels the copyright owner to grant a license, and royalties are determined by the amount provided in the statute. See the related term ASSIGNMENT.

LICENSEE See LICENSE.

LICENSOR See LICENSE.

MADRID CONVENTION ON INTERNATIONAL REGISTRATION OF TRADEMARKS An international agreement joined by various countries by which their nationals can submit registrations obtained within their own country to a central registry for recognition in all member countries. Each member country may accept or reject the mark registration.

MARKING The inclusion of a symbol or term on or in connection with material that is subject to an IP right. For example, © may be used in connection with material that is protected by copyright, ™ or ® may be used in connection with marks that are registered as trademarks or service marks, and "Patent Pending" or "Pat. Pend." may be used in connection with materials that are subject to patent protection. These marks serve to place the public on notice that the materials constitute protected IP and are subject to private rights, but they have little meaning in most countries today because marking is not a requirement of the international treaties that are intended to harmonize the treatment of IP rights. Some countries continue to enforce marking laws, however, and therefore local requirements should be checked before marketing IP protected items across a border.

NAFTA See NORTH AMERICAN FREE TRADE AGREEMENT.

NICE AGREEMENT See CLASSIFICATION (trademark). See Chapter 11, IP Rights in Multinational Forums.

NONDISCLOSURE AGREEMENT An agreement between a company and another party by which each party agrees not to disclose trade and industrial secrets to any other person or company without authority. Violation of a nondisclosure agreement gives rise to an action for breach of contract against the disclosing party. If any infringement has occurred because of the violation, the intellectual property owner can also sue to enjoin the commercial use of the intellectual property disclosed and to recover money damages.

NORTH AMERICAN FREE TRADE AGREEMENT (NAFTA) An agreement between Canada, Mexico, and the United States finalized in 1993 to eliminate trade barriers among these countries. NAFTA requires these countries to make certain provisions and to establish certain forums for the protection of IP rights in cross-border transactions.

NOTICE OF IP RIGHTS A notice that is displayed on or in connection with works, products, or other items that are protected as intellectual property. This notice is intended to make all third parties aware of your IP rights. Their knowledge will be implied if you have used the notice, and therefore they may be found to have acted in bad faith by copying and using your IP in commerce, even if they claim no actual knowledge of your rights. In some countries, a notice is mandatory and you may lose IP rights if you do not have the notice displayed. In most countries, use of a notice prior to registration of your IP rights gives rise to fines or other legal proceedings against you, and even to loss of your IP rights. The proper notice to be used varies from country to country. For example, some countries require the owner of a trademark to display the mark with the notice ®, some countries require use of ™, and other countries have no notice requirement at all.

PARIS CONVENTION A treaty by which the member countries have agreed to harmonize their treatment of various types of industrial property rights, including trademarks, service marks, and patents.

PARTY (to a transaction) An individual, group, or entity that represents one side of a question, contract, or dispute.

PASSING OFF DOCTRINE (mark) An act in bad faith by a party who uses a mark in such a way as to represent to consumers or the public at large that the party owns or has authority to use the mark when such is not the case, resulting in confusion as to the source of goods or services. This doctrine has been developed primarily in the courts to protect owners of trademarks against bad faith usage of their marks that may not qualify as statutory infringement. For example, Company A uses a trade name in small print to identify its distributorship, and that trade name is an identical or similar copy of the trademark of Company B. There is no direct infringement because the use of a trade name is distinct from the use of a trademark. However, Company B can sue for passing off on the ground that use of the trade name is likely to confuse consumers and the public at large and Company A intentionally selected the name to cause confusion.

PATENT The exclusive right granted to an inventor of a nonobvious and novel invention to use and develop the invention and to prevent others from using it.

PATENT COOPERATION TREATY (PCT) An international agreement signed by member states in 1970 to provide for efficient and uniform patent protection. A single PCT application must be filed with a central registry, and then national filings must be made in each member country.

PCT See PATENT COOPERATION TREATY.

PIRACY Any activity undertaken with intent to infringe on another's IP right or to acquire that right improperly.

PLAGIARISM (copyright) The deliberate copying of another's original expression or creative ideas and passing it off as one's own. Most plagiarism is not a violation of law, but merely an ethical or moral issue. However, if plagiarism is committed for commercial gain, it can be the basis of an infringement action.

POWER OF ATTORNEY A written or oral authorization by which one individual or entity (the principal) authorizes another (the agent) to perform stated actions on the principal's behalf. For example, a principal may sign a special power of attorney authorizing an agent to file an initial application to register a specific IP right or a general power of attorney authorizing an agent to file, process, and renew one or more IP rights.

PRINCIPAL An individual or legal entity that authorizes another individual or legal entity (the agent) to act on the principal's behalf. The principal will be bound by the agent's actions, provided such actions are within the scope of the authorization given.

See AGENCY; AGENT; POWER OF ATTORNEY.

PRIOR ART (patent) All inventions conceived and made public prior to the filing of a new patent application. A prior art reference is any written description or discussion of prior art that has been published—including in a periodical, prior patent application or registration, or other publication in any language printed anywhere in the world—prior to the filing of a new patent application.

PROVISIONAL PATENT A patent application allowed in some countries by which an inventor may file an interim application that sufficiently discloses the invention but that contains only part of the information required for a complete application. The provisional patent is not examined for its substantive content until a complete application is filed. It also has limited validity, and the application must therefore be revised and completed within a specific time or it will be deemed abandoned.

PUBLIC DOMAIN The rights and interests of the public at large, as opposed to the private rights and interests of an individual or company. Works and creations that enter the public domain are no longer the property of a particular private individual or company, and they no longer fall within the protection of intellectual property laws against infringement.

PUBLICATION A work, invention, or creation that has been displayed or distributed to the public at large is considered to have been published. For most types of IP rights, the rights must be secured prior to publication.

RACE STATUTE See FIRST TO FILE.

READ ON DOCTRINE A test developed and used by courts to determine whether a patent is being infringed based on whether the literal language of the patent claims are similar or identical to each element of the device or process alleged to be an infringement.

RESTRAINT OF TRADE A business activity that limits the free flow of commerce, such as an arrangement by which two businesses agree to fix prices (price fixing agreement), by which trade is restricted by geographical region (territorial restriction agreements) or by which a consumer must purchase one product as a condition of buying another product (tying arrangement). See related definitions at ANTI-TRUST LAWS and at COVENANT NOT TO COMPETE.

REVERSE ENGINEERING An examination of a product to find out its components and the method of manufacture. If IP is protected solely as a trade secret and another company through reverse engineering is able to determine the components and method of manufacture, the trade secret is considered public domain and cannot be protected. However, if the IP has been patented or copyrighted, then it remains protected regardless of discoveries made by means of reverse engineering.

SERVICE MARK A mark similar to a trademark, but a service mark protects services while a trademark protects goods (although the word "trademark" is often used to refer to marks that protect services, too.)

SHOP RIGHTS An employer's right to license its employee's invention when the employee has conceived and developed that invention within the scope of his or her employment. The employer's license is royalty-free, irrevocable, nonexclusive, and nontransferable. The employee retains ownership rights in the patent, including the right to issue nonexclusive licenses to other companies. Shop rights arise in the absence of an employment contract by which the employee has assigned all inventions to the employer.

SHRINK-WRAP LICENSE See LICENSE.

SITE LICENSE See LICENSE.

STATE OF THE ART The current technology, processes, standards, machinery, and other similar parameters existing as of a given moment in time for any particular industry or trade.

TANGIBLE MEDIUM OF EXPRESSION (copyright) A physical form or representation that can be perceived, reproduced, or otherwise communicated and that is more than transitory in duration. In most countries that offer copyright protection, a work is protected from the time it is reduced to a tangible medium of expression. Examples include paper, computer disk drives or diskettes, film, audio and video tape, and mediums for sculpture.

TRADE DESIGNS A shape, pattern, or other ornament applied to goods by an industrial process merely for appeal.

TRADE DRESS Exclusive rights claimed in the presentation of a product or service, such as the type, color, form, etc. of packaging, signage or sales materials.

TRADE NAME The name used to distinguish a business from other companies.

TRADE RELATED ASPECTS OF INTELLECTUAL PROPERTY RIGHTS (TRIPS) See GENERAL AGREEMENT ON TARIFFS AND TRADE (GATT).

TRADE SECRETS Creative works and compilations of information that give the creator or compiler a competitive advantage over other traders.

TRADEMARK An exclusive right to use a mark connected with goods and/or services in commerce for purposes of identifying and distinguishing the provider of the goods or services from other traders.

TRIPS See GENERAL AGREEMENT ON TARIFFS AND TRADE (GATT).

TYING ARRANGEMENT See RESTRAINT OF TRADE.

UNFAIR COMPETITION Commercial activities that are dishonest or fraudulent against the activities of other traders, such as fraudulent advertising, counterfeiting, and similar illegal trade practices.

UNIVERSAL COPYRIGHT CONVENTION (U.C.C.) An international treaty first signed in 1952 for protection of copyrights among the member nations. The members agree to offer national treatment to any work first published in any member country or by a national of any member country. The formalities that must be met to confer copyright protection on a work is merely the inclusion of the following notice: "© [year of first publication] [author's name]." This Convention applies in member countries that have not yet acceded to GATT and the Berne Convention.

UTILITY MODELS An exclusive right recognized in some countries to protect technical inventions from use by third parties. The novelty requirements are usually less strict for this type of right, and the term of the right is shorter.

UTILITY PATENT Most patents are utility patents, which refers to the requirement that the invention must be useful in an industrial or manufacturing application.

VALUE ADDED TAX (VAT) A tax based on the value added to a product at each stage of production and applied to foreign transactions. These taxes can also be applied to value added by services to a document or property right.

VOID AB INITIO Having no effect from the time of initiation. An IP right that is registered in bad faith may be considered void ab initio.

WIPO See WORLD INTELLECTUAL PROPERTY ORGANIZATION.

WORLD INTELLECTUAL PROPERTY ORGANIZATION (WIPO) A specialized agency of the United Nations that seeks to promote international cooperation in the protection of intellectual property, administers various treaties and unions of member countries, and offers arbitration forums for resolution of cross-border disputes among nationals of member countries.

WORLD TRADE ORGANIZATION (WTO) See GENERAL AGREEMENT ON TARIFFS AND TRADE (GATT).

WTO See GENERAL AGREEMENT ON TARIFFS AND TRADE (GATT).

CHAPTER 25

Resources

Aaker, *Managing Brand Equity: Capitalizing on the Value of a Brand Name* (Collier Macmillan, Toronto, Canada 1991)

Elias, *Patent, Copyright & Trademark* (Nolo Press, Berkeley, CA, 3d ed. 1999)
US-oriented overview of patent, copyright, trademark, and trade secret laws written in nonlegalistic terms, with points on the similarities and differences of laws in other countries.

Fishman, *The Copyright Handbook*
Step-by-step instruction and explanation of copyrights in the United States, including illustrative official forms.

Fishman, *Software Development: A Legal Guide*
Discussion of IP laws for companies, employees, and independent workers, complete with contracts on diskette.

Lindberg & Cohn, *The Marketing Book for Growing Companies That Want to Excel* (Van Nostrand Reinhold Co., New York 1986)
Includes discussion of the value of product and company names and the trend toward those names becoming generic.

Oathout, *Trademarks: A Guide to the Selection, Administration, and Protection of Trademarks in Modern Business Practice* (Charles Scribner's, New York, 1981)

Shippey, *Trademark Practice & Forms* (Ocean Publications, New York, 1996)
Country-by-country examination of trademark laws and procedures for registration and protection of trademarks.

http://www.bitlaw.com
Online source for the US Patent and Trademark Office's Acceptable Description of Goods and Services Manual, which is a detailed alphabetical listing of products and services with suggested descriptions and classification numbers useful for formulating the specification of goods required in applications for marks in most countries of the world.

http://www.execpc.com
News, trends, and developments on trade secrets.

http://www.tufts.edu/departments/fletcher/multi/trade.html
Links to international treaties for patents, trademarks, copyrights, and other IP protection.

http://lcweb.loc.gov/copyright
The website of the US Copyright Office, where you can find forms, laws, regulations, and guidelines on protection of copyrights.

http://www.uspto.gov
The website of the US Patent and Trademark Office, where you can search for patents and trademarks, file applications, and discover considerable information, news briefs, laws, and regulations related to intellectual property—for free.

http://www.wipo.org
Information on international IP treaties and trends, including links to government and country IP websites worldwide.